Neoliberalism and Education

The ongoing neoliberalisation of education is complex, varied and relentless. It involves increasingly diverse material and structural changes to curriculum, pedagogy and assessment and at the same time transforms how we are made up as educational subjects. It rearticulates what it means to be educated. This collection brings together creative and unanticipated examples of the adoption and adaptation of neoliberal practice, both collective and individual. These examples not only demonstrate the insidiousness of neoliberal reform but also suggest that its trajectory is uncertain and unfixed. The intention is that these examples might embolden education scholars and practitioners to think differently about education.

This book is shaped by a reading of the processes of the neoliberalisation of education as a dispositif. This heterogeneous dispositif encompasses and spans an uneven, miscellaneous and evolving network of educational regimes of knowledge, practice and subjectivities, as well as artifacts and non-human actants. The papers included address different aspects or points within this complex arrangement at different levels and in different sectors of education. They have been chosen to illustrate the evolving and multi-faceted penetration of market thinking and practice in education and also points of deflection and dissent. They also offer coverage of some of the uneven geography of neoliberalisation. They consider the potential for the production of subjectivities to provide the 'wriggle' room that can exist to refuse or subvert neoliberal identities. This book will have appeal across the social sciences and specifically to those working in education. The chapters included here were originally published in various Taylor & Francis journals.

Bronwen M.A. Jones received her PhD from University College London, Institute of Education, UK, in 2020. Her thesis entitled *Educating the Neoliberal Whole Child: A Genealogical Approach* was published by Routledge in 2021. She spent a number of years as Postgraduate Tutor on BA and MA programmes and continues to research and write on the construction of the child in neoliberal education policy.

Stephen J. Ball is Emeritus Professor of Sociology of Education at the University College London, Institute of Education, UK. He was elected Fellow of the British Academy in 2006 and is also Fellow of the Society of Educational Studies and a Laureate of Kappa Delta Phi; he has honorary doctorates from the Universities of Turku, Finland, and Leicester, UK. He is co-founder of the *Journal of Education Policy*.

Education and Social Theory

Series Editor: Stephen J. Ball, Institute of Education, University College London, UK

Social theory can help us to make sense of many aspects of contemporary education by providing analytic concepts and insights. Social theories are tools of analysis and interpretation for educational researchers that enable us to make sense of the processes, effects, and outcomes of educational experiences and institutions.

Drawing together selections from the best work previously published in Taylor and Francis journals to create powerful and effective collections, this series highlights and explores the social theories critical to educational writers, researchers and scholars. Each book focuses a different key writer or field of theory, with the overarching aim of providing an overview of the social theories important to education research, but also of showing how these theories can be applied in a practical manner in the current education landscape.

Foucault and Education
Putting Theory to Work
Edited by Stephen J Ball

Freud, Lacan, Zizek and Education
Edited by Claudia Lapping

The Education Assemblage
Edited by Greg Thompson

Bourdieu and Education
Edited by Diane Reay

Judith Butler and Education
Edited by Judith Butler

Nancy Fraser, Social Justice and Education
Edited by Carol Vincent

Basil Bernstein, Code Theory and Education
Women's Contributions
Edited by Parlo Singh

Globalisation and Education
Edited by Bob Lingard

Neoliberalism and Education
Edited by Bronwen M. A. Jones and Stephen J. Ball

Neoliberalism and Education

Edited by
Bronwen M. A. Jones and Stephen J. Ball

LONDON AND NEW YORK

First published 2023
by Routledge
4 Park Square, Milton Park, Abingdon, Oxon, OX14 4RN

and by Routledge
605 Third Avenue, New York, NY 10158

Routledge is an imprint of the Taylor & Francis Group, an informa business

Chapter 1 © 2023 Bronwen M. A. Jones and Stephen J. Ball

Chapter 2 © 2023 The Regional Studies Association

Chapter 4–11 © 2023 Taylor & Francis

Chapter 3 © 2018 Bob Jessop. Originally published as Open Access.

With the exception of Chapter 3, no part of this book may be reprinted or reproduced or utilised in any form or by any electronic, mechanical, or other means, now known or hereafter invented, including photocopying and recording, or in any information storage or retrieval system, without permission in writing from the publishers. For details on the rights for Chapter 3, please see the chapter's Open Access footnote.

Trademark notice: Product or corporate names may be trademarks or registered trademarks, and are used only for identification and explanation without intent to infringe.

British Library Cataloguing-in-Publication Data
A catalogue record for this book is available from the British Library

ISBN13: 978-1-032-18256-8 (hbk)
ISBN13: 978-1-032-18257-5 (pbk)
ISBN13: 978-1-003-25361-7 (ebk)

DOI: 10.4324/9781003253617

Typeset in Minion Pro
by codeMantra

Publisher's Note
The publisher accepts responsibility for any inconsistencies that may have arisen during the conversion of this book from journal articles to book chapters, namely the inclusion of journal terminology.

Disclaimer
Every effort has been made to contact copyright holders for their permission to reprint material in this book. The publishers would be grateful to hear from any copyright holder who is not here acknowledged and will undertake to rectify any errors or omissions in future editions of this book.

Contents

	Citation Information	vii
	Notes on Contributors	ix
1	Introduction: Neoliberalism is dead—Long live neoliberalism *Bronwen M.A. Jones and Stephen J. Ball*	1
2	Explaining (with) neoliberalism *Jamie Peck*	17
3	Neoliberalization, uneven development, and Brexit: further reflections on the organic crisis of the British state and society *Bob Jessop*	43
4	Neoliberalism, urbanism and the education economy: producing Hyderabad as a 'global city' *Sangeeta Kamat*	62
5	Neoliberalism and the demise of public education: the corporatization of schools of education *Marta Baltodano*	78
6	Fixing contradictions of education commercialisation: Pearson plc and the construction of its efficacy brand *Curtis B. Riep*	99
7	'Make money, get money': how two autonomous schools have commercialised their services *Jessica Holloway and Amanda Keddie*	118
8	Care of the self, resistance and subjectivity under neoliberal governmentalities *Stephen J. Ball and Antonio Olmedo*	131
9	Nuancing the critique of commercialisation in schools: recognising teacher agency *Anna Hogan, Eimear Enright, Michalis Stylianou and Louise McCuaig*	143

vi CONTENTS

10 Students as consumers? A counter perspective from student assessment as a
disciplinary technology 158
Rille Raaper

11 Preoccupied with the self: towards self-responsible, enterprising, flexible
and self-centered subjectivity in education 174
Kristiina Brunila and Päivi Siivonen

Index 189

Citation Information

The chapters in this book were originally published in various Taylor & Francis journals. When citing this material, please use the original page numbering for each article, as follows:

Chapter 2
Explaining (with) neoliberalism
Jamie Peck
Territory, Politics, Governance, volume 1, issue 2 (2013) pp. 132–157

Chapter 3
Neoliberalization, uneven development, and Brexit: further reflections on the organic crisis of the British state and society
Bob Jessop
European Planning Studies, volume 26, issue 9 (2018) pp. 1728–1746

Chapter 4
Neoliberalism, urbanism and the education economy: producing Hyderabad as a 'global city'
Sangeeta Kamat
Discourse: Studies in the Cultural Politics of Education, volume 32, issue 2 (2011) pp. 187–202

Chapter 5
Neoliberalism and the demise of public education: the corporatization of schools of education
Marta Baltodano
International Journal of Qualitative Studies in Education, volume 25, issue 4 (2012) pp. 487–507

Chapter 6
Fixing contradictions of education commercialisation: Pearson plc and the construction of its efficacy brand
Curtis B. Riep
Critical Studies in Education, volume 60, issue 4 (2019) pp. 407–425

Chapter 7
'Make money, get money': how two autonomous schools have commercialised their services
Jessica Holloway and Amanda Keddie
Discourse: Studies in the Cultural Politics of Education, volume 40, issue 6 (2019) pp. 889–901

Chapter 8

Care of the self, resistance and subjectivity under neoliberal governmentalities
Stephen J. Ball and Antonio Olmedo
Critical Studies in Education, volume 54, issue 1 (2013) pp. 85–96

Chapter 9

Nuancing the critique of commercialisation in schools: recognising teacher agency
Anne Hogan, Eimear Enright, Michalis Stylianou and Louise McCuaig
Journal of Education Policy, volume 33, issue 5 (2018) pp. 617–631

Chapter 10

Students as consumers? A counter perspective from student assessment as a disciplinary technology
Rille Raaper
Teaching in Higher Education, volume 24, issue 1 (2019) pp. 1–16

Chapter 11

Preoccupied with the self: towards self-responsible, enterprising, flexible and self-centered subjectivity in education
Kristiina Brunila and Päivi Siivonen
Discourse: Studies in the Cultural Politics of Education, volume 37, issue 1 (2016) pp. 56–69

For any permission-related enquiries please visit
http://www.tandfonline.com/page/help/permissions

Notes on Contributors

Stephen J. Ball is Emeritus Professor of Sociology of Education at the University College London, Institute of Education, UK.

Marta Baltodano is Professor in the Department of Teaching and Learning, School of Education Faculty, Loyola Marymount University, Los Angeles, USA.

Kristiina Brunila is Professor in the Department of Education, Teachers' Academy, Helsinki Institute of Sustainability Science (HELSUS), Finland.

Eimear Enright is Senior Lecturer in the School of Human Movement and Nutrition Sciences, Faculty of Health and Behavioural Sciences, University of Queensland, Brisbane, Australia.

Anna Hogan is ARC DECRA Research Fellow in the School of Teacher Education and Leadership, Queensland University of Technology, Brisbane, Australia.

Jessica Holloway is Senior Research Fellow and ARC DECRA Fellow in the Institute for Learning Sciences and Teacher Education, Research Centre for Digital Data and Assessment in Education, Australian Catholic University, Brisbane, Australia.

Bob Jessop is Professor Emeritus, Department of Sociology, University of Lancaster, UK.

Bronwen M.A. Jones received her PhD from University College London, Institute of Education, UK, in 2020.

Sangeeta Kamat is Professor and Grace Lee Boggs Faculty Fellow at the Center of Racial Justice and Youth Engaged Research, Department of Educational Policy, Research & Administration, College of Education, University of Massachusetts, USA.

Amanda Keddie is Professor of Education, School of Education, Deakin University, Australia.

Louise McCuaig is Honorary Associate Professor in the School of Human Movement and Nutrition Sciences, University of Queensland: Head Pastoral Programs (Health and Wellbeing), Matthew Flinders Anglican College, Queensland.

Antonio Olmedo is Associate Professor in Education Policy Sociology, Graduate School of Education, University of Exeter, UK.

Jamie Peck is Canada Research Chair in Urban and Regional Political Economy, University of British Columbia, Canada.

NOTES ON CONTRIBUTORS

Rille Raaper is Associate Professor and Deputy Director of Research in the School of Education, University of Durham, UK.

Curtis B. Riep is Graduate Student in the Department of Educational Policy Studies, University of Alberta, Edmonton, Canada.

Päivi Siivonen is Post-Doctoral Researcher, School of Educational Sciences and Psychology, University of Eastern Finland, Finland.

Michalis Stylianou is Senior Lecturer in the School of Human Movement and Nutrition Sciences, Faculty of Health and Behavioural Sciences, University of Queensland, Brisbane, Australia.

INTRODUCTION

Neoliberalism is dead—Long live neoliberalism

Bronwen M.A. Jones and Stephen J. Ball

As the ramifications of the COVID-19 pandemic continue to unfold, it appears that the death knell of neoliberalism is sounding. The call for the 'state' to step in and step up appears to signal the return of a Keynesian–lite approach to public finance and support.

> The political implications of COVID-19 will continue to unfold for months, perhaps even years. Ideologically, neoliberal proclamations about the imperative of 'fiscal austerity' and the limitations of public policy vanished faster than one could spell 'bankruptcy'. Intransigent Austrians and neoliberals of every hue hastily retreated into a half-baked Keynesianism, as they tend to do when economies tank: no one is enamoured of negative externalities or the downside of the 'free market'; in a crisis the first to grab the capacious teats of the Treasury wins the big prize and at the hour of economic need, state intervention is questioned only for what it has not yet done.
>
> (Saad-Filho, 2020, p. 477)

However, it would be hard to ignore the subtle and not so subtle insinuations of neoliberal practice into the story of the pandemic; the new 'opportunities' the virus has created for business interests, the influx of private equity into medical and health fields and the reanimation of interventionary, high-spending methods of population control and management.

It might be wise to be circumspect therefore, as obituaries of neoliberalism have been written before. The 2008 financial crisis and the votes for Brexit and Trump have all been cited as terminal ruptures of the neoliberal imaginary. However, here we are and it would appear that neoliberalism has not gone away and yet, 'neither does it remain what it was' (Peck, 2013, p. 133). Theorists continue to grapple with how best to understand this obstinate yet flighty phenomenon. We have had talk of 'zombie neoliberalism' (Peck, 2010) and 'mutant neoliberalism' (Callison and Manfredi, 2020) and Dean's 'militant thought collective' (2012, p. 86). Debate about the intransigent nature of neoliberalism has been rebooted and the questions about how best to make sense of its resurface and reform as well. So, although there are rumours that neoliberalism is entering the end game, it may be more prudent to brace ourselves for the start of another regeneration. With this in mind, this collection provides an opportunity to re-examine and re-assess how neoliberalism and neoliberalisation are understood and articulated. The papers suggest various ways to conceptualise and analyse how neoliberalisation continues to play out in education. Our suggestion evolves from a consideration of existing approaches and so we begin this introduction by briefly examining these.

It is hard not to concur with the key contributors in the field of neoliberal studies that as an analytic category, neoliberalism is a 'rascal concept' (Peck, 2013, p. 133), a 'rather overblown notion' (Dean, 2012, p. 70) with 'a perplexing mix of overreach and underspecification' (Brenner et al., 2010, p. 2). In addition to this, it is all too easy to be swayed by the drama of the apocalyptic tone that often accompanies the discussion of neoliberalism. Referenced as a 'big Leviathan' (Collier, 2012) and a 'slouching beast' (Ball, 2016), it has arguably become 'loose shorthand for a prevailing dystopian zeitgeist' (Venugopal, 2015, p. 168) and in certain quarters has evolved into 'a generic term of deprecation' (Thorsen and Lie, 2006, p. 9). There is no shortage of rhetorical flourish in the academic debate about neoliberalism; it is personified as sly and deceitful, insinuating itself into societal structures and governance – a cannibalising and colonising force programming the population to embrace the market and its concomitant social relations. Neoliberalism is often anthropomorphised as the villain in a grand narrative lamenting the global shift away from the golden era of the Keynesian welfare states (Barnett, 2005). Compelling though this story is, over-simplification and melodrama do little to help in exploring and understanding the multiplicity of ways in which neoliberal principles and practices have come to structure and been enacted in everyday life.

Conceptualising neoliberalism as a singular, definable and immutable theory is misleading and simplistic. If anything, as we shall see, it can be argued that the opposite is the case and this is not surprising given its 'origins'. The roots of neoliberalism as an active social movement are often traced to the Mont Pelerin Society, founded after the Second World War to debate the role of liberalism in building a new society that protected the rights of the individual. This eclectic endeavour included a range of economists, historians and philosophers who promoted laissez faire market economics in opposition to a centralised, collectivist state planning. Admittedly, over time they established a broad consensus on what constituted the 'neoliberal' economic perspective, but it would be inaccurate to claim it was consistently defined.

Indeed, Foucault, focuses on a different event as the beginning of contemporary neoliberalism – The Walter Lippmann colloquium (26–30 August 1938), held in France and including as participants Rüstow, Hayek and von Mises, with Raymond Aron acting as secretary. Beyond this Foucault traces the genealogy of neoliberalism, as part of a broader genealogy of the arts of government to specific features of liberal government in the 19th century, what he calls the 'phobia of the state', through two major iterations. One is German *ordoliberalism*, the other the '*anarcho-liberalism*' of the American Chicago School of economics. The former defined by *vitalpolitik*, the 'politics of life'; the latter by 'giving a new form to society according to the model of enterprise' – he adds that this model goes 'down to the fine grain of (the) texture' of society (Foucault, 2010, p. 241). Many accounts of neoliberalism ignore or avoid giving attention to localised variations or different historic versions, but as Ong (2007) demonstrates in the case of Asia, neoliberalism is a mobile and constantly adapting technology (see below).

As there is a lack of consensus regarding the roots of neoliberalism, it follows on from this that there is no equivocal neoliberal credo or manifesto, no declaration of beliefs that sets out definitively what the neoliberal project is. Whilst some reference the Washington Consensus as a 'quintessential expression' of neoliberalism (Hilgers, 2012, p. 81 cited in Collier, 2012, p. 192.) or Hayek's *Road to Serfdom* (1944) as a seminal text, doctrinal clarity and specificity is not a characteristic of neoliberalism. There is no ideal type or template, which serves as the model of neoliberal thinking or practice. And this is important because it means that the enactment of neoliberalism in the real world carries greater weight in helping to define and understand it.

The critical transition of neoliberalism into an active political project came in the late 1970s as a consequence of and response to the perceived failure of Keynesian economics, the Oil Crisis, stagflation in the 1970s. Neoliberal economics was positioned as an alternative to state planning and *ungovernability* (Jessop, 2016) and a route out of global crisis. In the US and the UK, this was pursued in combination with *neoconservatism* and became known as the politics of the New Right. The elections of Margaret Thatcher and Ronald Reagan inaugurated an era in which neoliberal thinking came to dominate and frame political thinking and practice in parts of the West (Hall, 2003; Jessop, 2004). Indeed, neoliberalism became a global project exemplified by the Washington Consensus and policies of structural adjustment promoted by the International Monetary Fund and World Bank. From the 1980s onwards, neoliberalism no longer existed solely on the page or in the minds of radical thinkers, it took form and became something 'actually existing' (Peck et al., 2018) with all the accompanying epistemological and ontological complications that 'actually existing' bring. As neoliberalism became a tangible and observable project, it became necessary for researchers and commentators to account for and understand the continuities and coherences, differences and contradictions that characterise neoliberalism in practice. Enactments of neoliberalism across the world in multiple, different ways intensified the debate about how best to understand it. The 'spread' of neoliberalism appeared to be rapid and extensive, but its practices were uneven and diverse. It seemed that neoliberalism was everywhere and yet hard to pin down (Peck and Tickell, 2002). To capture this complexity, scholars turned their focus to the processes of *neoliberalisation* or neoliberalism as an on-going 'process, not an end-state' (ibid., p. 383), as practice rather than theory.

Jessop (2018) defines neoliberalisation as 'a variegated series of processes with a core policy set that comprises: liberalization, deregulation, privatization, re-commodification, internationalization, reductions in direct taxation, and decriminalization of predatory economic activities'. This is a useful orientation and goes some way towards helping us to identify and analyse many of the changes that have taken place globally in countries that vary considerably in terms of their economic, political and cultural make-up. The particular concern here is to identify and analyse the extent to which these processes have played out in the field of education and changed the meaning and experience of education for its participants over the past three decades. We want to spend some time considering the way in which different accounts or theories of neoliberalisation have enabled us to understand such change.

Neoliberalisation is often presented as a process that operates at two key levels. Firstly, there are political and economic changes and reforms that occur at a macro structural, 'big picture' level, referred to as big N neoliberalism or 'neoliberalism writ large' (Ong, 2007, p. 14). In these accounts, 'neoliberalization as a common process' (Peck, 2013, p. 141) is stressed. This leans towards a presentation of neoliberalism as a monolithic, coherent free market project whose practices of deregulation and privatisation and reduction or reformation of the state extend globally. This level of analysis stresses the commonalities in processes of neoliberalisation and sits at the heart of studies that identify fundamental structural patterns that have been repeated globally and assumed a kind of 'orthodoxy'.

These can be traced back to early 'New Right' education reforms introduced in the US and England and Wales (Fuller and Stevenson, 2019, p. 1) and to the principles articulated and debated at the Walter Lippmann colloquium and the Mont Pelerin meeting. In the field of education, this is most clearly represented by Sahlberg's evocation of GERM – Global Education Reform Movement. GERM outlines five defining features of the global manifestation of neoliberal practice and approaches to education: standardisation, a focus on core subjects, low-risk teaching methodologies, corporate management models and test-based accountability practices. Sahlberg's acronym-come analogy also neatly conveys the reifying tendency of scholarship with regard to neoliberalism, conceptually constructing neoliberal reforms as 'an epidemic that spreads and infects educations systems through a virus' (Sahlberg, nd).

This kind of analysis has also helped to 'stage' the cumulative and extensive nature of the structural changes many education systems have undergone. Peck and Tickell (2002) reference this as a move from 'roll back' to 'roll out' neoliberalism. Put simply, this captures a common pattern of neoliberalisation that begins with the 'deregulation and dismantlement' of the Keynesian-welfare state or its equivalents and proceeds to an 'emergent phase of active state building and regulatory reform' as neoliberal principles are enacted more extensively and creatively (Peck and Tickell, 2002, p. 384). Indeed, as the roll out phase of neoliberalism continues, it solidifies as a new form of governance, which suggests that the terminology of 'rolling back' may not be helpful or accurate. The enterprise form that increasingly characterises the field of education is indicative of a change in the structure of the polity. Far from representing a shrinking of the state, this brings about a reconfiguration of the state as the proliferation of new agencies and actors, organisations and businesses, charities and foundations becomes involved in both public service provision and policy. In some ways, this new mode of governance can make it seem that neoliberalism has broken free from the state or rendered it redundant, but we only have to consider the role and impact of the relentless and on-going production of new education policy to appreciate the facilitative role of the state as a 'market maker'. Indeed, the state is reborn and reinvigorated, and Foucault alerts us to a neoliberal government that is 'dense, frequent, active and continuous' (2010, p. 145) and 'multiple, vigilant and omnipresent' (ibid., p. 160) and works to construct a whole 'social fabric' that involves 'the generalisation of the economic form of the market' (ibid., p. 243)

This approach to neoliberalisation offers an overview of how neoliberal reform proceeds. However, it has been critiqued as implying that neoliberalisation involves the rolling out of an ideal template of neoliberal practice. Increasingly, as neoliberal educational practices have been adopted in countries around the world, researchers have observed that this has not been a uniform and standardised process. To encapsulate the variations, contingencies and discrepancies in the way neoliberalisation has proceeded, academics refer to small 'n' approaches that explore the 'flux and diversity' of neoliberalism (Brenner et al., 2010, p. 183). These challenge the image of neoliberalisation as a top-down application of homogenous reforms. Peck et al. iterate '[n]eoliberalism has not and does not pulsate out from a single control center or heartland; it has always been *relationally* constituted across multiple sites and spaces of "co-formation"' (2009, p. 106). Ong is an exemplar of this approach with her analyses of the way neoliberal strategies have been taken up by East and Southeast Asian states as exceptions to their usual practices. In this schema, neoliberalisation occurs not as an imposition but as an interaction with pre-existing social, political and cultural conditions to give rise to varied and diverse manifestations. This mirrors the more general notion of *glocalisation* (Robertson, 1995) as opposed to globalisation. This 'low flying' (Brenner et al., 2009, p. 199) case study approach works with an understanding of political power not as a 'hegemonic, thoroughly structurant, state dwelling power' (Cotoi, 2011, p. 110) but as a form of governance where neoliberalism co-exists with alternative or even competing government rationalities. There is an acknowledgement that neoliberalism 'is never the *entire* story' (Peck, 2013, p. 150) and is not always discerning in its choice of bedfellows. Indeed, room is created for 'friction, double movements, resistance [and] alternatives' (ibid., p. 150). In terms of neoliberal reform in education, this approach has placed greater emphasis on variations in the manifestation of neoliberal influence within national education systems. These approaches point to a more complex process of policy borrowing and policy mobility that acknowledges the variations in the pace, extent and convolution of neoliberal reform (Ball, 2017). Studies of school choice and accountability in particular have evidenced the diversity and adaptability of neoliberal practice to its contingent political and social environments. While there are nations in which the incursions of neoliberalism into education policy and practices have been minimal, over and against existing political histories and local cultures, at the other extreme Chile is undoubtedly the most complete example of a neoliberal system of education. In Chile, a military coup mounted against the elected government of Salvador Allende created a break with history and a space in which a national neoliberal experiment became possible. Among many other neoliberal reforms, the military government of Pinochet (1974–1990), directly advised by Chicago School free market economists, introduced a system of vouchers that could be used by parents either in the public school system or in the private sector. This stimulated the opening of large numbers of private schools, and by 1980 there were almost 3000 in operation, almost all of which were seeking to derive profit from the voucher system. Over time, the patterns of parental choice, the geographical distribution of schools and the charging of top-up fees, of different amounts, by the private schools, produced a dramatic social segregation of students, with socially disadvantaged students massively over-represented in the residual public sector (Valenzuela et al., 2014). England with policies of local management of schools, school choice, devolved budgets and direct employment of teachers and the more recent development of Academies and Free schools is another but different social laboratory of neoliberal adoption (Gunter, 2011). Here, the development of a market culture of competition, commercialisation and marketisation that accompanied policies of school choice and accountability succeeded in making educational institutions business-like and like businesses. This endogenous privatisation in turn paved the way for and made thinkable and doable the introduction of private firms, companies, organisations and individuals as providers of services within the education marketplace (exogenous privatisation). The result is a system of choice and a diversity of provision that involves complex networks of private, public, voluntary organisations in the field of education – all of which operate within the ethic of enterprise. The key is that whilst a global spread of choice policies is evident, increasingly research has identified the idiosyncrasies and specificities of the way they are taken up and enacted (Lingard, 2010; Wu, 2014). For example, Tan's (2019) adoption of Ong's approach to characterise Shanghai's neoliberal school choice and assessment policies as 'neoliberalism with Chinese characteristics' offers an interesting case of the way this level and style of theoretical analysis works.

Big N and little n approaches are valuable as ways of making sense of the processes by which education systems around the world have been subject to various different patterns of neoliberal reform. However, their emphasis tends to fall on the structural reforms and practices that are hi-vis manifestations of neoliberalisation. In doing so, it seems that a critical aspect of the neoliberalisation of education, felt so strongly by those involved in education, does not receive the attention it deserves. We are referring to a process of neoliberalisation that occurs not just 'out there' in a myriad of differing practices but a process that takes place 'in there' – in the way we understand education, its purpose and value and the way we understand ourselves and others as people involved in education. These are the two aspects of Foucault's 'social fabric', and they constitute what he refers to as (neo)liberalism as 'a general style of thought, analysis and imagination' (2010, p. 219) and a 'principle of intelligibility and a principle of decipherment of social relationships and individual behaviour' (2010, p. 243). For Foucault, this points to/constitutes a new form of government – governmentality – peculiar to neoliberalism. From this perspective, neoliberalism is a grid or network of individual identity, social and political meanings and human functioning within which some practices and relations are made possible and even necessary and others are excluded. That is, a positivity and a modality of government that 'produces, limits, excludes, frames, hides, scars, cuts, distorts' (Olssen, 2009. p. 86).

Certainly, a great deal of research has born witness to the transformation in the social, personal, cultural and ethical relations of education as a result of neoliberal reform. Researchers and academics have analysed discourses and practices of marketisation (Bowe et al., 1994; Gewirtz et al., 1995; Whitty and Power, 2000), managerialism (Gewirtz and Ball, 2000; Lynch, 2014), commercialisation and entrepreneurship (Ball, 2018; Peters, 2001; Wilkinson, 2006). The implementation of standardised testing and league tables have been understood as processes, or technologies, of performativity and accountability (Ball, 2003; Lingard and Sellar, 2013; Sellar and Lingard, 2014). The changing experience of being a teacher and what it means to teach have been critiqued (Codd, 2005; Gewirtz et al., 2009; Jeffrey and Woods, 1998). The role of parents and students as consumers of education has been explored from pre-school childcare to higher education (Olmedo and Wilkins, 2017; Rowe and Lubienski, 2017; Vincent et al., 2008; Wilkins, 2010).

These studies explore the neoliberalisation of the social, ethical and personal experience of education, the way in which neoliberal reform has prompted new relationships and ways of being and relating to education. They probe the social, cultural and ethical transformation of education as strategically fundamental to the promotion and production of particular kinds of neoliberal subjectivities. Ball discusses the manifold ways in which neoliberal education policy reworks us into neoliberal subjects (2003, 2012, 2016) – as Ball (2003) asks 'are we all libertarians now?' Further studies extend this kind of analysis to explore neoliberalisation as a process that effects the formation of neoliberal subjectivities across education (Bailey, 2015; Bradbury, 2019; Spohrer et al., 2018).

This kind of analysis is important. It concerns one of many critical points where neoliberalism touches us profoundly, shaping our relation to the world, others and ourselves. It is not however always easy to situate it in relation to those big N and little n approaches that have dominated our understanding of neoliberalisation. Perhaps therefore the time has come to take stock of our understanding and conceptualisation of the neoliberalisation of education.

There is value in adopting a theoretical approach that offers a different emphasis, a different sightline on how neoliberalisation proceeds and what neoliberalisation can look like. In particular, one that centres issues that have tended to be either side-lined or have now become more pressing. That is to say, we need an approach that adequately addresses *how* neoliberalisation changes the personal, social and ethical selves and relations of education. How is it that we are made up as neoliberal subjects sometimes against our best efforts and wishes? Further, it seems that the perennial rejuvenations and restructurings of neoliberal education are increasingly flighty, uneven and sometimes unexpected, suggesting a bumpier pattern of reform and adaptation that is more challenging to map. Allied to this whilst neoliberalism has often had 'strange bedfellows', it is clear – in education at least – that its sometimes antagonistic existences need exploring not just as a context of localised versions of neoliberalism but as very real challenges to its principles and practices. Certain divergent practices and ideologies are not necessarily support acts providing colour and interest to the star turn, but they are providing 'push back' and offering glimpses of alternative futures. This needs charting and documenting in a way that notes not only the tension and antagonisms but also the unpredictability of the next step. We concur with Peck et al. that it is unlikely that any one 'crisis' will prompt the 'irretrievable collapse' of neoliberalism in a 'Berlin Wall moment' (2009, p. 95) – the crisis of 2008 left neoliberalism virtually unscathed. Nevertheless, the time has come to pay more attention to the fringes of neoliberal influence where it sometimes meets its match or hits the buffers. We need to be able to track and trace the more finessed and fine adaptations where it is not clear whether what we see is a fizzling out or deeper absorption of neoliberal values.

Centring these issues means adopting a theoretical construct which makes much less of the big N-little n divide and embraces the sprawling yet tightly and multiply connected processes of neoliberalisation as they evolve, intensify and dissolve. This is not easy! The fundamental challenge is that neoliberalism rests upon, brings about and flourishes not simply on the basis of a set of tenets or principles, or through a set of changes in systems of delivery, or in the enactment of new forms of social relations but in and through a complex arrangement and ensemble of practices, methods, ethics, interactions and subjectivities. It involves 'the coupling of a set of practices and a regime of truth' (Foucault, 2010, p. 19) that 'form an apparatus (dispositif) of knowledge-power that effectively marks out in reality that which does not exist' (ibid., p. 19). Finding a way or ways to think about, visibilise and analyse this not only requires a methodological approach that is flexible and multi-modal but that also identifies coherences and continuities across different places and levels of enactment. We need to be able to take seriously both the alignments and affinities and the contradictions and anomalies that are evident in neoliberal educational thinking and practice. We must acknowledge that there are sometimes very significant points of resistance to and failures of neoliberalism, places and times where neoliberalising tendencies have been squashed or subverted or simply dissipated. Equally, we need to find a way to explicate how neoliberalism has become sedimented and embedded as a social fabric and how it has disappeared from sight not because it has moved on but because we can no longer spot it. It has become part of who we are and how we are – it is integral to how we see the world, ourselves and others and how we understand education and its purpose – it catches us and forms us unawares.

Below, we suggest adopting Foucault's notion of the dispositif as a way of theorising neoliberalism and neoliberalisation. We set out what we think the value of this approach is and go on to explain how the concept of the dispositif has directed the selection of articles for this collection.

The dispositif

Foucault describes the dispositif as a:

> thoroughly heterogeneous ensemble consisting of discourses, institutions, architectural forms, regulatory decisions, laws, administrative measures, scientific statements, philosophical, moral and philanthropic propositions–in short, the said as much as the unsaid.
>
> (1980, p. 194)

This heterogeneous and polymorphic ensemble is cohered and connected by a particular web of meaning, a theme, a concept – in this case 'the economization of the entire social field' (Foucault, 2010, p. 242). Whilst its individual building blocks consist of varying practices, processes, technologies, discourses, buildings, gestures, signs, etc., it is the relations between such diverse items that visibilise the dispositif and are critical to naming it. The construct of the dispositif takes seriously the materiality of thought, power and knowledge, tracking the instantiation and reiteration of truths as they cohere to produce a tangible and identifiable regime of truth. Identifying and analysing a dispositif involves tracing a network of policies, practices and discourses and establishing patterns of connection and coherence across material and discursive and macro and micro levels of enactment while at the same time attending to gaps, mismatches and clashes. In education, these neoliberal tropes are played out repeatedly in a wide variety of discourses and practices and are supported by and trigger multiple connected and aligned truths. However, this coherence is found not only in more obvious forms of market thinking and market practices, it exists in the fundamental epistemological and ethical framework that runs through multiple components of the dispositif. The consequence of this is the production of a powerful milieu which shapes meaning, identities and relationships. This milieu comes to both constitute and shape our common sense understanding of ourselves and the world. And this, according to Foucault, can be understood as a manifestation and facilitation of a distinctive liberal form of government – government that founds and establishes 'the principle of rationalization of the art of government in the rational behaviour of those who are governed' (Foucault, 2010, p. 312). To briefly elucidate.

Different policies and practices of school choice and varying and diverse systems of accountability have produced multiple forms of commodification; the commodification of education as a private rather than a public good, the commodification of the child as a bearer of academic results as schools find ways to admit children who will boost their rankings place and the commodification of the self as children and teacher alike are exhorted to see themselves as sites of investment and projects to be worked upon. Not only have these commodifications changed the way in which education is understood, but also they have changed the way we both see and value ourselves and others. Education is instrumentalised by the prioritisation of examination results and is no longer something to be valued in its own right. Relationships are imbued with an ethics of instrumentalism as others become a means to an end. This is a circuit of educational practice and experience that is cohered by a form of instrumental ethics which shapes our understanding of education, others and ourselves. We are all enterprises now, all entrepreneurs of the self, and this is the normalised rational behaviour through which Foucault claims we are governed. The dispositif helps us to foreground and connect the multiple ways in which iterations of neoliberal tropes interact to sustain this common-sense rationalisation (See Jones, 2021).

Whilst identifying patterns of coherence between the multivalent components of the dispositif is fundamental, it is important to trace its boundaries as well and this is not straightforward. This is particularly so in the case of neoliberalism inasmuch that it rests on 'the possibility of giving a strictly economic interpretation of a whole domain previously thought to be non-economic' (Foucault, 2010, p. 219) More and more of our social, cultural and emotional life, even those most intimate parts are opened up to the market creating manifold shifting boundaries of the dispositif. The constituents of the dispositif each have their own genealogy and different potential trajectories. Whilst being connected by strategic objectives and conjoined at specific 'points of contact', they are also subject to 'strategic elaboration' in ways that may be unforeseen, contradictory or both. The dispositif as a method of research and analysis allows us to identify these strategic affiliations, elaborations and relations and examine how they support and play into a neoliberal regime of truth.

Returning to consider practices of choice and accountability in education, it is clear that they are reiterated and supported by other discourses. This epistemological and ethical coherence extends beyond market logic to include powerful discourses of the economy, science and the number. Numerical knowledge – quantitative research methodology, statistical analyses of test results, student and teacher performance, league tables and rankings – plays into and reiterates commodification and instrumentalism. It makes commodification of relationships and experiences that are complex and fragile easy and lends that commodification an aura of neutrality and facticity. The learner is made visible and calculable and thus governable. Numbers define our worth, measure our effectiveness and in a myriad of other ways work to inform or construct what we are today. We are subject to numbers and numbered subjects. This intensifies the ethics of instrumentalism by fixating on a numerical return that can be presented as or worse translated into failure or success. The d(iscourse) of the knowledge economy supports the commodification of knowledge and education as private goods that can be exchanged for success in a competitive job market. Practices of school choice and accountability are circumscribed and supported by wider discourses with which they share an epistemological and ethical continuity. We can see multiple overlapping processes that replay and relay commodification and instrumentalism to circumscribe and reconstruct how education happens, how it is understood and how it positions and defines us.

However, it is equally important is to identify the frayed edges of a dispositif, the points at which coherence is lost and power shifts and dissipates. They are the points where the neoliberal dispositif butts up against other regimes of truth. As tightly cohered as the neoliberal dispositif is, there are still 'cracks, silent shocks, malfunctions' (Foucault, 1990, p. 156) and these represent possibilities for alternative trajectories and different ways of thinking and being.

The dispositif enables us to visibilise processes of neoliberalisation in a way that makes connections across multiple arenas of experience. It allows us to probe more deeply how structural change is imbricated in ethical and social change and in making us up as neoliberal subjectivities by pointing to different levels of coherence. Further, it encourages an exploration of the peripheries of neoliberal reform, which may help us to probe more meaningfully some of the unforeseen consequences, more savvy adaptations and quiet refusals of neoliberal practice that are so tricky to theorise. These are all issues/areas that are highlighted in this collection.

This collection is the collation of a body of scholarship that supports and explicates the theorisation of the neoliberalisation of education as a dispositif. The articles explore and examine the evolving penetration of market thinking and practice in education at different levels and in different ways. They highlight the sometimes-unanticipated ways in which neoliberal reform is experienced and at the same time identify points of deflection and dissent where neoliberalism appears to have overreached itself. They address the formation of subjectivities and social and pedagogical relationships in the context of neoliberal reform that are ambiguous and complex – difficult to pigeon hole as either resistance or subjugation.

Introduction to the articles

The first two articles address in greater detail some of the difficulties involved in conceptualising and analysing neoliberalism particularly in light of the economic, social and political upheavals of the 2008 global economic crash, austerity and Brexit. According to Peck, far from signalling the end of neoliberalism as many had forecast, the global crises have simply 'thrown the explanatory chips into the air' (Peck, p. 18) and driven theorists back to the drawing board to ponder 'renovated' conceptions of neoliberalism (ibid., p. 19). In a far more extensive and detailed account than we have begun here, Peck confronts head on the difficulties that surround the often-polarised accounts of neoliberalisation into 'context-rich, agent centred and difference-finding approaches' and 'political-economic or macroinstitutional approaches' (ibid., p. 10). Peck points to the fact that there is never a 100% realised enactment of neoliberalism; it is 'an always-thwarted totalisation' (ibid., p. 38), and as such, it always exists relationally among others and is 'never the *entire* story, never the *only* causal presence' (ibid., p. 35). He concludes optimistically that the consequence of this is that it therefore lives alongside 'actually existing alternatives' (ibid., p. 36) and this sets the scene for some of the articles that follow as they document instances of individual and collective challenges to neoliberal practice. The second article by Jessop embraces the notion of neoliberalism as a variegated, partial and hybrid process. He sets out clearly different typologies and stages of neoliberalisation tracing in detail the uneven development that sits at the heat of the neoliberal project. Jessop situates Brexit as part of the trajectory of neoliberalism and hence problematises and claims that Brexit sounds the beginning of its demise.

The collection then splits into two key foci. The first focus includes a set of articles that tie the diverse material, practical and structural changes of neoliberal reform to the contingent environments in which they operate. They explore the various and connected shifts in the understanding of education that they prompt and reiterate. They include creative and unanticipated examples of the adoption and adaptation of neoliberal practice and in some cases point to alternative visions of education or accounts of collective/individual resistance to neoliberal reform.

Kamat's examination of neoliberalisation in Andhra Pradesh and Hyderabad focuses on the role of Higher Education in transforming the local economy. Her close analysis explores the inextricable relationship between the neoliberal globalisation, the evolution of the education sector and the socio-economic transformations in the region. Specifically, she focuses on the conjuncture of caste histories, class relations and uneven, post-colonial geographies showing how they integrate with the specific evolution of the education sector to become part of the story of neoliberal globalisation in Andhra Pradesh. Significantly, Kamat concludes with an account of the local inequalities and social and class contradictions that have accompanied the developments he describes. She examines student protests and a broader political 'nativist' movement that appears as a rejection of the neoliberal model of development. Whilst this in turn raises uncomfortable questions surrounding the growth of populist movements, Hyderabad and Andhra Pradesh represent an evolving example of 'actually existing neoliberalism' and 'actually existing alternatives' that merits attention.

Baltodano examines the political and economic policies that have altered the structures and practices of teacher education in the US. She identifies 'multiple and concurrent' tactics of neoliberalism (p. 90) – policies and practices of commodification and marketisation, systems of accreditation and a culture of managerialism – to show how they have cumulatively shaped the provision and nature of teacher education in the US. Her argument extends beyond these observations to draw out how these policy developments and structural alterations have worked together to undermine the notion of education as a public good, sweeping aside 'the intended democratic goals of public education' (p. 86). By way of a conclusion, albeit it one intended as the starting point of a debate, Baltodano draws on Nussbaum's and Andrzejewski et al.'s collective vision for social justice to propose a model of education that challenges and counteracts the neoliberal imaginary. Her hope is that this model might be the start of a conversation or lead to the launch a movement 'to reclaim education as a public good' (p. 93).

Riep's and Holloway and Keddie's articles address the practices of commercialisation and marketisation that are characteristic of neoliberalised education systems but they do so in unusual and different ways. Together both document the way in which policies of privatisation shape evolving educational practices, relationships and culture. The articles show clearly that these practices and relationships are not static and involve actors who are able to adapt and extend market thinking and practices in novel ways and to different ends. Both articles introduce us to actors that exhibit a serpentine neoliberal logic but whose motivations and objectives differ dramatically. Holloway and Keddie's article in particular raises some difficult questions about how we are positioned by neoliberal practice and how our understanding of what constitutes a neoliberal subjectivity cannot be fixed or clear.

The commercialisation of education for profit still sits uneasily with many and Riep tackles the way this discomfort is ameliorated by a key player in the education market. Focusing on Pearson plc. 'the world's leading learning company', he explores what he sees as their attempt to legitimate, justify and therefore secure their commercial activities and profit in the face of the fundamental contradictions inherent in profiting from education. He argues that their *Efficacy Framework* – designed to measure the performance of the companies' educational products and services – operates as a 'social fix', which frames how the company is perceived and judged. By stressing the transformative impact that an educational commodity can have on the learner's or consumer's life, Pearson manages the way it is perceived. In unpicking the way in which Pearson is able to delimit what its customers understand about its products in order to secure its market position, Riep gives us a concrete example of the way that the neoliberal global education industry works to adapt and overcome 'crisis – tendencies' (Riep, p. 102). This is neoliberalism on the go, flight of foot and adapting to a changing situation to ensure survival, success and profit.

Holloway and Keddie's article exemplifies the connectedness of endogenous and exogenous privatisations illustrating the way in which practices are compounded and escalate as neoliberal reform takes hold. Focusing on the Independent Schools Programme initiative in Queensland, Australia, designed to promote school autonomy, they examine how two different schools have responded creatively to their autonomy to undertake novel ways of raising funds. In the context of a quasi-market in which edu businesses and private companies sell services to schools, Holloway and Keddie show how these two schools have disrupted this model to commercialise and marketise their own best practices and position themselves as both for-profit providers and consumers. They show us teachers who are able to imaginatively adopt market practice and successfully monetise their pedagogical practice in order to secure resources for their students and their communities. The article reveals innovative and unexpected forms of teacher agency, but Holloway and Keddie sound a note of caution that speaks to the mutability and tenacity of neoliberal tropes. Whilst these schools have undoubtedly been able to reap the benefits of commercialisation, they have also established that schools can profitable. Holloway and Keddie note that this may pave the way for the view that they should be profitable. As commercialisation introduces new norms for what schools can and should do, this impacts what education is and what is becoming. There is no simple answer to this: the article shows us a commercialisation of education that implies that neoliberalism has been hoist by its own petard, but perhaps the fact remains that it is many ways simply an extension of neoliberal practice.

The second series of articles follows closely on from the difficult questions raised about neoliberal subjectivities in Holloway and Keddie's article. These articles look more closely at how these evolutions in the educational milieu prompt and rest upon the generation of new subjectivities. These subjectivities are explored as both sites of governance and sites of resistance, as the 'wriggle' room that can allow for the subversion or rejection of neoliberal subjectivities.

Ball and Olmedo's article introduces the focus for this section with a reconsideration of what resistance to neoliberalism might look like. Rather than considering traditional collective political resistance, they explore and locate resistance to neoliberalism at the level of the subject. They examine the daily experiences and practices of individual teachers who find ways to refuse the neoliberal subjectivities that certain practices and games of truth promote. Examining a series of email exchanges, Ball and Olmedo draw on Foucault's conception of the care of the self to understand these teachers' daily struggles with and refusals of neoliberal practices of performativity. By acting 'irresponsibly', these teachers take responsibility for themselves and open up the possibility of thinking differently about education and their roles. Ball and Olmedo locate resistance to or refusal of neoliberalism at the level of the individual subject's dissatisfaction, unresponsiveness and recalcitrance. It is at this level of individual enactment, or failure to enact, that the neoliberal dispositif butts up against discreet but discrepant ethical positions.

Hogan et al. continue the theme of teacher's subjectivities but return us to the topic of commercialisation. Focusing on the role of commercialisation in the provision of Social and Emotional Learning (SEL) in Australian schools, they examine the way teachers use and value commercial resources. They argue that far from being seduced by commercialisation, teachers exert and display professional agency in a mix and match approach to commercial products motivated by a concern to offer a bespoke learning experience for their students. They offer and call for a more sophisticated analysis of the role and impact of commercialisation in schools that, referencing Ball, 2016, recognise teachers as 'courageous counterpoints' (p. 153). This research demonstrates the danger of making assumptions about the nature of the impact of neoliberal reform. Following on from Ball and Olmedo's study, it recognises individual subjects as important points of inflection who creatively interact with policies and practices.

Raaper uses Foucault's conceptualisations of power to analyse student experiences of higher education in two different universities – one in the UK and one in Estonia. She considers the ways in which students have been positioned as consumers by neoliberal education policies focusing particularly on the impact of this for their experience of assessment. In showing the continuing importance of traditional and less traditional manifestations of disciplinary power in assessment practices, Raaper argues that students are not always created as neoliberal 'consuming' subjects in quite the way that might be expected. She explores the various tactical responses students adopt to assessment but ultimately argues that despite the significance of a globally dominant consumerist policy, the student experience of assessment remains constrained. The article demonstrates the uneven impact of neoliberal policy and the way in which neoliberal discourses can sit comfortably alongside or even inhabit practices that confound it. Further, it points to the finesse with which individual subjects negotiate their relationship with different neoliberal policies and practices.

By contrast, although retaining the emphasis on the less anticipated effects of neoliberal discourse, Brunila and Siivonen explore the way the seemingly distinct discourses of therapy and enterprise work together to produce neoliberal subjectivities in adult education. Building on the work of Foucault, Rose, and Ecclestone and Hayes, they argue that therapeutic discourses claim to produce a subject freed from 'psychic and emotional chains' who is able to take up their position as the rational autonomous subject required by discourses of enterprise. Rather, they claim that therapeutic discourses produce a fragile and vulnerable subject that when tied to the notion of individual responsibility and enterprise produces a competitive survivor. Brunila and Siivonen demonstrate how these two discourses work together 'linking political rhetoric and regulatory programmes to the self-steering capacities of the subjects themselves' (p. 185). These discourses chime in their removal of the social fabric as a fundamental support for those who are disposed. They play into each other to reiterate neoliberal tropes and undermine the idea of young adults as socially responsible citizens.

Neoliberalisation is located at the level of structural reform, reform that has been replicated globally and adapted locally. It is also located at an ethical, social and personal level, which involves a transformation in how education is understood and how we understand ourselves and others. On multiple fronts, neoliberal reform can be erratic, unpredictable and patchy and it is not always clear when it has been resisted or when it has successfully co-opted its critics. It can be confusing and difficult to straddle these different directions and levels of reform and retain the sense of coherence that is necessary if neoliberalism is to make any sense at all as an analytic construct. Our suggestion is that conceptualising neoliberalism as a dispositif might offer an opportunity to connect more idiosyncratic practices of neoliberal reform to their wider 'family resemblances' (Peck et al., 2018). In addition, it can begin to visibilise the multiple ways in which educational discourse and practices sustain a neoliberal milieu whose edges are unclear. In this collection, we have brought together articles that spotlight the sometimes-unanticipated ramifications of diverse structural reforms and the canny adaptations of and resistances to neoliberal practice that challenge theorisation. We do not claim that the dispositif is a theoretical panacea or performs a 'methodological abracadabra' (Peck, 2013, p. 151), but it shifts the emphasis and sightlines so that we can trace the full dimensions of neoliberalisation. It directs our attention to multiple, layered points of cohesion and affinity that also serve to reveal points of incongruity and dissonance.

References

Bailey, P. (2015). Consultants of conduct: New actors, new knowledges and new 'resilient' subjectivities in the governing of the teacher. *Journal of Educational Administration and History* **47**, 3, 232–250.

Ball, S. J. (2003). 'Social justice in the head: Are we all libertarians now?' Social justice, identity and education. In C. Vincent (Ed.), *Social Justice, Education and Identity*, London: RoutledgeFalmer.

Ball, S.J. (2012). Performativity, commodification and commitment: An I-Spy guide to the neoliberal university. *British Journal of Educational Studies* **60**, 1, 17–28.

Ball, S.J. (2016). Subjectivity as a site of struggle: Refusing neoliberalism? *British Journal of Sociology of Education* 37, 8, 1129–1146.

Ball, S.J. (2017). *The Education Debate*. Bristol: The Policy Press.

Ball, S. J. (2018) The tragedy of state education in England: Reluctance, compromise and muddle— a system in disarray, *Journal of the British Academy*, 6, 207–238.

Barnett, C. (2005). The consolation of neoliberalism. *Geoforum* **36**, 1, 7–12.

Bowe, R., Ball, S.J. and Gewirtz, S. (1994). 'Parental Choice', Consumption and social theory: The operation of micro-markets in education. *British Journal of Educational Studies* **42**, 1, 38–52.

Bradbury, A. (2019). Making little neo-liberals: The production of ideal child/learner subjectivities in primary school through choice, self-improvement and 'growth mindsets'. *Power and Education* **11**, 3, 309–326.

Brenner, N., Peck, J. and Theodore, N. (2010). Variegated neoliberalization: Geographies, modalities, pathways. *Global Networks* **10**, 2,182–222.

Callison, W. and Manfredi, Z. (Eds.) (2020). *Mutant Neoliberalism: Market Rule and Political Rupture*. New York: Forham University Press.

Codd, J. (2005). Teachers as 'managed professionals' in the global education industry: The New Zealand experience, *Educational Review* **57**, 2, 193–206.

Collier, S.J. (2012). Neoliberalism as big Leviathan, or...? A response to Wacquant and Hilgers. *Social Anthropology* **20**, 2, 186–195.

Cotoi, C. (2011). Neoliberalism: A Foucauldian perspective. *International Review of Social Research* **1**, 2, 109–124.

Dean M. (2012). Free economy, strong state. In D. Cahill, L. Edwards and F. Stilwell (Eds.), *Neoliberalism: Beyond the Free Market* (pp. 69–89). Cheltenham: Edward Elgar.

Foucault, M. (1980). The confession of the flesh. In C. Gordon (Ed.), *Power/Knowledge: Selected Interviews and Other Writings 1972-1977 by Michel Foucault* (pp. 194–228). Sussex: The Harvester Press.

Foucault, M. (1990). Practicing criticism. In L.D. Kritzman (Ed.), *Michel Foucault: Politics, Philosophy, Culture: Interviews and Other Writings* (pp. 152–156) *1977–1984*. London: Routledge.

Foucault, M. (2010). *The Birth of Biopolitics: Lectures at the College de France 1978–1979*. Basingstoke: Palgrave Macmillan.

Fuller, K. and Stevenson, H. (2019). Global Education Reform: understanding the movement. *Educational Review* **71**, 1, 1–4.

Gewirtz, S., Ball, S. J. and Bowe, R. (1995). *Markets, Choice and Equity*. Milton Keynes: Open University Press.

Gewirtz, S. and Ball, S. (2000) From 'Welfarism' to 'New Managerialism': Shifting discourses of school headship in the education marketplace. *Discourse: Studies in the Cultural Politics of Education* **21**, 3, 253–268.

Gewirtz, S., Mahony, P., Hextall, I. and Cribb, A. (Eds.) (2009). *Changing Teacher Professionalism: International Trends, Challenges and Ways Forward*. London: Routledge.

Gunter, H.M. (2011) Introduction: Contested educational reform. In H.M. Gunter (Ed.), *The State and Education Policy: The Academies Programme* (pp. 1–18). London: Continuum.

Hall, S. (2003). New Labour's double shuffle. *Soundings* **24**, 10–24.

Hayek, F.A. (1944). *The Road to Serfdom*. Abingdon: Routledge.

Jeffrey, B. and Woods, P. (1998). Testing Teachers: The Effect of School Inspections on Primary Teachers. London: Routledge.

Jessop, B. (2004). New Labour's doppelte Kehrtwende: Anmerkungen zu Stuart Hall und eine alternative Perspektiv zu New Labour. *Das Argument* **256**, 494–504.

Jessop, B. (2016). *The State: Past, Present, Future*. Cambridge: Polity Press.

Jessop, B. (2018) Neoliberalization, uneven development, and Brexit: further reflections on the organic crisis of the British state and society. *European Planning Studies* **26**, 9, 1728–1746.

Jones, B.M.A. (2021). *Educating the Neoliberal Whole Child: A Genealogical Approach*. London: Routledge.

Lingard, B. (2010). Policy borrowing, policy learning: Testing times in Australian schooling. *Critical Studies in Education* **51**, 2, 129–147.

Lingard, B. and Sellar, S. (2013). 'Catalyst data': Perverse systemic effects of audit and accountability in Australian schooling. *Journal of Education Policy* 28, 5, 634–656.

Lynch, K. (2014). New managerialism: The impact on education. *Concept* **5**, 3, 1. Available at: http://concept.lib.ed.ac.uk/article/view/2421.

Olssen, M. (2009). *Toward a Global Thin Community: Nietzsche, Foucault and the Cosmopolitan Commitment*. Boulder, CO: Paradigm.

Olmedo, A. and Wilkins, A. (2017). Governing through parents: A genealogical enquiry of education policy and the construction of neoliberal subjectivities in England. *Discourse: Studies in the Cultural Politics of Education* **38**, 4, 573–589.

Ong, A. (2007). Neoliberalism as a mobile technology. *Transactions of the Institute of British Geographers* **32**, 1, 3–8.

Peck, J. (2010) Zombie neoliberalism and the ambidextrous state. *Theoretical Criminology* **14**, 1, 104–110.

Peck, J. (2013). Explaining (with) neoliberalism. *Territory, Politics, Governance* **1**, 2, 132–157.

Peck, J. and Tickell, A.T. (2002). Neoliberalizing space. *Antipode* **34**, 3, 380–404.

Peck, J., Brenner, N. and Theodore, N. (2009). Postneoliberalism and its malcontents. *Antipode* **41**, S1, 94–116.

Peck, J., Brenner, N. and Theodore, N. (2018). Actually existing neoliberalism. In D. Cahill, M. Cooper, M. Konings and D. Primrose (Eds.), *The SAGE Handbook of Neoliberalism* (pp. 3–15). US: Sage Publications Ltd.

Peters, M. (2001). Education, enterprise culture and the entrepreneurial self: A Foucauldian perspective. *Journal of Educational Enquiry* **2**, 2, 58–71.

Robertson, R. (1995). Glocalization: Time-space and Homogeneity- Heterogeneity. In M. Feathersone, S. Lash, & R. Robertson (Eds.), *Global Modernities*. London: Sage.

Rowe, E. and Lubienski, C. (2017). Shopping for schooling or shopping for peers: Public schools and catchment area segregation. *Journal of Education Policy* **32**, 3, 340–356.

Saad-Filho, A. (2020). Covid and the end of neoliberalism. *Critical Sociology* **46,** 4–5, 477–485.

Sahlberg, P. Global educational reform movement is here. Available at: https://pasisahlberg.com/global-educational-reform-movement-is-here

Sellar, S. and Lingard, B. (2014). The OECD and the expansion of PISA: New global modes of governance in education. *British Educational Research Journal* **40**, 6, 917–936.

Spohrer, K., Stahl, G. and Bowers-Brown, T. (2018). Constituting neoliberal subjects? 'Aspiration' as technology of government in UK policy discourse. *Journal of Education Policy* **33**, 3, 327–342.

Tan, C. (2019). PISA and education reform in Shanghai. *Critical Studies in Education* **60**, 3, 391–406.

Thorsen, D.E. and Lie, A. (2006). What is neoliberalism? Department of Political Science: University of Oslo Retrieved June, 2020 from http://folk.uio.no/daget/What%20is%20Neo-Liberalism%20FINAL.pdf

Valenzuela, J.P. Bellei, C. and de los Ríos, D. (2014). Socioeconomic school segregation in a market-oriented educational system. The case of Chile, *Journal of Education Policy*, vol. 29, 1, 217–241.

Venugopal, R. (2015). Neoliberalism as concept. *Economy and Society* **44**, 2, 165–187.

Whitty, G. and Power, S. (2000). Marketization and privatization in mass education systems. *International Journal of Educational Development* **20**, 93–107.

Wilkins, A. (2010) Citizens and/or consumers: mutations in the construction of concepts and practices of school choice. *Journal of Education Policy* **25**, 2, 171–189.

Wilkinson, G. (2006). Commercial breaks: An overview of corporate opportunities for commercializing education in US and English schools. *London Review of Education* **4**, 3, 253–269.

Wu, X. (2014). *School Choice in China: A Different Tale?* London: Routledge.

Explaining (with) Neoliberalism

JAMIE PECK

ABSTRACT The paper takes the form of a reflection on the explanatory status of neoliberalism, before and since the global crisis of 2008. Prior to the crisis, political-economic conceptions of neoliberalism as a hegemonic grid and as a relatively robust regime of state-facilitated market rule were being received with growing skepticism by some poststructural critics, while some ethnographers found the accompanying conceptual tools rather too blunt for their methodological purposes. The fact, however, that the global crisis—far from marking an inauspicious end to the regime of market rule—seems to have brought about something like a redoubling of its intensity and reach has prompted a reconsideration, in some quarters, of the explanatory and political status of neoliberalism. This, in turn, has opened up some new avenues of dialog between structural and poststructural treatments of neoliberalism, and between ethnographic and political-economic approaches, while at the same time highlighting a series of continuing tensions, both epistemological and ontological. The paper provides a critical commentary on this emerging terrain.

EXTRACTO Este artículo sirve de reflexión sobre el estado explicativo del neoliberalismo, antes y desde la crisis global de 2008. Antes de la crisis, los conceptos político-económicos del neoliberalismo, en forma de un entramado hegemónico y un régimen relativamente sólido de la ley del mercado facilitada por el Estado, eran recibidos con un creciente escepticismo por parte de algunos críticos postestructuralistas, mientras que algunos etnógrafos consideraban que las herramientas conceptuales complementarias no eran lo suficientemente precisas para sus objetivos metodológicos. Sin embargo, la crisis global—lejos de marcar un final desfavorable al régimen de la Ley del Mercado—parece haber causado un aumento en su intensidad y alcance, lo que ha llevado a reconsiderar en algunos círculos la explicación y el estado político del neoliberalismo. Esto, a su vez, ha abierto nuevas vías de diálogo entre los tratamientos estructurales y postestructurales del neoliberalismo, y entre los planteamientos etnográficos y político-económicos, resaltando al mismo tiempo una serie de tensiones continuas, tanto epistemológicas como ontológicas. Este artículo es una observación crítica sobre este terreno emergente.

摘要 本文反思新自由主义于2008年全球危机之前及之后的解释状态。在危机之前，政治经济学将新自由主义概念化为一种霸权网络，以及一个由国家促进的市场规则所构成的相对稳健之制度，但此一概念亦逐渐伴随着部分后结构批评的质疑，而民族志研究者亦发现，其所附带的概念化工具，对于达到他们的方法论目的而言显得过于拙钝。但与市场规则制度的终结相反的是，此一全球危机事实上似乎再次强化了市场规则的强度与广度，因而在一些地方促发了对于新自由主义的解释及政治状态的重新考量。此一趋势因而开创了结构主义与后结构主义新自由主义取径之间、以及民族志与政治经济学取径之间的崭新对话途径，却也同时突显了认识论与本体论层面一系列持续存在的紧张关系。本文便针对此一发展中的领域提出批判性的评论。

RÉSUMÉ Cet article constitue une réflexion du statut explicatif du néolibéralisme avant et après la crise mondiale de 2008. Avant la crise, certains critiques post-structuraux considéraient avec un scepticisme croissant des notions politico-économiques du néolibéralisme comme un réseau hégémonique et un régime relativement solide de l'économie de marché d'État, tandis que des ethnographes considéraient les outils qui les accompagnaient plutôt peu tranchants quant à leurs fins méthodologiques. Cependant, le fait que la crise mondiale—loin de mettre une fin de mauvaise augure à l'économie de marché—semble nécessiter que l'on redouble, plus ou moins, son intensité et sa portée a provoqué un réexamen dans certains milieux du statut explicatif et politique du néo-libéralisme. À son tour, cela a ouvert de nouvelles pistes de dialogue entre les traitements structuraux et post-structuraux du néolibéralisme, et entre les façons ethnographiques et politico-économiques, tout en soulignant également une série de tensions à la fois épistémologique et ontologique. L'article fournit une analyse critique de ce débat naissant.

INTRODUCTION: DEFLATING NEOLIBERALISM?

Neoliberalism has always been an unloved, rascal concept, mainly deployed with pejorative intent, yet at the same time apparently increasingly promiscuous in application. For some, it is the spider at the center of the hegemonic web that is worldwide market rule. For others, it is a bloated, jumbo concept of little utility, or worse, a cover for crudely deterministic claims tantamount to conspiracy theorizing or closet structuralism. Poststructuralist critics, even those that use the term, are wont to argue with some justification that the concept of neoliberalism is too often 'inflated' or 'overblown' (COLLIER, 2012; DEAN, 2012), and that it is frequently deployed in a manner that less than convincingly 'accelerates', in explanatory terms, from specific circumstances to large claims (LATOUR, 2007). The advent, successively, of the Wall Street crash, the Great recession, and the age of austerity have amongst their many other consequences thrown the explanatory chips into the air once again. These events manifestly did not mark the end of neoliberalism, as a contradictory regime of market-centric rule, and neither have they resulted in the retirement of the associated, still-emergent concept, which has barely reached middle age on many counts. Premature announcements of the death of neoliberalism, in the thick of the financial crisis, proved to be variously wishful and deceitful, though the crypto-regulationist contention that neoliberalism was passing into its zombie phase—spasmodically lurching in roughly the same direction, anti-socially pursuing many of the same warm-blooded targets, but largely dead from the neck up, as a program of intellectual and moral leadership (PECK, 2009)—seems to have retained a certain morbid currency.

In the political-economic twilight world that has been taking shape 'after' the crisis, it appears that neoliberalism—both as a political-economic-cultural phenomenon, and as an explanatory concept—has not gone away, but neither does it remain what it was. The sobering failure, to date anyway, of postneoliberal 'alternatives' to gain much meaningful traction, either extra-locally or in mainstream discourse, has meant that neoliberalism appears to have scored a most audacious (yet at the same time hollow) victory. It now sits as a lonely occupant of an ideological vacuum largely of its own making. In this afterlife, the arch-advocates of market reform in the global power centers may sound somewhat more circumspect, their rhetorical hubris, intellectual cant, and technocratic self-assurance having been tempered, but for the most part they remain in post. As CENTENO and COHEN (2012, p. 312) conclude, in their recent survey of the perplexing arc of market rule, '[t]he crisis and ensuing Great Recession may have shaken neoliberalism's supremacy, but it remains unchallenged by serious alternatives and continues to shape post-2008 policy.'

Many of these policies—hewing toward the familiar line of regulatory restraint, privatization, rolling tax cuts, and public-sector austerity—are in fact being pursued in an even more sternly necessitarian fashion than before. After doubling up, neoliberalism has doubled down. This unmistakable doggedness itself commands a certain kind of attention, even for those who might have preferred just to be rid of the concept. But in truth, explanations of neoliberalism have been evolving along with their mutating *explanandum*. Evidence of what looks like an ideological resurgence of a brusquely renovated version of neoliberalism, coupled with the roughly simultaneous arrival of probing intellectual histories that have leavened the old conspiracy theories with some new conspiracy facts (see MIROWSKI and PLEHWE, 2009; JONES, 2012), has led some to contemplate a grudging recuperation of the concept. More skeptical than most, perhaps, of 'leftist Don Quixotes tilting at ideological windmills', Dean's perceptive tour of the post-crisis horizon reaches the conclusion that neoliberalism must now be correctly seen as 'a militant thought collective, many of whose innovations and ideas have become embedded in the techniques of various regimes of national and international government over the last thirty years' (2012, p. 69, 86).

Yet there remains a certain unease about the explanatory status of the concept of neoliberalism, perhaps amplified by what for most critics is an essentially unwanted, continued relevance. As Hall has reflected,

> The term 'neo-liberalism' is not a satisfactory one ... Intellectual critics say the term lumps together too many things to merit a single identity; it is reductive, sacrificing attention to internal complexities and geo-historical specificity. I sympathize with this critique. However, I think there are enough common features to warrant giving it a provisional conceptual identity, provided this is understood as a first approximation. Even Marx argued that analysis yields understanding at different levels of abstraction and critical thought often begins with a 'chaotic' abstraction; though we then need to add 'further determinations' in order to 'reproduce the concrete in thought'. I would also argue that naming neo-liberalism is politically necessary to give the resistance to its onward march content, focus and a cutting edge. (2011, p. 706)

The fact that the meaning, and in some quarters the very existence, of neoliberalism continues to be debated, several decades after its ascendancy as a (euphemistically styled) governmental project, and almost as long after the term's lagged emergence as a social-scientific signifier, must be telling us something.

Is neoliberalism, as more 'inflationist' accounts tend to have it, an expansive and adaptable ideological project, jointly constituted with prevailing forms of financialized capitalism, a project that variously frames, legitimates, and necessitates a paradigmatic package of policies? (Here, neoliberalism represents a codification of the prevailing rules of the globalizing-capitalist game.) Or does it designate but one strand of a diffuse complex of individualized post-social governmentalities, a never more than small-n, flexible assemblage of technologies, routines, and modes of conduct, as more 'deflationist' and particularized analyses are more inclined to argue? (Here, neoliberalism is but one transformative pulse among many, and not necessarily the dominant one.) Does it really define the principal ideological power grid of the contemporary world, or is its invocation a manifestation of post-Keynesian yearning, a consolatory figment of the left-structuralist imagination? These are not trivial, or merely semantic, questions. If neoliberalism really has risen again, following its near-death experience the Wall Street crash of 2008, and if its lingering aftermath has yet to give rise to a recognizable 'post-neoliberal' successor, what is to be made of the austere netherworld that the increasingly normalized crisis has apparently wrought? What (renovated) conceptions of neoliberalism might be put to work in such circumstances? And *how* might they be put to work?

In pursuit of these questions, the paper proceeds in four steps. First, some of the conditions of 'actually *still* existing' neoliberalism, in this post-crisis afterlife, are briefly examined. Next, by way of a retro-methodological reflection on the politics of Thatcherism, and contending accounts of those politics then and now, some critical questions are raised about 'catch-all' explanatory maneuvers, even under conditions of neoliberal hegemony. Third, moving toward the definition of more positive methodological (pro) positions, an argument is sketched for situating processes of neoliberalization within 'discrepant' formations—which, it is suggested, more closely resemble their normal, rather than exceptional, conditions of existence. A fourth section takes this a step further, proposing that neoliberalism, whether or not it is understood to be hegemonic, must be theorized amongst its others—that is, amongst others *of* neoliberalism that are not only elsewhere and 'out there', but also right here, side by side in mongrel forms of market rule, and amongst others *to* neoliberalism, its various competitors, would-be successors, and alternatives. This entails some rethinking of neoliberalism 'inside/out', with particular implications for the conduct of (critical) urban and regional studies, both methodologically and politically (cf. PECK *et al.,* forthcoming). Finally, the paper is concluded with a comment on the longing to get over neoliberalism, which might be considered to be a scholarly as well as social condition in these twilight times.

NEOLIBERALISM: UNDEAD

One some counts, it lasted barely six months. That was the length of the ideological service interruption experienced in the global power centers, when the Wall Street crash of 2008 shorted out some of the primary circuits of financialized capitalism. For a while, this temporary power failure was deeply disorienting, not least for those corporate, financial, and media elites whose actions were amongst the proximate causes of the overload. There followed a brief fling, in mainstream circles, with alternative rationalities, ruses, and remedies, as even Keynes was exhumed, if not entirely rehabilitated, as a justification for once again saving capitalism from the capitalists (see PECK *et al.,* 2010; BLYTH, 2013). The 'system' duly saved, almost entirely at public expense and with hardly any strings attached, it was not long before business was being conducted almost as usual in the epicenters of the crisis in Washington, New York, and London. The moment of ideological free-fall, which had begun in the Fall of 2008, quickly passed into a normalized crisis, managed in the barely reformed terms of a neoliberal *resettlement.* By the time of the London G20 summit in April 2009, as the *Guardian*'s LARRY ELLIOT (2011, p. 22) later observed, the 'flirtation with alternative thinking was over', global elites having 'returned to the pre-crisis mindset with remarkable speed'. Never mind that (even) internal assessments would not only reveal, but effectively *confess to,* debilitating levels of 'groupthink' and 'intellectual capture' in multilateral agencies like the International Monetary Fund (see IEO-IMF, 2011), very little had changed.

What might be incautiously labeled 'the system' was brazenly rebooted with more or less the same ideological and managerial software, complete with most of the bugs that had caused the breakdown in the first place. And even in the midst of neoliberalism's unlikely reincarnation, there were ominous signs that its post-crisis mutations might be yet more anti-social than their predecessors, imposing the rule of markets in more intensely disciplinarian ways, and substituting still more coercive and necessitarian strategies for the politics of consent and compromise. A new normal was taking shape, as the costs of restructuring and insecurity were visited (once again) on the poor and the vulnerable, as austerity programming, entitlement cutbacks, and radical reforms of the public sector were once again raised to the status of non-negotiable imperatives. The watchwords in the western economies at the center of the crisis have since been growth restoration, deficit reduction, and budgetary restraint, but macroeconomic conditions have remained dangerously sluggish on both sides of the Atlantic.

The period of panic-induced 'stimulus' having apparently passed, both Europe and the USA have been resorting to internally administered forms of structural adjustment amid growing evidence that this is merely perpetuating the anemic and faltering conditions of 'recovery'. In the USA, budget debates in Washington are more and more resonant of the End Times, stalemated between anti-tax nihilism on one side and concession bargaining on the other, while fiscal discipline is 'devolved' downward onto cities and states (PECK, 2012). Hovering on the brink of a currency crisis, Europe has been imposing long-term austerity measures on the lagging economies of the Mediterranean, while tightening public-spending spigots just about everywhere else. In the process, the financial crisis seems to be 'transforming the European Union overnight', as KALB (2012, p. 318) has caustically put it, 'from a self-declared civic alternative for US-style capitalism into a transnational debt collection agency'.

Widespread public opposition to post-crisis austerity measures and cuts to social programs has brought hundreds of thousands onto the streets of European cities, perhaps most conspicuously in the *indignados* protests in Spain. Initially, the grassroots response in the USA could hardly have been more different, as the tea-party movement's fiscal fundamentalists rallied to the noble cause of tax cuts and deregulation, demanding even less government, not more. But the subsequent electoral resurgence of the Republican Party,[1] coupled with the timidity-cum-paralysis that gripped the first-term Obama Administration, would promptly generate gyrations and counter-movements of its own. The US Republicans seem to have overplayed their hand, suffering a humbling defeat in the 2012 Presidential elections, while retaining belligerent control of Congress, and caught between the unruly spirits of the tea-party caucus and the unforgiving arithmetic of a practically stalled legislative process. The Democrats, on the other hand, have the hollow victory of (narrow) electoral advantage in the absence of a governing program. Meanwhile, the proudly leaderless Occupy movement funneled dissent toward systemic forms of socioeconomic inequality and the predatory behavior of financial, corporate, and governing elites, helping to stimulate a belated but still-inconclusive public dialog around a wide array of alternatives. (The next steps, however, remain unclear.) Tens of thousands marched against public-sector cuts and union busting in Wisconsin. The incomplete revolutions across the Arab world might be considered more-or-less distant precursors to these social mobilizations, although their political consequences are clearly far from straightforwardly additive—or for that matter predictable. Something similar might be said about the now-daily uprisings against dispossession and exploitation across China. Perhaps these really do amount to a 'global mass upheaval in fragments' (KALB, 2012, p. 318), but viewed as a potentially anti-systemic movement, the whole has yet to exceed the sum of the parts. As Davis has reflected on the turbulent protest politics of 2011:

> As the fates of previous journées révolutionnaires warn us, spring is the shortest of seasons, especially when the communards fight in the name of a 'different world' for which they have no real blueprint or even idealized image [...] But perhaps that will come later. For the moment, the survival of the new social movements—the occupiers, the indignados, the small European anti-capitalist parties and the Arab new left—demands that they sink deeper roots in mass resistance to the global economic

> catastrophe, which in turn presupposes—let's be honest—that the current temper for 'horizontality' can eventually accommodate enough disciplined 'verticality' to debate and enact organizing strategies. It's a frighteningly long road just to reach the starting points of earlier attempts to build a new world. But a new generation has at least bravely initiated the journey. (2011, p. 5)

Meanwhile, many of the same hands remain on the levers of power; indeed, the grip may in some ways be even tighter. In distributional terms, neoliberal reformers have largely prevailed in the initial stages of their freshly hatched plans for social-state retrenchment and enforced austerity. And what is austerity, BLYTH (2013) asks, if not a program of large-scale regressive redistribution? Much of the opposition is understandably defensive—more a politics of protest than a counter-paradigm in the making—which may be sharply focused in its critical opposition to neoliberalism but remains diffuse and inchoate when it comes to alternatives. There is cold comfort, moreover, in the massive imbalances in the global economy, where desperate efforts to maintain export-led growth across the BRIC (Brazil, Russia, India, China) economies remain precariously reliant on indebtedness and productive hollowing out across the world's final markets, and where endemic problems of social and ecological unsustainability remain largely unaddressed. Meanwhile, the late-neoliberal 'freedoms' conferred on corporations and financial speculators continue to be actively defended as the only legitimate (or practical) means of growth restoration by national governments in Washington, London, and elsewhere. In the name of markets, corporate monopolization continues to deepen …

These highly asymmetrical conditions, of hegemonic rearmament on the one hand and inchoate resistance on the other, seem to broadly affirm those first readings of the initial fallout of the Wall Street crash and the Great Recession, that this conjuncture was not immediately propitious for ideological regime change—for all the evident culpability of the bankers and (de)regulators. Rather than an imminent, postneoliberal turn to the left and to renewed social-statism, the crisis seemed set to play into the hands of established corporate, financial, and political interests, setting the stage for a host of reactionary responses and presentational makeovers (see BOND, 2009; PECK *et al.,* 2010). Second readings may have been somewhat more circumspect, though the optimism of the progressive intellect remains distinctly tempered. When Colin CROUCH (2011, p. 179) rhetorically asks, 'what remains of neoliberalism after the financial crisis', his soberly delivered answer is 'virtually everything'. While the neoliberal model has been undeniably tarnished, the social structure on which the program was predicated, Crouch maintains, is still largely intact (in marked contrast, it should be noted, to the broadly *simultaneous* crises of Keynesianism, a generation ago, as a governing ideological project, as a dominant mode of economic science, and as an institutionalized social contract). Crouch's worldly conclusion, from what is a broadly transatlantic vantage point, is that the realistic scope for (moderately) progressive politics hardly exceeds the goal of moderating the most egregious excesses of the entrenched neoliberal nexus of corporate, financial, and market power. Some reboot of the third way is, realistically, what is on offer here.

Alternatively (quite literally, one might say), Emir Sader's view from Latin America, while no less worldly in its own way, sees the potential for incrementally opening up a series of pragmatically postneoliberal pathways, where these can be constructed on the foundations of 'transitional' social settlements, such as those that have been developing in Brazil. For SADER (2011, p. 104), 'grasp[ing] the reality of the existing political landscape' means focusing strategically on 'where the right is located and the dangers it poses', rather than 'confus[ing] a moderate, contradictory ally [such as the Brazilian Workers' Party] with the real enemy'. Correspondingly, he maintains that the challenge for a renewed, broad left is to pursue struggles that are 'anti-neoliberal in the sense of combatting all forms of submission to the market [but also] post-neoliberal in [promoting] alternatives centered on the public sphere'; and that are strategically targeted on a 'refounding of the state' (SADER, 2011, pp. 105, 132). Reclaiming the state, however, remains a controversial strategy in many left circles, where more energy seems to be focused on grassroots and 'horizontalist' efforts, usually outside (and antagonistic to) formal structures (see WAINWRIGHT, 2003; HARVEY, 2012).

If there is a familiar ring to post-crisis restatements of the nefarious logic of neoliberalism, it must be acknowledged that the dialog around alternatives also seems to be stuck in the same grooves. More than postneoliberal pipedreams, these must confront the fact that alternative designs (whether reformist or radical, pragmatic or utopian) must in some way or other gain traction on the inhospitable terrain of the now. Yet more prosaically, they must also confront—from what at this remove looks more and more like a Wall Street *correction*, rather than a serious ideological rupture—the possibility that neoliberalism may not, in fact, meet its ultimate end by disappearing into an apocalyptic black hole of its own construction. Neoliberalism's rude return from what was widely interpreted, for a time anyway, as a terminal event—a very public financial crisis, striking at its central nervous system—represents a sobering lesson about both the dogged persistence of market rule and the challenges of effecting various kinds of progressive turn. Perhaps neoliberal policy preferences are now just too deeply embedded in the dominant circuits of corporate, financial, and political power? Perhaps the array of progressive alternatives is destined to remain, in the short- to medium-term at least, too disparate and isolated, advocated by social forces generally short on political leverage, strategic capacity, and institutional resources? Recurring questions such as these, it must be said, are finding few compelling answers.

Meanwhile, many are interpreting these dispiriting conditions as a lurch backwards to a different kind of neoliberal future. In countries like the USA and the UK, where some may have thought they had seen the worst of neoliberalism's excesses, attacks on the social state are being pursued with new-found fervor. A US Republican Party that moved sharply to the neoliberal right during the Reagan years has continued to hurtle in this direction, first through the Gingrich realignment of the 1990s and then further still under the influence of the tea party/Fox News/Grover Norquist axis. President Obama may have raised a laugh, at the Democratic Convention, by parodying the Republicans' anti-tax fundamentalism, though the Democrats' own forms of triangulated timidity on these questions—as measured in action, rather than merely in words—might also have prompted some self-satisfied smirks on the other side:

> Our friends at the Republican convention were more than happy to talk about everything they think is wrong with America, but they didn't have much to say about how they'd make it right. [A]ll they have to offer is the same prescription they've had for the last thirty years:
> Have a surplus? Try a tax cut.
> Deficit too high? Try another. (LAUGHTER)
> Feel a cold coming on? Take two tax cuts, roll back some regulations, and call us in the morning.[2] (APPLAUSE)

In Britain, where even third-way accretions of Blairite neoliberalism are being rolled back, the reserves of gallows humor may be running low. As JOHN HARRIS (2011, p. 29), a commentator for the *Guardian*, has forlornly asked, 'If you're old enough to remember the Thatcher years, you may have an answer to this question, but it's still worth asking: in living memory, have thousands of us on the left ever felt so bleak?'

WHAT THATCHER DID

'I blame Thatcher' was an almost reflexive retort on the British left in the 1980s, since passing into cliché status. Beyond its function as a mobilizing slogan, the phrase also performed explanatory work, of a kind. It pointed unambiguously, of course, to a root cause, personalizing and politicizing at the same time. By implication, it suggested a remedy for various ills that (at least in principle) was simple: remove Thatcher and then ... Whatever the depressing *explanandum* (the deindustrialization of northern Britain, management failure across the public services, the social breakdown of inner-city communities, or 'loadsamoney' loutishness in the South East of England), 'I blame Thatcher' could serve as a universally applicable and pithy explanans. However, setting aside for the moment the question of the proper positioning of Thatcherism in the long and geographically checkered history of transnational neoliberalization, its meaning and salience as a political-economic and cultural phenomenon divided even the most astute analysts of the time (JESSOP *et al.*, 1988; HALL and JACQUES, 1989; SKIDELSKY, 1989). Stuart Hall and Bob Jessop have since agreed that Thatcherite neoliberalism has been the dominant, if not defining, force in British politics since the 1970s, though they differ on the extent of its cultural hegemony (Hall characterizes Thatcherism as 'epochal', in that it established a new political stage; Jessop insists that British neoliberalism has been more unstable, less consensual), and they continue to disagree over the role of historical and external constraints on the effective availability of governing strategies, which Jessop emphasizes and Hall downplays (HALL, 2003; JESSOP, 2004). They also diverge on the question of whether the New Labour project of Blair and Brown represented an asymmetrical hybrid of neoliberalism and social democracy, in effect an attenuated form of Thatcher's 'full-blown' neoliberalism (HALL, 2003), or the contradictory consolidation of neoliberal accumulation strategies and ameliorative socio-institutional 'flanking', secured in conjunction with a deformed resurrection of Christian socialism (JESSOP, 2004). Even now, the question of what Thatcher did remains contested.

What does seem to be clear, however, is that neither she, nor her successors, were acting alone. Neoliberalization, even when it is dominant, never secures a monopoly. As a frontal project, it always exists amongst its others, usually antagonistically. So Thatcher forged a governing strategy across the fault lines of neoliberalism and traditional British Toryism and little-Englander anti-Europeanism; Blair reworked the interface between an inherited neoliberal settlement and social democracy or Christian socialism (take your pick), while separating from the labor movement; and Cameron's coalition since 2010 can be seen as a volatile cocktail of Blairism and Thatcherism, remixed in the context of weak leadership and even more deeply financialized times. Meanwhile, the institutions of the British welfare state (and its allies) did not disappear altogether, even if they have been relentlessly eroded and restructured for more than three decades now. Neoliberalism has evidently been much more than a sinewy presence here, but its shapes have kept shifting and it has never been the *only* occupant of the political stage.

As a result, although this may be analytically inconvenient, neoliberalism can only be found amongst its others, in a state of messy coexistence. Likewise, the contemporary cry, 'Neoliberalism did it', should never be taken at face value as an omnibus 'first cause' (TICKELL and PECK, 2003, p. 179; FERGUSON, 2010, p. 171), since it will always be found amongst other causes, not to say other culprits, while both its form and consequences can *only* be revealed in conjuncturally specific ways. 'Globalization' often performs this questionable role as first or primary cause in more orthodox analyses (cf. PIVEN, 1995, on 'globaloney'); there is no excuse for propagating parallel forms of 'neoliberaloney', as a kind of all-determining mega-cause, bluntly attributed. Establishing causality necessitates the *specific* consideration of cases, conjunctures, and contexts, no less in situations where neoliberalism is understood to be incipient or subordinate, as in some analyses of contemporary China (cf. NONONI, 2008; CHU and SO, 2010), than in those where it is considered to be dominant, normalized, or to occupy the leading position (cf. GAMBLE, 1988; HALL, 2011). The evocation of 'hybridity' in this context is more than a poststructuralist tic, but an indicator of the inescapably impure forms in which neoliberalizing tendencies are found.

Since neoliberalization is always an incomplete process (and frustrated yet frontal project), these circumstances of contradictory cohabitation represent the rule, rather than the exception. Chronically uneven spatial development, institutional polymorphism, and a landscape littered with policy failures, oppositional pushbacks, and stuttering forms of malregulation are all consequently par for neoliberalism's zigzagging course; incomplete or partial neoliberalization is not some way-station on the path to complete neoliberalism, so it represents a category error to evaluate neoliberalism against the yardstick of absolute market rule (BRENNER *et al.,* 2010). As a result, cities, regions, or countries must not be classified in the wrongheaded terms of 'degrees' of neoliberalization, as if lined up on an historic (down?) escalator 'full' neoliberalism. Neoliberalism may be present in this or that regional formation. It may even be almost *omni*present. But it can only be present in conjuncturally hybrid forms. Statistically, there may be a good chance that 'neoliberalism did it', where this historically specific mode of market rule is hegemonic or dominant, but the contextual circumstances of such acts are more than background scenery, since neoliberalism is never found alone and it never acts alone. Even hegemonies, Stuart Hall reminds us, are incomplete and contradictory.

> [I]s neo-liberalism hegemonic? Hegemony is a tricky concept and provokes muddled thinking. No project achieves a position of permanent 'hegemony'. It is a process, not a state of being. No victories are final. Hegemony has constantly to be 'worked on', maintained, renewed and revised. Excluded social forces, whose consent has not been won, whose interests have not been taken into account, form the basis of counter-movements, resistance, alternative strategies and visions ... and the struggle over a hegemonic system starts anew. They constitute what Raymond Williams called 'the emergent'—and the reason why history is never closed but maintains an open horizon towards the future ... Neo-liberalism is in crisis. But it keeps driving on. However, in ambition, depth, degree of break with the past, variety of sites being colonized, impact on common sense and everyday behaviour, restructuring of the social architecture, neo-liberalism does constitute a hegemonic project. (HALL, 2011, pp. 727–728)

The manner in which neoliberalism has kept 'driving on', at least so far, is in this respect never preordained. And in real-time analyses of urban and regional restructuring, an (analytical) context in which 'neoliberalism' is now regularly invoked—clearly *too regularly* for some—if and how *particular* events, actions or movements are connected to the contradictory reproduction of neoliberal hegemony must always be an empirical and political question. The establishment of straight-line connections to a singular global Neoliberalism represent more than analytical shortcuts, in this context; they also misrepresent the constructed and contradictory nature of neoliberalization as a transformative process.

Even those skeptical of the claim that neoliberalism represents a globally hegemonic 'common sense' (cf. HARVEY, 2005), can perhaps accept the proposition that a 'common thread' (HALL, 2003, p. 22) has been identifiable for some time, across a whole raft of political-economic, social, and cultural (trans)formations. This would include the somewhat cumulative ideological/institutional realignments of the Thatcher–Blair–Cameron, Reagan–Clinton–Bush–Obama, or the Deng–Jiang–Hu kind, in which the strategies of each successor borrow selectively from and react selectively against those before them; but it would also extend to the relational interpenetration of governing logics and routines, across sites and territories, through such means as structural adjustment, normative isomorphism, and competitive discipline, across transnational space. Whether one leans toward heavily qualified readings of neoliberalism-as-contextualized exception, or bolder notions of neoliberalization-as-common-process, some of these lines of connection and 'cross-formation' are widely recognized. Analytically, however, the next steps can be quite divisive.

In fact, it is almost as if there is a fork in the road, between those who would take a political-economic or macroinstitutionalist path and those pursuing more particularized approaches, often in a poststructuralist and/or ethnographic vein (with the latter being *different* paths to the usually more-provisional recognition of neoliberal influences or inflections in particular or localized settings). The former are inclined to emphasize extra-local disciplines and (always) 'out there' forces, expressed through structurally unequal power relations; the latter will tend to find neoliberalism, if at all, as just one of many pulses, in more frail and provisional forms, in closely observed 'in here' situations. For the former, neoliberalism possesses a structural and more-than-the-sum-of-its-parts quality, even as attention is duly paid to 'the diversity of "actually existing" neoliberalisms, and why and how the diffuse system of power that lends them a certain unity has managed to implant itself with such apparent success in such a wide range of circumstances [across] both neoliberalism and its counter-movements' (GLEDHILL, 2004, p. 336; see also BRENNER and THEODORE, 2002; SAAD-FILHO and JOHNSTON, 2005). For the latter, pertinent questions are more reflexively defined, oftentimes self-consciously *against* those 'paradigms that envision neoliberalism as a coherent, unitary force or treat it as a monolith acting upon the world [and] the project of identifying neoliberalism's unifying strands across disparate contexts', and in favor of difference-finding approaches that foreground the 'contingent, contradictory, and unstable character of neoliberal processes, examining historically and geographically contextualized situations through grounded studies of concrete places, people, and institutions' (TRETJAK and ABRELL, 2011, p. 29; see also ONG, 2006; KINGFISHER and MASKOVSKY, 2008a).

There are sound reasons to take such poststructuralist injunctions seriously, just as (for different but in some cases overlapping reasons) there is an indispensible role for investigations in various ethnographic registers. Despite more than a decade of efforts to develop constructive dialogs between these more context-rich, agent-centered, and difference-finding approaches on the one hand, and political-economic or macroinstitutional approaches on the other (see LARNER, 2003; PECK, 2004), and notwithstanding some recent attempts to rethink the terms and terminology of such engagements (see BRENNER *et al.,* 2010; DEAN, 2012; FAIRBANKS, 2012), for various reasons this division has been a recurring motif. Some prefer to tune out of what has been characterized as '[the] "normal science" for economic geography—studies of neoliberal this and that' (GIBSON-GRAHAM, 2008, p. 620); others have observed that a neoliberal-centric position can inadvertently reproduce a narrowed analytical and political gaze (LEITNER *et al.,*

2007a). For a range reasons, though, there is a now a rather large catalog of studies of neoliberal this and that, loosely programmatic in character, which in turn are connected to various theoretical understandings of neoliberalism and neoliberalization, themselves also (and still) evolving.

If there is an analytical fault line here, this is exposed when more nuanced and contingent accounts come *at the expense of* an appreciation of the commonalities and connections across ('local') neoliberalisms; if they are positioned at an ironic distance from the more-than-local ideational and ideological constitution of neoliberalism *qua* hegemonic formation; or if they are detached from the normative networks, policy frames, and power relations that recursively secure the parameters for (or limits on) local or national action. There is, after all, surely little dispute, amongst critical analysts, that neoliberalism remains a 'thwarted totalization' (KINGFISHER and MASKOVSKY, 2008b, p. 118), and that the vagaries of neoliberal policy depart routinely and raggedly from the pristine vision of neoliberal ideology (FERGUSON, 2010, p. 171).[3] Indeed, KINGFISHER and MASKOVSKY (2008a, p. 119) characterize their approach, constructively, not as the antithesis but the 'flipside' of GLEDHILL'S (2004) stated project of tracing connections and commonalities across different cultural formations, seeking to place these analytical traditions in conversation rather than merely in tension (see also FAIRBANKS, 2012). In other situations, however, this can flip over into more practiced ambivalence, invoking neoliberalism effectively as a foil, at arm's length and in scare quotes, where exceptionalist-particularist readings of small-n neoliberalism are set up as weakly contingent formulations of an under-specified other, in a field of unpatterned difference, *against* the (mis)conception of a 'uniform global condition of "Neoliberalism" writ large' (ONG, 2006, p. 14, 2007), sometimes concretized as American capitalism.

The comparative advantage of close-focus, experience-near, low-flying methods is their facility for finding and placing neoliberalism in muddy hybrids, in fraught and often frustrated forms of partial or distorted realization. They bring neoliberalism to earth, in all kinds of ways, both literally and metaphorically (see COLLIER, 2011; FAIRBANKS, 2012). Here, pulses and traces of neoliberalizing tendencies are deeply contextualized, often in quite idiosyncratic 'local' formations. On the other hand, such accounts typically have less to say about the (more macro and trans-local) context of this (more immediate and usually local) context. They are unable readily to address (and sometimes actually demur from) issues related to the spatial patterning and historical evolution of neoliberal strategies and fronts *across* cases and contexts; though they differ on the question of whether such macroanalytical work is a different-but-complementary exercise, or a worrisome structuralist hangover. Partly conceding this point, COLLIER quite reasonably counters that '[t]o say that [poststructuralist] approaches fail to grasp the "context of context" … or the "macro-spatial rules" that structure neoliberalisation processes' is only an argument against doing so in a rather tautological sense, since it restates 'the fact that a non-structural approach is a non-structural approach' (2012, p. 189; cf. BRENNER *et al.,* 2010). But if supposed islands of hybrid neoliberal practice exist, at least in part, in mutual relation to one another, and if the reproduction of neoliberalism as a more-than-local regime of rules, disciplines, and incentives occurs, at least in part, through 'out there' circuits, domains, and logics (such as competitive pressure, prescriptive policy modeling, and fiscal constraints), then a non-structural approach, for all its other virtues, will be missing something if it is *anti*-structural, either by commission or omission.

In this respect, while there is a great deal to be gained from deeply contextualized and methodologically skeptical investigations that purposefully set out to put neoliberalism in its place (amongst other forces, formations, dynamics, and tendencies), there is much to be lost if such analyses reflexively spurn more abstract and/or macro formulations. It is not sufficient to stereotype analyses of the recurring, structural forms of neoliberalization processes—their more-than-the-sum-of-the-parts and more-than-local qualities—as no more than another invocation of the Big Picture (à la LATOUR, 2007, p. 187), and to follow this with the deliberately flattening questions, 'in which movie theatre, in which art gallery is [this picture] *shown*? Through which optics is it *projected*?' Problematizing the issues of how local neoliberalizations articulate with one another, of how family resemblances connect hybrid formations, of how mid-level and higher abstractions can be generated and interrogated, and of how macro patternings emerge across multiple cases and conjunctures is not merely a matter of 'staging the totality', as Latour puts it, of preemptively positioning every 'local neoliberalism' in a preconceived box, enslaved to an unchanging Master Narrative. Rather, it is a matter of confronting the question of how, in practice, market hegemonies are being continuously remade through uneven spatial development (not instead of it), and of recognizing the ways in which all such local formations are jointly constituted, not only with distant others but also with formative networks (for example, of technocratic expertise and policy norms) and differently scaled relations (for example, of a fiscal or geopolitical nature). Methodologically, it is unhelpful to be 'voluntarily blind' (LATOUR, 2007, p. 190) to such cumulative, multi-locale rationalities and to the constitutive outsides of neoliberalization processes, or to pass them off as merely Big Picture fantasies.

Just as it is never adequate to characterize neoliberalism only in reference to its fanciful self-representation, it is also misleading to position supposed deviations and exceptions only in relation to some imagined, overbearing norm (of Neoliberalism as rigid and mechanically imposed Global Hegemon), the very existence of which is effectively denied. The fear seems to be that the incautious capitalization of the phenomenon might bring on a bout of stealth-structuralism, sweeping all and sundry in its omnipotent sway, so protection is sought in the methodological swaddling of hyper-contingency. In the process, self-consciously small-n treatments of neoliberalism tend to render their local objects of analysis into conceptual and political orphans, separated from all of their 'relatives'). Against such maneuvers, which are more likely to obfuscate the meaning and consequences of neoliberalism than they are effectively to *position* it, relative to actually existing variants and alternatives, process-based interpretations of neoliberalization seek to specify the *patterning* of contingencies across cases, with no expectation of imminent regulatory monopoly or incipient socioinstitutional convergence, just as they problematize uneven development itself as a (defining) characteristic of this process, not as a mere side-effect of 'blocked' liberalization. These approaches do not, however, presume that neoliberalism exists exclusively in 'out there', quasi-global settings, as if to play some sneaky neo-structuralist trump card. Rather, they propose, as a central methodological challenge, the problem of empirically connecting and dialectically relating 'in here' conditions, projects, struggles, and alternatives with 'out there' rule regimes, disciplinary pressures, competitive constraints, and so forth. Rather than floating offshore as a detached but all-determining superstructure, out-there neoliberalism is seen to be jointly constituted through all of the various in-heres, even as this more-than-local phenomenon can be shown to be disproportionately animated by certain centers of calculation and sites of conjunctural power. An additional aspect of this dialectical commitment, to *always* positioning the local, is an abiding skepticism concerning attempts detach or bracket off—for whatever reason—the in here from the out there.

As a restructuring paradigm and frontal ideological project with a global reach, neoliberalism cannot be separated from those extra-local domains that contribute to its reproduction, nor is it advisable to imply that neoliberalization is natural and normal in some places but an alien or aberrant presence in others. Neoliberalism is found, almost overwhelming empirical evidence now shows, in all manner of forms and formations, but it can *never* be found in a pristine state, implemented on a *tabula rasa* or social blank slate, in a fashion that is entirely unobstructed or unmediated. And there is no ideal type or institutional template against which hybrids can be singularly evaluated. The problematic of variegated neoliberalization (BRENNER *et al.*, 2010; PECK *et al.*, forthcoming)—while hardly a receipt, admittedly, for an easy methodological life—entails the relational analysis of hybrids amongst *other* hybrids. More like an ideological parasite, neoliberalism both occupies and draws energy from its various host organisms—bodies politic ranging from post-Soviet states to East Asian developmental regimes and European welfare states—but it cannot, ultimately, live entirely without or outside them. (So again, the out-there and the in-here are jointly constituted—pretty much inescapably.) Understanding the effects of such 'parasitical' infections and mutations must involve the diagnostic study of many patients, not just a few of the more (or less) susceptible to the deregulatory bug. This also necessitates an understanding of the 'ecological' conditions and preconditions (cf. JESSOP, 2000) that have enabled the emergence and spread of such viral forms, their favored sites of incubation, their swarming behavior, their modes of reproduction, and their various mutations.

NEOLIBERALISM IN DISCREPANT FORMATIONS

As a discrepant, contradictory, and shape-shifting presence, found in a wide range of political-economic settings, governance regimes, and social formations, neoliberalism will not be fixed. In some respects, it is more appropriate to define neoliberalism—or the process of neoliberalization—through its recurring contradictions and uneven realization than in reference to some presumed, transcendental essence (see PECK and ZHANG, forthcoming). At its contradictory heart, as an ongoing process of regulatory transformation, lies the discrepancy between the galvanizing utopian vision of freedom through the market, discursively channeling competitive forces that are far from imaginary, and the prosaic realities both of earthly governance and endemic governance failure. Hence the now well-understood gulf between neoliberalism as ideology, as a strong discourse of market progress, and the much less prepossessing array of actually existing neoliberalisms (BOURDIEU, 1998; BRENNER and THEODORE, 2002). In abstract terms, this gulf exists because the neoliberal worldview rests on the fundamentally mistaken understanding that it is possible somehow to 'liberate' markets from their various institutional moorings and social entanglements, to disembed and purify social life as (if) a projection of utilitarian rationality (POLANYI, 1944). In concrete terms, the gulf exists because neoliberal restructuring schemes, while often damagingly consequential, will always be incomplete. They are inescapably associated with negative externalities and with downstream consequences that prompt their own counter-flows, resistances, recalibrations, adjustments, alternative mobilizations, and occasional u-turns. And in their tendency to overreach and overflow (in the absence of a theoretical 'brake' on what are rolling programs of marketization, privatization, dispossession, deregulation, commodification …) will inadvertently prompt double-movement counteractions of various sorts. These counteractions, however, may be either regressive or progressive; and they may impede neoliberalization or enable its (nonlinear, adaptive) reproduction. In practice, the course of neoliberalization almost never describes a tidy arc from regulated to deregulated markets, or big government to smaller states, but is more likely to result in a plethora of gyrations across the terrains of social regulation.

The messiness of these revealed outcomes should not be naively taken as grounds for dispensing with theories of neoliberalization; on the contrary, it means that they are all the more necessary, and that they are necessarily contextual. But of course, *critical* theories of neoliberalization must not be confounded by what the neoliberal medicine doctors choose to write on their own bottles ('Miracle cure: shrinks the state, grows the economy, frees the people!'). Neoliberalization cannot be reduced to a unidirectional process of enacting a master plan cooked up by Hayek and friends at their mountain resort in Mont Pelerin, deviations from which stand as variants or refutations of 'neoliberal theory'. Neither should it be expected that processes of neoliberalization are working inexorably toward the 'destination' of a particular institutional formation, or that they express an incipiently coherent institutional logic (cf. WACQUANT, 2012). Rather, the dynamic mapping of inescapably mongrel formations and mutative flows —that is, tracing the uneven spatial development of neoliberalization *amongst its others* —holds the key to understanding how neoliberalism has been reproduced, systematically, through discrepant formations (PECK, 2010; PECK and THEODORE, 2012b). This is difficult, if not impossible, absent some appreciation of the distinctive hegemonic form of neoliberalism, as HALL (2011) has argued. Cahill likewise observes:

> neoliberal doctrine is best understood as an ideology—a doctrine which provides only a partial representation of the world and whose misrepresentations mask material processes which benefit dominant class interests. When read as an ideology, a clearer picture can be formed of the relationships between neoliberal doctrine and the practices which have generally been labelled 'neoliberal'. (2012, p. 177)

Cahill goes on to note three significant (and recurring) anomalies in subsequent neoliberal statecraft, where revealed practice diverges, time and time again, from the official script—that the aggregate 'size' state has not significantly been reduced since the 1970s; that the scope or reach of the state has been extended in some realms; and that there has been extensive recourse to coercive and authoritarian powers. His means of addressing this apparent paradox is a Polanyian one: 'the discrepancy between neoliberal theory and practice [lies in] the failure of neoliberal theory to recognize the inherently socially embedded nature of the capitalist economy' (CAHILL, 2012, p. 115). The contradictions, in other words, are part of the package.

The fact that all neoliberal experiments are antagonistically embedded means that they can only exist as unstable, mongrel formations; in practice, there can be no 'purebred' neoliberalisms. Critical theories of neoliberalization must therefore be purposefully addressed to the contradictory dynamics *between* neoliberal theory and practice; neither purely abstract-ideational nor purely concrete-institutional analyses will alone suffice. Neoliberal theory will always be frustrated, yet at the same time it has the (demonstrated) capacity to inspire, direct, and prioritize programs of socioeconomic transformation and state restructuring; the effect is to invoke a utopian destination, even if this is unattainable, as a means to sustain a transformative *direction* in reform and restructuring efforts. (In so far as neoliberalism 'works', as a frontal ideological program, this appears to be its *modus operandi*.) Neoliberal practice necessarily diverges from this same (flawed) theory, yet it does not merely exist 'downstream' from the ideological commanding heights; neoliberal nostrums have been perpetually adjusted, strategically, in dialog with the vagaries of practice and comingled with others, even as they continue to resound to a certain matrix of idealized commitments. The contradictions, again, are part of the package.

On these grounds, one can support HILGERS' (2012, p. 81) assertion that neoliberalism 'can never be understood in radical separation from historical configurations', even while questioning his earlier claim that it is only when neoliberalism touches down, in particular grounded formations, that it becomes properly the subject of anthropological investigation (HILGERS, 2011). As COLLIER (2012, p. 194) has countered, not only is it a self-limiting error to sequester ethnographic practice in such a way, there is 'no reason that an anthropological investigation of neoliberalism as an original movement of thought ... could not be linked to policy programmes, to trans-local channels of circulation carved by powerful institutions or peripatetic experts, [and] to patterns of adoption and adaptation in various countries and sectors', even if these extra-local concerns have not been of paramount concern in the field to date. It is not that neoliberalism only becomes sociologically complex in grounded, local, and lived settings, while its founding principles and global logics can be somehow cordoned off as an automated realm of iron-clad economic laws and fixed philosophical principles. There is a need for *no less* situated and sociological analyses of the origins, tenets, and imperatives of neoliberalism—before, 'above', outside, and beyond this or that 'local' configuration, actually existing neoliberalism, hybrid assemblage, etc.—and although COLLIER (2012, p. 194), for his part, is skeptical that these are 'reconcilable' with more structural accounts of neoliberalism, to rule out what could be a fruitful conversation seems like another form of sequestering (cf. MIROWSKI and PLEHWE, 2009; PECK, 2010). If exceptionalist local studies of hybrid neoliberalism really are incompatible with understandings of the phenomenon-cum-process in cross-situation, more-than-local terms, or if such studies can only be positioned at ironic distance from (or in nondialectical tension with) processual understandings, then perhaps they are using the wrong terminology?

'Template' models of neoliberalism have been rightly questioned by structural and non-structural analysts alike (see BRENNER *et al.,* 2010; PECK *et al.,* forthcoming). It follows that the problematic of neoliberalization is never 'quite as simple as lining up a list of attributes of neoliberalism, such as privatization, deregulation and the limited state, and showing whether or not they correspond to the current "institutional reality" of state' (DEAN, 2012, p. 75). As a rolling and somewhat revolutionary program of macrosocial and macroinstitutional transformation, neoliberalization *acts on and through* these institutional landscapes; this is not a static neoliberal*ism,* a classificatory category that can be cleanly determined to be more or less commensurate with different state or social forms. It follows that theorizing more or less exclusively within the domain of concrete state or social forms, or in the realm of hybrid assemblages, can only generate partial explanations. It may indeed be wise to heed the Foucauldian injunction that neoliberalism should not be *presumed* to display unity or coherence as a governing doctrine-cum-political program; yet a reflexive presumption of disarticulated *incoherence* hardly stands as a meaningful methodological axiom. As Dean has recently reflected,

> the most significant limitation of the early governmentality approach to neoliberalism is the very concept of 'advanced liberalism' itself. [I]ntellectual historians have established that neoliberalism can be regarded as a thought collective with a frontal character and indeed a social and political movement. The enduring significance of that movement and the degree of its coherence *qua* movement is something which is systematically underestimated by approaching 'advanced liberalism' as simply a diverse and contingent 'assemblage' of techniques and rationalities bearing at best a 'family resemblance'. (2012, p. 79)

There is a parallel risk in those low-flying approaches that effectively prioritize deviations from a supposed (big-N Neoliberal) global norm, focusing on ostensibly more distant hybrid forms, while remaining deeply ambivalent (or even antagonistic) to political-economic conceptions of neoliberalism. Such approaches risk methodological myopia if they are dismissive of, or blind to, cross-local patternings, to recurrent strategies, to extra-local constraints, incentives and disciplines—simply lumping these into the indefensible bogey-category of 'monolithic' conceptions of Neoliberalism (cf. PECK and TICKELL, 2012). The risk that they run is one of systematically underestimating the frontal and programmatic character of the neoliberal offensive, by reducing it to even less than the sum of its parts. This, as George W Bush might have said, would be to 'mis-underestimate' neoliberalism.

After all, for all its mixed achievements on the ground, the hegemonic grip of neoliberal ideology continues to be manifest in the form of unrelenting political pressure for market-oriented and voluntarist modes of governance, based on the principles of devolved and outsourced responsibility, along with a correspondingly circumscribed regulatory solution space. (This is how neoliberalism frames, brackets, and preemptively narrows the field of the politically visible and tractable.) It follows that invocations of (dynamic) neoliberalization rather than (static) neoliberalism represent more than analytical sophistry; rather, they seek to capture the underlying character of this transformative process, as a 'directional' and not a 'destinational' form of liberal-capitalist political economy. (This is one reason why the Gramscian metaphor of the hegemonic front seems appropriate in this context.) This may also help to explain the mood, or temper, of the neoliberal reformer—endlessly frustrated, impatient, seeing (potential) setbacks at every turn and socialist-interventionists under every bed, and as a result always (re)targeting obstacles to, and opponents of, the rolling program of market-oriented transformation. History may ultimately judge neoliberalism, as a result, as rather more efficacious in dismantling and disabling alien and contesting social formations (like collective provisions, systems of social redistribution, planning regimes) than in effectively sustaining its self-identified Jerusalem of market freedoms. Denied their utopian destination, pathways of neoliberalization invariably describe a vagarious and crisis-strewn course, markedly away from preceding social formations, such as the developmental state or Keynesian-welfare state, but hardly describing some beeline to the neoliberal nirvana. Hence the significance of Hayek's portrayal of neoliberalism as a 'flexible credo', and Milton Friedman's recurrent complaint that the aggregate size of government has been extremely difficult, historically speaking, to shrink. By virtue of the radical non-availability of the destinational dream of the zero-state society, one of absolute deregulation and unsullied market freedom, neoliberal reformers are condemned to dwell in the purgatories of governance. Their guiding philosophy provides a framework for action in these circumstances (which is why they repeat many of the same mistakes), but it delivers few (if any) sustainable solutions.

This is a principal reason for the messiness, and incompleteness, of trajectories of neoliberal restructuring. And it also accounts for the fact that neoliberalism has never been associated with a fixed policy repertoire or tendential institutional core, but instead improvises within ideological and fiscal parameters, resorting routinely to experimentation, opportunism, and trial through costly error—albeit in the broad context of a pattern of socio-regulatory selectivity favoring market-based and market-like strategies, coupled with an allowance for corporate states of exception. So, over time, the strategy of outright privatization has blurred into a myriad of murky arrangements like public–private partnerships; strict monetarism was succeeded by inflation targeting and fiscal vigilance; bootstrapping exhortations to the poor, the unemployed and other blamed victims gave way to a feel-good emphasis on human and social capital building, even community empowerment; Thatcher's infamously blunt 'there's no such thing as society' mutated into the smoke-and-mirrors rhetoric of David Cameron's Big Society. Some might see this as a softening of the hard-edged version of 1980s neoliberalism, or the mainstreaming of the accompanying political project. There may be some truth in these arguments, but they also call attention to the ways in which the project of neoliberalism continues to evolve, both as a governing strategy and as a policy package. This has happened both as a result of its own limitations and blindspots (such as a tendency to speculative excess and indifference toward social externalities) and as a response to crises, frequently of its own making. It also reflects a proclivity for working around, selectively undermining, and tactically targeted sources of opposition and resistance.

For some considerable time now, it has been an article of faith on the left that neoliberalism would eventually succumb to its own contradictions (PECK and TICKELL, 1994; ALBO, 2007). The Wall Street crash and its aftermath may have finally put paid to this myth, to the expectation that the entrenched and polymorphic phenomenon of neoliberalism might somehow still be vulnerable to a form of total 'system failure' (PECK *et al.,* 2010). While there would have been poetic justice in the final crisis of neoliberalism being incubated in New York City, an appropriately inauspicious end to the free-market doctrine of neoliberalism and its culture of deregulation, this kind of singular, terminal event may be increasingly unlikely. Local failures—even 'big' ones—will continue to animate the moving landscape of neoliberalization, as for the time being at least will be localized adaptations in these and other places. Analytically, single-site case studies, either of an affirmative or a dissenting character, cannot properly capture what is a multi-sited, relational process of reproduction.

The Wall Street crash and its sobering aftermath can also be seen as an explanatory corrective to a certain kind of structural overreading of neoliberalism, which underestimates the plural adaptability of the project, especially the capacity to improvise provisional regulatory fixes, workarounds, mediations, displacements, deferrals—to variously maintain a directional momentum even in the face of significant obstacles, serial failures, and sporadic forms of resistance. By the same token, the doggedness of neoliberalism, its demonstrated capacity to surf through successive waves of crisis, and the unmistakable patterning of regulatory responses to the Great Recession, all stand as an explanatory challenge to those who would have preferred to do away with the concept of neoliberalism altogether. Refusing to use the word, even *sans* capital-N, will not make these conditions go away. What to do, then, if neoliberalism is indeed 'once more the dominant, nay self-evident, policy paradigm' (KALB, 2012, p. 320)?

NEOLIBERALISM INSIDE/OUT

The awkward reality, perhaps, is that it is difficult to live either with, or without, macrological concepts such as neoliberalization (see CLARKE, 2008). On the one hand, the concept's apparent promiscuity, and its ready availability as a plausible source of ultimate causality, means that it is readily prone to inflation into a blunt, omnibus category. On the other hand, dismissing neoliberalism (or Neoliberalism) as a structuralist fantasy or regulationist folly, while instead to taking recourse to the 'exceptionalist' analyses deliberately detached from the consideration of macro-scale constraints and incentives, extra-local forces, hegemonic formations, trans-local rules of the game, cross-case connections, family resemblances, and so forth, is to privilege localist-particularist forms of explanation over relational-conjunctural ones. What COLLIER (2012, p. 186) poses as a choice between a more hierarchical, political economy-style reading of neoliberalism as 'macro-structure or explanatory background' and flatter, more poststructural and horizontalist approaches to 'neoliberalism as though it were the same size as other things', is not one that is amenable to reconciliation in some happy, friction-free synthesis. There are real tensions between what are different ontological and epistemological understandings of neoliberalism, but this does not mean that there is no scope for dialog (see KINGFISHER and MASKOVSKY, 2008a; FAIRBANKS, 2012).

The potential contribution of variegated neoliberalization approaches, in this context, lies in their overlapping concern with 'how neoliberalism is specified in a variegated landscape of institutional, economic and political forms' (BRENNER et al., 2010; COLLIER, 2012, p. 191; PECK and THEODORE, 2012b). In the terms summarized in Figure 1, this means embracing a conception of neoliberalism based on the twin principles of relationality and connectivity. Relational approaches can be distinguished from gradational ones in that they call attention to the mutual constitution and qualitative interpenetration of 'local' neoliberalisms, rather than drawing more/less distinctions of a quantitative kind between supposed 'degrees' of neoliberalization, or measuring near/far distances relative to some imagined 'heartland'. And approaches that emphasize (global) connectivity over (local) exceptionality likewise problematize the linkages, interconnections, and more-than-local patterns revealed by neoliberalization processes; they work between internalist treatments of neoliberalism (as a characteristic of, say, particular institutions or territorialized political regimes) and externalist conceptions of global hegemony, instead to problematize what might be called inside/outside relations.

From a Foucauldian perspective, COLLIER (2012, p. 191) recognizes that neoliberalism 'is a concept we cannot do without', and therefore that operationalization of this concept must imply definitional parameters; while the position 'neoliberalism can be just anything' is manifestly indefensible, wary of inflationary tendencies, COLLIER is equally concerned that expansionist conceptions can become indiscriminate theories of 'everything'.

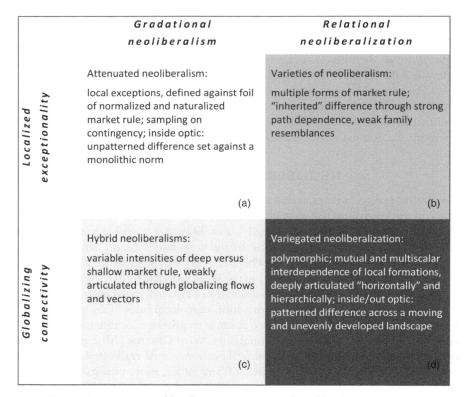

Figure 1. Between neoliberalism as exception and neoliberalism inside/out.

These are sensible (if not commonsensical) admonitions. Even though they only represent a first step toward methodological operationalization, the fact that such propositions (still) need to be stated is itself revealing. If a minimalist point of departure is that neoliberalism is never everything—either 'within' a particular social formation, governance regime, or territorial space, or in the realm of extra-local relations—then it is clearly imperative that neoliberalism must, inescapably and in every situation, be located amongst its others. Even where neoliberalism is demonstrably hegemonic, it is never the *entire* story, never the *only* causal presence; it never acts alone. Furthermore, friction, double movements, resistance, alternatives are ever-present. While a case can be made that neoliberalism possesses an inherent expansionary logic (since it actively targets new spaces and fronts for marketization, while unleashing loosely bounded deregulatory imperatives), 100% monopoly status is impossible, even in theory. And this is not just a matter of 'local differences'. Even globally, neoliberalism exists among other forces and conditions. With reference to what KALB (2012, p. 319) unapologetically calls 'the jumbo questions [of] global capitalism', for example,

> the interconnected key issues of global transformation, such as the financialisation of Western capitalism, the insertion of China, in particular, into the global capitalist assembly line, the tripling of the world proletariat since 1989, including the associated urbanisations, migrations and related competitive pressures, and the rolling eclipse of Western hegemony, cannot be explained by, or reduced to, a reigning policy paradigm or even a state calculus called 'neoliberalism', even though it is multiply entangled with such calculus and paradigm.

That these global conditions were in part enabled by earlier rounds of neoliberalization (such as the selective deconstruction of 'barriers' to the flows of trade, capital, and labor), and that they also establish conditions for the further entrenchment of neoliberal regulation (for instance, in terms of exacerbation of interjurisdictional competition, inducing more 'entrepreneurial' postures on the part of local actors, coupled with downward pressure on taxes, wages, and costs, which in turn redouble pressures for entrepreneurial responses and competitive adjustment), clearly does not mean that all these phenomena should be rolled into an all-inclusive catch-all notion of Global Neoliberalism, at which point the quest for explanation ceases. The indiscriminate cry that 'Neoliberalism did it' belongs in the same family as the 'I blame Thatcher' denunciations of old; who did what, to whom, where, and how must be specified in social, economic, and institutional terms. In the global or extra-local realm, this means teasing out neoliberalizing tendencies (again, among their others) in particular settings, circuits, and fields—such as decision-making cultures within multilateral agencies; channels of policy learning and mobility; the rules of regulatory regimes in investment, trade, and finance; the operations of epistemic communities and technocratic networks; governance at a distance through financial instruments, indexing and benchmarking systems, model-building and best-practice emulation; and so forth. Neoliberalism has different valences, registers, capacities, and contradictions across these (and other) fields, circuits, and settings; they are not all neatly fitting components of a singular, global template. Theoretically informed, and informing, empirical work on these issues is consequently essential for the refinement even of relatively abstract understandings of neoliberalization, which cannot be divined unilaterally from founding theories or germinal texts.

Correspondingly, neoliberalism will also be found amongst its others within local or national territorial formations. It may occupy a dominant or subordinate position in these formations, but even under conditions of dominance the qualitative form of the process is likely to change, evolve, mutate—as for example in Stuart HALL's (1988, 2003, 2011) successive analyses of cumulative neoliberalization through the Thatcher, Blair, and Cameron regimes. And because there are still others (and counter-tendencies) to neoliberalization even where it is dominant, properly conjunctural analyses must take account not only of internal relations and characteristics but external connections and contradictions. This cannot reduced to a binary choice between situations in which neo-liberalism is allegedly 'exceptional' and those where it is supposedly normal and unex-ceptional, for this implicitly naturalizes neoliberalism in some settings, while preempting questions of its contextualization and trajectory in others (see BRENNER *et al.,* 2010). Likewise, all 'local' neoliberalizations exist in a relational global field, not as islands. None are entirely isolated, just as none should be reduced to mere reverbera-tions of a global logic:

> [N]eoliberalisms are not merely locally variegated instantiations of global ideas but fully lived realities in which people and states have their own theories, and elaborate their own discourses and critiques, about the worlds they inhabit and the ways in which these should be organised. 'Actually existing neoliberalism(s)' are more than curious local manifestations of global norms. (GOLDSTEIN, 2012, p. 305)

As Goldstein's work in Bolivia after Morales clearly shows, however, (anti)neoliberal strategies are never freely chosen either. While Morales' platform and key elements of his governing program have been (pronounced as) *contra el neoliberalismo,* elsewhere this has been compromised by the way that his administration has been 'caught up in the sticky business of global capitalism', not to mention the vagaries of domestic politics (WEBBER, 2011; GOLDSTEIN, 2012, p. 307). The point here is to judge such configurations both in their own terms and in relation to their others, near and far, not to hold them up against an imagined singular yardstick of absolute neoliberalism (which does not, and could not, exist anywhere), against some supposedly crystalline evocation of its logic (whether read from the list of Washington consensus policy commandments, *ur*-texts like the *Road to serfdom,* or the secret transcript of the Mont Pelerin meetings), or against allegedly para-digmatic or first transitions (such as those of Chile, New Zealand or the UK). It is meth-odologically axiomatic that variegated neoliberalism can only be fully understood *across* sites, texts, institutions, and so forth, rather than being theorized (as deviations from) a privileged center, ultimate form or pure theory, however that might be defined (PECK and THEODORE, 2012b; PECK and TICKELL, 2012). As an especially crisis-prone pattern of social regulation, neoliberalism might be considered somewhat deviant wherever it is found.

To do so, of course, is not simply to (re)embrace an unthinking style of neoliberal-centrism. It calls for methodological strategies that are pitched somewhere between, on the one hand, those finely granulated studies of local neoliberalizations, that are characteristically light on extra-local referents or invoke the concept only ambivalently, and on the other hand, those sweeping accounts of neoliberal hegemony that are largely abstracted from any kind of social or textural specificity and which gloss over uneven development and contradictory hybridity. Operating in between (and in and between) these methodological poles involves turning neoliberalism, as a real-world process, inside/out. There is no readily available methodological abracadabra here, indeed a plurality is strategies is called for rather than a singular fix. But some of the well-established rationales for (extended) case selection (cf. BURAWOY, 2011; PECK and THEODORE, 2012a) seem appropriate in this context: selecting and theorizing cases in an orthogonal or awkward relation to emergent explanatory conceptions, in order both to interrogate and reconstruct those conceptions. This means positioning local cases in relational and conjunctural terms, rather than terrain of typicality or exception. It means striving to make part–whole connections, while recognizing that this more-than-the-sum-of-the-parts phenomenon only exists by dint of its parts. It means uncovering local constitutions of global forces, rather than resorting to top-down 'impact' models. And it means rendering the moving landscapes of neoliberalization as theoretical problematics in their own right (rather than placing these in the shadow of presumed convergence), probing power centers and vulnerable flanks, mapping the spatialities of consent and conflict, and tracing interdependencies through hierarchies and networks. In this context, the functioning of neoliberalism as an operational matrix, as a form of regulatory hegemony always in the (re)working, would not reside, unquestioned, as an article of critical faith, but would rendered anew as an object of sustained, reflexive and dialectical interrogation.

In this respect, there may be scope for different kinds of conversation between approaches to variegated neoliberalization rooted in geographical political economy and more situated treatments of neoliberalism found in some stripes of Foucauldian and post-structural scholarship. In rather different terms, a parallel conversation might also emerge between analysts of neoliberalism as an ideological and/or macroinstitutional phenomenon, on the one hand, and those on the other hand who have been more concerned with its more granulated, grounded, and provisional forms, often unearthed ethnographically or through intensive case studies. Anxious to dismantle jumbo-scaled, template-like models of neoliberalism, COLLIER nevertheless recognizes that:

> As an analytical term, neoliberalism draws meaningful conceptual interconnections among a range of historical experiences and contemporary problems in a way that is essential; methodologically speaking, we need it. (2011, p. 247)

For COLLIER, the empirical reality of evidently diverse social and geographical manifestations of neoliberalism/its others is not a reason to abandon the concept altogether, but an invitation rigorously to refine it. The 'significance of neoliberalism', he writes, 'must be sought, at least in part, in the disparate experiences in which neoliberal styles of reasoning, mechanisms of intervention, and techniques have played a significant role in shaping the forms of government'; where he has a problem, understandably, is with those analyses that, to recall the Foucauldian objection, do not 'pay the full price' of establishing the interconnections and commonalities to which their definitions implicitly adhere (COLLIER, 2011, p. 12). Quite right. But there is a price, too, to be paid for invocations of neoliberalism that are *only* local, which are distanced and detached from extra-local domains, referents, and spaces of reproductive circulation. 'Inside' manifestations of neoliberal logics—a privatization program in Macedonia, say, or a conditional welfare initiative in Indonesia—are locally embedded and constitutively contextual, to be sure, but they must not be shorn of their constitutive outsides, such as the actually existing and imagined 'reform families' to which they belong, as near or distant relatives to other and earlier projects, experiments, and models. This underlines the need for a continuing concern with neoliberalism's *family* misfortunes.

CONCLUSION: GETTING OVER NEOLIBERALISM

To say that neoliberalism is still with us is not the same as saying that this is a permanent condition or that neoliberalism is always, transcendentally, the same. This is one reason why simple invocations of neoliberalism as an all-purpose, omnibus explanation for the contemporary condition can never be enough. Citing the process of neoliberalization must not be a substitute for explanation; it should be an *occasion* for explanation, involving the specification of particular causal mechanisms, modes of intervention, hybrid formations, social forms and foibles, counter-mobilizations, and so forth. It might be said that the concept does define a problem space and a zone of (possible) pertinence, and as such represents the beginning of a process of analysis. But it is here that the task of excavating contextual forms and connective flows really begins; it is here that analysts really have to 'pay the full price' of invoking this more-than-local concept.

If 'neoliberalism did it' should never be a fig leaf for preemptive explanation, neither should invocations of neoliberalism be a prelude to unbounded analytical (or indeed political) fatalism, of the 'we're all doomed to endless market rule' variety. As an always-thwarted totalization, the neoliberal circle is never squared. Even hegemonies have their outsides and others; their construction is a continuing and contradictory process, not a fixed condition. Those skeptical of the utility of the concept of neoliberalism sometimes complain that its deployment, even the dropping of the name, somehow throws gasoline on the flames while effectively denigrating alternatives, both actual and potential. Some of this skepticism, clearly, stems from a deeper concern with all forms of explanation that invoke structural rationalities, big processes, and hegemonic forces, but quite often these are stereotyped as mechanistic forms of template theorizing rather than for what they actually are. Process-based approaches to neoliberalization, in fact, work explicitly with *and across* difference, problematizing the (re)production of that difference, and they are no less attentive to the contradictions and limits of neoliberalism in both theory and practice. These approaches do not necessitate the automatic or preemptive dismissal of non-neoliberal alternatives or postneoliberal trajectories, but they do require that such (emergent) developments are understood, in the current context at any rate, *in relation to* hegemonically neoliberalized fields of power and their associated domains of transformative practice. Searching questions are therefore likely to be raised about one-sided projections of enclavist alt-models, if the advocacy of these is detached from an assessment of the challenges of scaling up or networking out. 'Alternatives' must be analyzed relationally too, not in utopian isolation (see PECK, forthcoming).

Squaring up to neoliberalism, in such a context, need not mean genuflecting before the altar of limitless market rule (see LEITNER *et al.*, 2007b). Applying the principles of relationality 'all the way down' (or all the way out), however, calls for an understanding of the ways in which hegemonic forms of neoliberalization both inhabit, and tendentially remake, the field of difference. There are few bright lines, these days, between neoliberalism and its others, irrespective of whether these others are progressive or conservative, liberal or authoritarian. So it is ill-advised to code the world 'beyond' neoliberalism in blanket terms, as a space of somehow untouched alternatives or as a generalized zone of resistance. Two conditions of neoliberalism's contradictory existence—its apparent facility for shape-shifting survival and the fact that perhaps its signal, enduring achievement has been the incapacitation of bases for ideological opposition—suggest that it may be less likely to meet its ultimate end in some epic, dialectical contest between a muscular Neoliberalism in the blue corner and plucky Resistance in the red. Perhaps it is still likely that the contradictions of neoliberalism will get it in the end, but the end may well be a protracted one—maybe one in which the complex of neoliberal projects and programs is eventually exhausted, and incrementally outflanked or exceeded. Meanwhile, if no big-bang failure of neoliberal rule is imminently expected, then what are currently styled as alternatives will have to do more (even) than stand their ground in local enclaves; they will have to stake claims on enemy territory while rewriting the rules of extra-local redistribution, reciprocity, and competition.

Optimism of the will can and must be replenished by the diverse alternatives, real utopias, and counter-projects to neoliberalism, many of which are to be found at the local scale, but pessimism of the intellect should also caution that neoliberalism's 'permanent economic tribunal' (FOUCAULT, 2008) continues to exhibit a capacity to crimp, contain, and co-opt these more progressive others, *especially* where they issue a challenge to the governing imperatives of financialized and corporatized market rule (see CROUCH, 2011). Meanwhile, neoliberalism itself is never static, but as a flexible credo constantly reanimated by crisis and contradiction is persistently generating market-friendly alternatives of its own. As long as neoliberal rules continue to hold sway at the scale of inter-local relations, 'local' alternatives are likely to remain just that, local. (Indeed, it might provide a clue as to why they are local in the first place.) The intensifying capillary, infrastructural, and normative reach of market rule at the transnational scale (cf. MANN, 1984; SIMMONS *et al.*, 2008), threatens to further entrench, as one of the many perverse outcomes of the crisis, the 'dull compulsion' of competitive relations and the pernicious logic of regulatory undercutting.

Doing away with the concept of neoliberalism will not do away with the conditions of its still-hegemonic existence; neither, on its own, would it render alternatives any more realizable. Rather, it is imperative that the array of alternatives—from the reformist though to the radical—are positioned relationally in ideational, ideological, and institutional terms. This is not, then, a plea for a relentlessly 'neoliberalocentric' perspective, for it is arguably more important than ever to ensure that the reach and ambition of critical endeavors—methodological, theoretical, and political—extend across the *entire field* of socioeconomic difference, a task in which Polanyian forms of comparative socioeconomics, for instance, might have constructive roles to play (see PECK, forthcoming). Consistent with such an approach is the observation that the necessary incompleteness of the neoliberal program of free-market reform means that it must always dwell among its others, along with the rather cold comfort that its ultimate destination is unattainable. Actually existing alternatives (progressive and otherwise) will never be completely expunged. The residues of preexisting social formations will never be entirely erased or rendered inert. Double movements against the overextension of market rule will not only continue, but can be expected to intensify, presenting new challenges but also opening up new moments for social action. Crises, in forms old and new, will recur. Realistically speaking, it is on this uncertain and uneven terrain that all forms of postneoliberal politics will have to be forged. And there is analytical work to be done too, not least across the interdisciplinary field of critical urban and regional studies. There is much to be gained from this work being conducted across, as well as within, methodological traditions and theoretical registers, although a particularly important contribution remains to be made by the 'ethnographic archeologist', as BURAWOY (2003, p. 251) dubbed them some time ago, 'who seeks out local experiments, new institutional forms, real utopias if you wish, who places them in their context, translates them into a common language, and links them one to another across the globe'.

Acknowledgements – I thank Catherine Kingfisher, Michael Flower, and two anonymous referees for their constructive and probing comments on an earlier draft of this paper. The arguments here have benefited from ongoing conversations with Neil Brenner, Rob Fairbanks, and Nik Theodore, and in the Geography 560 seminars at UBC. I am solely responsible for what is here, however.

NOTES

1. In the 2010 mid-term elections, the Democrats lost 63 seats in the US Congress and 6 in the US Senate; the Republicans also gained 6 governorships and some 680 seats in state legislatures, securing the party's strongest position at the state level since 1928.
2. Barack Obama; Obama's speech to the Democratic National Convention. *Washington Post*, 6 September, accessed at http://www.washingtonpost.com/politics/dnc-2012-obamas-speech-to-the-democratic-national-convention-full-transcript/2012/09/06/ed78167c-f87b-11e1-a073-78d05495927c_story.html.
3. These have also long been staple observations in political-economy accounts of neoliberalism, although this is often lost in critical translation.

REFERENCES

ALBO G. (2007) Neoliberalism and the discontented, in PANITCH L. and LEYS C. (Eds) *Global Flashpoints*, pp. 354–362. Merlin Press, London.

BLYTH M. (2013) *Austerity: The History of a Dangerous Idea*. Oxford University Press, New York.

BOND P. (2009) Realistic postneoliberalism—a view from South Africa, *Development Dialogue* **51 (1)**, 193–211.

BOURDIEU P. (1998) *Acts of Resistance*. Polity, Cambridge.

BRENNER N. and THEODORE N. (2002) Cities and the geographies of "actually existing neoliberalism", in BRENNER N. and THEODORE N. (Eds) *Spaces of Neoliberalism: Urban Restructuring in North America and Western Europe*, pp. 2–32. Blackwell, Oxford.

BRENNER N., PECK J. and THEODORE N. (2010) Variegated neoliberalization: geographies, modalities, pathways, *Global Networks* **10(2)**, 1–41.

BURAWOY M. (2003) For a sociological Marxism: the complementary convergence of Antonio Gramsci and Karl Polanyi, *Politics and Society* **31(2)**, 193–261.

BURAWOY M. (2011) *The Extended Case Method: Four Countries, Four Decades, Four Great Transformations, and One Theoretical Tradition*. University of California Press, Berkeley.

CAHILL D. (2012) The embedded neoliberal economy, in CAHILL D., EDWARDS L. and STILWELL F. (Eds) *Neoliberalism: Beyond the Free Market*, pp. 110–127. Edward Elgar, Cheltenham.

CENTENO M. A. and COHEN J. N. (2012) The arc of neoliberalism, *Annual Review of Sociology* **38 (1)**, 317–340.

CHU Y. and SO A. Y. (2010) State neoliberalism: the Chinese road to capitalism, in CHU Y. (Ed.) *Chinese Capitalisms: Historical Emergence and Political Implications*, pp. 73–99. Palgrave Macmillan, Basingstoke.

CLARKE J. (2008) Living with/in and without neo-liberalism, *Focaal* **51(1)**, 135–147.

COLLIER S. J. (2011) *Post-Soviet Social: Neoliberalism, Social Modernity, Biopolitics*. Princeton University Press, Princeton.

COLLIER S. J. (2012) Neoliberalism as big Leviathan, or …? A response to Wacquant and Hilgers, *Social Anthropology/Anthropologie Sociale* **20(2)**, 186–195.

CROUCH C. (2011) *The Strange Non-death of Neoliberalism*. Polity, Cambridge.

DAVIS M. (2011) Spring confronts winter, *New Left Review* **72**, 5–15.

DEAN M. (2012) Free economy, strong state, in CAHILL D., EDWARDS L. and STILWELL F. (Eds) *Neoliberalism: Beyond the Free Market*, pp. 69–89. Edward Elgar, Cheltenham.

ELLIOT L. (2011) Three years on, it's as if the crisis never happened, *The Guardian*, 30 May, 22.

FAIRBANKS R. P. (2012) On theory and method: critical ethnographic approaches to urban regulatory restructuring, *Urban Geography* **33(4)**, 545–565.

FERGUSON J. (2010) The uses of neoliberalism, *Antipode* **41(1)**, 166–184.

FOUCAULT M. (2008) *The Birth of Biopolitics*. Palgrave, Basingstoke.

GAMBLE A. (1988) *The Free Economy and the Strong State: The Politics of Thatcherism*. Macmillan, London.

GIBSON-GRAHAM J.-K. (2008) Diverse economies: performative practices for "other worlds", *Progress in Human Geography* **32(5)**, 613–632.

GLEDHILL J. (2004) Neoliberalism, in NUGENT D. and VINCENT J. (Eds) *A Companion to the Anthropology of Politics*, pp. 332–348. Blackwell, Oxford.

GOLDSTEIN D. M. (2012) Decolonialising "actually existing neoliberalism", *Social Anthropology/Anthropologie Sociale* **20(3)**, 304–309.

HALL S. (1988) The toad in the garden: Thatcherism among the theorists, in NELSON C. and GROSSBERG L. (Eds) *Marxism and the Interpretation of Culture*, pp. 35–57. University of Illinois Press, Urbana, IL.

HALL S. (2003) New Labour's double shuffle, *Soundings* **24**, 10–24.

HALL S. (2011) The neo-liberal revolution, *Cultural Studies* **25(6)**, 705–728.

HALL S. and JACQUES M. (Eds) (1989) *New Times*. Lawrence & Wishart, London.

Harris J. (2011) The world needs a new Marx, but it keeps creating Malcolm Gladwells, *The Guardian*, 8 June, 29.

HARVEY D. (2005) *A Brief History of Neoliberalism*. Oxford University Press, Oxford.

HARVEY D. (2012) *Rebel Cities*. Verso, London.

HILGERS M. (2011) The three anthropological approaches to neoliberalism, *International Social Science Journal* **61(202)**, 351–364.

HILGERS M. (2012) The historicity of the neoliberal state, *Social Anthropology/Anthropologie Sociale* **20(1)**, 80–94.

IEO-IMF [INDEPENDENT EVALUATION OFFICE OF THE INTERNATIONAL MONETARY FUND] (2011) *IMF Performance in the Run-Up to the Financial and Economic Crisis*. IEO-IMF, Washington, DC.

JESSOP B. (2000) The crisis of the national spatio-temporal fix and the tendential ecological dominance of globalizing capitalism, *International Journal of Urban and Regional Research* **24(2)**, 323–360.

JESSOP B. (2004) New Labour's doppelte Kehrtwende: Anmerkungen zu Stuart Hall und eine alternative Perspektiv zu New Labour, *Das Argument* **256**, 494–504.

JESSOP B., BONNETT K., BROMLEY S. and LING T. (1988) *Thatcherism*. Polity, Cambridge.

JONES D. S. (2012) *Masters of the Universe: Hayek, Friedman, and the Birth of Neoliberal Politics*. Princeton University Press, Princeton.

KALB D. (2012) Thinking about neoliberalism as if the crisis was actually happening, *Social Anthropology/Anthropologie Sociale* **20(3)**, 318–330.

KINGFISHER K. and MASKOVSKY J. (2008a) Introduction: the limits of neoliberalism, *Critique of Anthropology* **28(2)**, 115–126.

KINGFISHER K. and MASKOVSKY J. (Eds) (2008b) The limits of neoliberalism, *Critique of Anthropology* **28(2)**, 115–255.

LARNER W. (2003) Neoliberalism?, *Environment and Planning D: Society and Space* **21(5)**, 509–512.

LATOUR B. (2007) *Reassembling the Social*. Oxford University Press, New York.

LEITNER H., SHEPPARD E. S., SZIARTO K. and MARINGANTI A. (2007a) Contesting urban futures: decentering neoliberalism, in LEITNER H., PECK J. and SHEPPARD E. S. (Eds) *Contesting Neoliberalism: Urban Frontiers*, pp. 1–25. Guilford, New York.

LEITNER H., PECK J. and SHEPPARD E. S. (2007b) Squaring up to neoliberalism, in LEITNER H., PECK J. and SHEPPARD E. S. (Eds) *Contesting Neoliberalism: Urban Frontiers*, pp. 311–327. Guilford, New York.

MANN M. (1984) The autonomous power of the state: its origins, mechanisms and results, *Archives Européennes de Sociologie* **25(2)**, 185–213.

MIROWSKI P. and PLEHWE D. (Eds) (2009) *The Road from Mont Pèlerin*. Harvard University Press, Cambridge, MA.

NONONI D. M. (2008) Is China becoming neoliberal?, *Critique of Anthropology* **28(2)**, 145–176.

ONG A. (2006) *Neoliberalism as Exception: Mutations of Citizenship and Sovereignty*. Duke University Press, Durham, NC.

ONG A. (2007) Neoliberalism as a mobile technology, *Transactions of the Institute of British Geographers* **32(1)**, 3–8.

PECK J. (2004) Geography and public policy: constructions of neoliberalism, *Progress in Human Geography* **28(3)**, 392–405.

PECK J. (2009) Zombie-Neoliberalismus und der beidhändige Staat, *Das Argument* **282**, 644–650.

PECK J. (2010) *Constructions of Neoliberal Reason*. Oxford University Press, Oxford.

PECK J. (2012) Austerity urbanism: American cities under extreme economy, *City* **16(6)**, 626–655.

PECK J. (Forthcoming) For Polanyian economic geographies, *Environment and Planning A*.

PECK J. and THEODORE N. (2012a) Follow the policy: a distended case approach, *Environment and Planning A* **44(1)**, 21–30.

PECK J. and THEODORE N. (2012b) Reanimating neoliberalism: process geographies of neoliberalization, *Social Anthropology/Anthropologie Sociale* **20(2)**, 177–185.

PECK J. and TICKELL A. (1994) Searching for a new institutional fix: the after-Fordist crisis and global-local disorder, in AMIN A. (Ed.) *Post-Fordism: A Reader*, pp. 280–316. Blackwell, Oxford.

PECK J. and TICKELL A. (2012) Apparitions of neoliberalism: revisiting "Jungle law breaks out", *Area* **44(2)**, 245–249.

PECK J. and ZHANG J. (Forthcoming) A variety of capitalism … with Chinese characteristics?, *Journal of Economic Geography*, DOI: 10.1093/jeg/lbs058.

PECK J., THEODORE N. and BRENNER N. (2010) Postneoliberalism and its malcontents, *Antipode* **41(1)**, 94–116.

PECK J., THEODORE N. and BRENNER N. (Forthcoming) Neoliberal urbanism redux?, *International Journal of Urban and Regional Research*.

PIVEN F. F. (1995) Is it global economics or neo-laissez-faire?, *New Left Review* **213**, 107–115.

POLANYI K. (1944) *The Great Transformation*. Beacon Press, Boston, MA.

SAAD-FILHO A. and JOHNSTON D. (Eds) (2005) *Neoliberalism: A Critical Reader*. Pluto Press, London.

SADER E. (2011) *The New Mole: Paths of the Latin American Left*. Verso, London.

SIMMONS B. A., DOBBIN F. and GARRETT G. (2008) Introduction: the diffusion of liberalization, in SIMMONS B. A., DOBBIN F. and GARRETT G. (Eds) *The Global Diffusion of Markets and Democracy*, pp. 1–63. Cambridge University Press, New York.

SKIDELSKY R. (Ed.) (1989) *Thatcherism*. Blackwell, Oxford.

TICKELL A. and PECK J. (2003) Making global rules: globalization or neoliberalization?, in PECK J. and YEUNG H. W-C. (Eds) *Remaking the Global Economy: Economic-Geographical Perspectives*, pp. 163–181. Sage, London.

TRETJAK K. and ABRELL E. (2011) Fracturing neoliberalism: ethnographic interventions, *New Proposals* **4(2)**, 29–32.

WACQUANT L. (2012) Three steps to a historical anthropology of actually existing neoliberalism, *Social Anthropology/Anthropologie Sociale* **20(1)**, 66–79.

WAINWRIGHT H. (2003) *Reclaim the State: Experiments in Popular Democracy*. Verso, London.

WEBBER J. R. (2011) *From Rebellion to Reform in Bolivia*. Haymarket Books, Chicago, IL.

ᵃ OPEN ACCESS

Neoliberalization, uneven development, and Brexit: further reflections on the organic crisis of the British state and society

Bob Jessop ⓘ

ABSTRACT
Neoliberalization is a variegated series of processes with a core policy set that comprises: liberalization, deregulation, privatization, recommodification, internationalization, reductions in direct taxation, and decriminalization of predatory economic activities. Compared to the era of Atlantic Fordism and Spatial Keynesianism, neoliberalization promotes uneven development in the name of competitiveness and pursues policies that largely neglect its adverse economic, social, and political repercussions. Growing inequalities of income, wealth and life-chances have been ascending the political risk agenda and, through works such as Piketty's *Capital in the twenty-first Century*, have been 'conversationalized'. Yet little concrete action occurs to remedy the results of uneven development in societies undergoing neoliberal regime shifts. This contribution relates these issues to Brexit as a symptom of the organic crisis of British society, marked by manifold economic, political and social crises, and the continuing failure to address uneven development. The referendum question falsely posited that Brexiting would resolve many of these problems. However, the real issue should have been 'in' or 'out' of neoliberalism. Failure to deliver the anticipated benefits of Brexit will interact with the continuing crisis of British society to reinforce environmental, economic, social, and political crises and provide further grounds for right-wing populist mobilization.

Introduction

My contribution explores the genealogy and development of neoliberalism in its Anglo-Saxon and European heartlands and relates it to the recent changes in the world market, the world of states and a still emerging global society. As is common nowadays, I examine neoliberalization as a variegated, partial and hybridized process (cf. Peck & Theodore, 2012). I elaborate this approach in two main ways: the first is to present a taxonomy of neoliberalization; the second is to outline a periodization of one taxon, namely, principled neoliberal regime shifts in their Anglo-Saxon heartland. The best-known and most-studied cases of such shifts are the United States of America and United Kingdom; several others exist, including, most egregiously, Iceland. Next, I suggest that

---

This is an Open Access article distributed under the terms of the Creative Commons Attribution License (http://creativecommons.org/licenses/by/4.0/), which permits unrestricted use, distribution, and reproduction in any medium, provided the original work is properly cited.

neoliberalization is a major driving force of uneven development. Indeed, it is a feature, not a bug, of the neoliberal project. I examine this within a multi-temporal, multi-spatial analytical framework. There is an interesting contrast with Ordoliberalism. For, whereas neoliberalization promotes disruption to boost competition and competitiveness, Ordoliberalism seeks to achieve these goals by establishing a stable institutional framework. This contrast is reflected in the greater propensity of neoliberal regime shifts to crisis-tendencies, 'blowback' effects, and resistance. I illustrate this from the Brexit process, but other cases are the rise of US populism and the actions (and inactions) of the Trump Presidency. I conclude with some comments on the likely consequences of Brexit for the ongoing crisis in Britain's economy, state, and society.

Neoliberalism and neoliberalization

Given the polyvalence of the core terms, we find diverse typologies of neoliberalism and/or neoliberalization. None is the best entry-point for all theoretical and practical purposes. For this anniversary issue of *European Planning Studies*, I begin with its economic and political dimensions rather than its pre-history or other salient aspects of neoliberalism. From this perspective, neoliberalization is an economic, political, and social project that tends to judge economic activities in terms of profitability and social activities in terms of their contribution to accumulation and seeks to promote this vision through institutional redesign, encouraging new forms of subjectivity and conduct, and establishing new spatio-temporal fixes. This interpretation might suggest that it promotes the spontaneous operation of market forces. However, neoliberalization actually depends on the exercise of political power to establish and consolidate its various forms and, when confronted with crisis, to rescue them. As such it involves all three of Max Weber's types of 'political capitalism': unusual deals with political authority, accumulation through force and domination, and predatory economic activities (Weber, 2009). Thus one might argue that it entails a primacy of the political (understood here to include the polity, politics, and policy) rather than free market as envisaged in 'theoclassical' economics. The argument below builds on this analysis.

Based on theoretical considerations and historical observation, four main forms of neoliberalism can be distinguished analytically. These may exist in hybrid forms and, depending on their contradictory and crisis-prone evolution, different forms may also succeed each other in the same economic and political space.[1]

First, the most radical form was *neoliberal system transformation* in post-Soviet successor states. Russia and Poland provide two contrasting cases: Chicagoan 'creative destruction' induced by neoliberal shock therapy and a more Ordoliberal 'market therapy without shock'.

Second come *neoliberal regime shifts*. Breaking on principle with post-war Atlantic Fordist class compromise, at least six neoliberal policies were pursued in order to modify the balance of forces in favour of capital. These policies comprise: (1) liberalization to promote free market competition or at least greater market competition to the detriment of monopoly or state monopoly competition; (2) deregulation, based on a belief in the efficient market hypothesis and the prudential, self-preserving instincts of companies and financial institutions; (3) privatization to roll back the frontiers of the polity in favour of the profit-oriented, market-mediated economy and the efficient allocation of resources and dynamic innovative potential that markets are expected to deliver; (4) the introduction of market proxies in the residual state sector to favour efficient, effective, and economical delivery of public services, thereby reducing the scope for non-market logics in the public sector, especially when combined with cuts in state budgets; (5) reductions in direct taxation on corporate income, personal wealth, and personal income – especially on (allegedly) entrepreneurial income – in order to boost incentives for economic agents to earn, save, invest, innovate, create, and accumulate individual and corporate wealth rather than have the state determine the level and content of the national output; and (6) the promotion of internationalization to boost the free flow of goods and services, profit-producing investment and technology transfer, and the mobility of interest-bearing capital, all with a view to completing the world market. One might add to this list the decriminalization of financial crime (Black, 2014). Thatcherism and Reaganism are well-known cases but similar shifts occurred in Australia, Canada, Cyprus, Eire, Iceland, and New Zealand. While often identified with right-wing parties, these shifts have also been initiated, maintained or backed by centre-left parties, sometimes under a 'Third Way' label.

Type three comprises economic restructuring and regime shifts that occurred in response to inflationary and/or debt crises in economies pursuing import-substitution growth. These changes were imposed from outside by transnational economic institutions and organizations backed by leading capitalist powers and backed by partners among domestic political and economic elites in the countries affected. Neoliberal reforms were a condition for financial and other aid to crisis-ridden economies in parts of Africa, Asia, Eastern and Central Europe, and Latin America. While the second and third types often pursue similar policies in the (semi-)periphery of the global economy, they have analytically distinct roots.

Fourth, we observe a more pragmatic, partial, and potentially reversible set of neoliberal policy adjustments. Not all of the six (or seven) neoliberal economic policies are adopted in such cases because this type involves more modest and piecemeal changes deemed necessary by governing elites and their social base(s) to maintain existing economic and social models in the face of specific crisis-tendencies and the challenges generated by growing world market integration. In Europe, the Nordic social democracies and Rhenish capitalism provide examples. However, such adjustments can cumulate despite the fluctuating political fortunes of the parties that back them and, as if by stealth, lead to neoliberal regimes (witness Germany in the last 25 years). Moreover, following the North Atlantic Financial Crisis (hereafter, NAFC) and the Eurozone crisis, these cumulative changes have become harder to reverse as global pressures and the approach to crisis-management in Europe tend to reinforce neoliberalization. This can be seen in efforts to institutionalize neoliberalism in a succession of pacts and crisis-management responses in the Eurozone economies. One response is the rise of nationalist and populist blowback in core and periphery alike.

Periodization of neoliberal regime shifts

Neoliberalization in its Anglo-Saxon heartlands has involved seven main stages to date. The first is its pre-history as an intellectual, ideological and political movement up to 'the point of no return', i.e. when the momentum behind a neoliberal regime shift made it highly likely that a political party committed to neoliberal policies would enter office with a popular mandate or through negotiations with other parties to form a coalition government. Stage two sees the formation of a government committed to a neoliberal agenda and efforts to consolidate control over the legislature and executive branch in the face of opposition inside the government itself or from other forces acting within or at a distance from the state. Consolidation initially focused on shifting the balance of forces through a mix of short-term concessions, passive revolution, and concerted efforts to win hegemony or, in extremis, use of police powers to overcome resistance. This process may overlap with the third stage, namely, attempts to roll back the institutions and institutionalized compromises associated with different versions of the Atlantic Fordist post-war settlement. A key aim of stages two and three was to translate the discursive politics of free markets and a liberal state into substantive policy initiatives to remove obstacles to the neoliberal project. Fourth come efforts to roll forward neoliberal institutions, consolidate the shift in the balance of forces, and constitutionalize neoliberal principles nationally and, where possible, regionally and globally – making them harder to reverse even were the political conjuncture to turn temporarily against continued neoliberalization.

The fifth stage was blowback as an unintended but inevitable effect of a one-sided emphasis on serving mobile export-oriented profit-producing capital and interest-bearing capital. This led to resistance from disadvantaged capitals, intensified uneven development, increasing inequalities of income and wealth, debt-default-deflation dynamics (cf. Rasmus, 2010), and resistance from subaltern groups. This is the moment of the 'Third Way' and analogous attempts to provide flanking and supporting mechanisms to maintain the momentum of neoliberal regime shifts.

Stage six was initiated by the irruption of the NAFC. This initially signified a crisis *of* finance-dominated accumulation regimes but did not produce a crisis *of* neoliberalism in the US and UK. Indeed, this only occurred in Iceland, where the weight of the hypertrophied financial sector far exceeded that in the UK and radical measures imposed the costs of crisis-management on financial capital (Cyprus's implosion came later as part of the Eurozone crisis). However, in the first two cases, while financial capital may have lost some credibility, it continued to dominate the accumulation regime, the state apparatus, and, in the USA, the legislature. It could therefore exploit the crisis, ensuring that it did not, in Rahm Emanuel's words, 'go to waste'. Indeed, central banks and states in the neoliberal heartlands intervened massively to rescue imprudent and predatory banks that were deemed too systemically important or too well-connected politically to be allowed to fail. Toxic assets and losses were socialized at the expense of households, the public debt, and industrial capital. Financial crisis was translated discursively and practically into public debt and fiscal crises and intensified neoliberal vilification of state spending, with calls for further austerity measures.

Stage seven emerged in the context of the sixth stage. Thanks to its dominance in the power bloc, financial capital was able to manoeuvre to delay, dilute, and otherwise weaken attempts to re-regulate its operations at the expense of the public purse and future crises. This created the conditions to transform a crisis of finance-dominated accumulation into a crisis in this accumulation regime. At the same time, efforts continued to transform neoliberal austerity policies and politics into a permanent, constitutionalized state of austerity that undermine the institutions and practices of liberal democracy (Bruff, 2014; Jessop, 2016b, 2018). These are partly aimed at limiting and defeating resistance to neoliberalism and its effects. This resistance has taken increasingly vocal populist forms marked by strong exclusionary discourses, practices, and effects. These measures and the new forms of resistance indicate the continuing primacy of politics in neoliberalization.

The economic significance of neoliberalization

Neoliberalization promotes ever more forcefully (and, in many cases, forcibly) the completion of the world market and the correlative, but increasingly contradictory, subordination of all social relations to the competitive logic of capital accumulation. Rhetorically, its proponents aim to overcome the frictions of national boundaries, open national economies to foreign competition, intensify the global division of labour, and enhance the role of mobile financial capital in equalizing profit rates on a global scale and, indeed, equalizing the return on all commodified assets. Ever more rarefied forms of fictitious capital (including derivatives) are crucial vectors of this process. While the goal of completing the world market seems to privilege market forces its advancement, consolidation, crisis-management, and defence against resistance depend on the primacy of the political. Substantively, neoliberalization privileges some capitals and spaces over others, enabling them to appropriate superprofits at the expense of less powerful economic agents and less attractive spaces. Among other effects, world market integration in the shadow of neoliberalism enhances capital's capacity to defer and/or displace the effects of its internal contradictions by increasing the global scope of its operations, reinforcing its capacities to disembed certain of its operations from local material, social, and spatio-temporal constraints, enabling it to deepen the spatial and scalar divisions of labour, thereby expanding opportunities to relocate across spaces and places and move up, down, and across scales. It also collapses time horizons by commodifying and securitizing the future. All of these processes have their specific contradictions and crisis-tendencies.

To establish why neoliberal regime shifts, cumulative neoliberal policy adjustments, and the politics of neoliberalization prove resilient rather than retreat in the face of their respective crisis-tendencies, we must look beyond their intellectual appeal and domestic and international political backing to the economic logic of neoliberalization. This is related to the distinction between the use-value and exchange-value aspects of the elementary form of value, namely, the commodity. The commodity is both a use-value and an exchange-value: without use-value, it would not be purchased; without exchange-value, it would not be produced. Analogous properties are found in other forms of the capital relation. The worker is both a concrete individual with specific skills, knowledge, and creativity *and* an abstract unit of labour power substitutable by other such units (or, indeed, other factors of production); the wage (including the social wage) is both a source of demand *and* a cost of production; money functions both as a 'national' currency circulating within a monetary bloc where it is subject to state control *and* as an international money exchangeable against other monies in currency markets; profit-producing capital is a more or less concrete stock of time- and place-specific assets undergoing valorization according to their specific properties *and* abstract value in motion (notably as realized profits available for re-investment); land, defined to include all natural resources, is a free gift of nature *and* a monopolistic claim on revenues in the form of rent; knowledge circulates as part of the intellectual commons *and* can also become the object of intellectual property rights; and so forth.

In each case, neoliberalization privileges the exchange-value aspect over the use-value aspect of a given form of the capital relation. It emphasizes cost reduction and cost recovery and subjects all economic activities to profit-oriented logic regardless of any negative externalities. This structural privileging of exchange- over use-value not only favours capital over labour but also benefits hypermobile profit-producing and interest-bearing capital at the expense of other capitals that are embedded in broader sets of social relations and/or that must be valorized in particular times and places. Mobile profit-producing capital gains to the extent that it can plausibly threaten to reorganize its production chains to avoid barriers to differential accumulation that arise from state intervention and/or pressure from subaltern classes and social movements. This intensifies the influence of the logic of capital on a global scale as the global operation of the law of value commensurates local conditions at the same time as it promotes the treadmill search for superprofits that exceed the prevailing world market average rate of profit. The same phenomenon can be seen at smaller scales, such as the European Union, where a combination of enlargement and increased integration inside the single market enabled European and, even more, non-European capital to exploit national, regional, and local differences and demand fiscal, financial, or material concessions to attract investment. In turn, interest-bearing capital is the most abstract and general expression of exchange-value not only in the capitalist mode of production itself but also in capitalist social formations more generally. It gains from the full set of neoliberal policies (including de-criminalization) which facilitate, inter alia, financial innovation (e.g. securitization), unregulated speculation, and predatory finance. In this sense, compared to the largely intermediary roles of finance in Fordist regimes and, likewise, in the much-heralded (if somewhat lagging or lacking) productivist, post-Fordist knowledge-based economy (KBE), neoliberalization promotes not a benign form of finance-led growth but a predatory finance-dominated accumulation regime.

Such one-sided treatment can overlook or deny, but not suppress, the significance of the use-value aspects of the above-mentioned forms of the capital relation. Eventually their vital role in capitalist (and societal) reproduction becomes evident and, absent appropriate ways to handle the contradictions between use- and exchange-value, crises emerge that may forcibly re-impose the unity of the capital relation, typically through a more or less sudden and destructive process of devalorization. This one-sided treatment also increases inequalities of wealth and income that undermine demand and also generate growing popular resistance – issues recognized in largely neoliberal spaces such as the World Economic Forum as major threats to prosperity, social cohesion, and political stability and 'mainstreamed' by texts like Piketty (2014). But neither crises nor elite hand-wringing can easily reverse or otherwise redress the *structural* impact of neoliberal measures since the 1980s and their juridico-political consolidation through neoliberal constitutionalism and authoritarianism. This would require a favourable balance of forces and concerted action in a period when mainstream opposition parties and movements have been weakened and further demobilized by the neoliberal mantra of 'no alternative'. This has created the space for extreme populist blowback against neoliberalization.

Neoliberalization and uneven development

Uneven development occurs in all modes of production and social formations but assumes different forms in each. In capitalism, it is shaped by a distinctive political economy of time, by disjunctions among labour time, production time, circulation time, turnover time, and naturally necessary reproduction time within and across different sectors, and by the dialectic of time–space compression and distantiation. While the world market as both the presupposition and posit of capital accumulation is the final frontier and ultimate horizon of uneven development, the latter is better seen as a series of fractal processes that occur in self-similar but not identical ways, cross-cutting and interweaving territories, places, scales, and networks and producing complex multi-spatial and multi-temporal effects (cf. Jessop, 2016a).

Together these economic and extra-economic mechanisms provide conditions for uneven production of absolute and relative-surplus value and its redistribution in form of superprofits and quasi-rents tied to spatial and/or political advantages (Hadjimichalis, 1987, 2018). Institutional and spatio-temporal fixes shape the forms and effects of uneven development, including the scope for combined development. But structural effects and strategic interventions are mediated in complex, ultimately uncontrollable, ways by inherited institutions, competing strategies, the shifting balance of forces, and creative destruction. This emphasizes, as Hudson notes, 'the decisive role of distinctive subnational couplings of economic structures and modes of governance and regulation' (Hudson, 2003, p. 50).

The pattern of uneven development varies with the differential articulation of economic, political and social spaces into a variegated world market. For example, there is a significant contrast between the heartlands of Atlantic Fordism in its heyday and today's neoliberal heartlands regarding strategies and policies towards uneven development. Atlantic Fordism was associated with measures to limit and/or compensate for uneven development (e.g. through spatial Keynesianism, cf. Brenner, 2004). The political and policy focus in this period was on creating the conditions for a Fordist dynamic (with significant variation among economies in the circuits of Atlantic Fordism), integrating national economic space, generalizing norms of mass consumption, and spreading the benefits of Fordist growth through infrastructural investment, collective bargaining, collective consumption, and welfare state measures. This required measures to compensate for the uneven sectoral, regional and social impact of post-war growth to promote the virtuous cycle of Fordist accumulation. In contrast, the rise and consolidation of neoliberal regimes was marked by neglect of uneven development and/or measures to reinforce it by actively freeing market forces. These measures involved rolling back policies and apparatuses concerned to counteract uneven development and rolling forward policies and reorganizing apparatuses to support sectoral and regional winners rather than to sustain losers or compensate sectors or regions that lose from the new neoliberal strategy. Two related aspects of this approach are: identify cities and regions that can serve as national (or EU-wide) champions; and induce, persuade or force declining regions to compete on neoliberal criteria for limited funds that might facilitate regeneration. Both aspects intensify uneven development, especially when declining regions are blamed for their own decline, required to make themselves attractive to capital based on mobilizing their own resources, or left to rot. More generally, whether promoting strong competition based on dynamic efficiency or weak competition based on a race-to-the bottom, global, European, national, regional, and local competitiveness took precedence over inter-regional and societal cohesion. This is because the neoliberal policy set prioritizes exchange-value and the rights of capital over hard-won economic, juridico-political and social rights for workers and citizens or a broader sense of national solidarity. Its destructive impact is reinforced by accumulation through dispossession (especially the plundering of public assets and the intellectual commons to benefit capital), regulatory arbitrage, and the limited mobility of productive capitals that have to be valorized in particular times and places.

Uneven development in the United Kingdom

Neoliberal measures since 1979 reinforced the ongoing pattern of de-industrialization and, where core industries survived, contributed to their balkanization, i.e. their splitting up among rival foreign capitalist interests. Successive governments have declared Britain to be 'open for business' (and takeover), leading to competing and uncoordinated ties to foreign capital, including, recently, Chinese, Indian, and Russian interests alongside 'the usual suspects'. Without the economic, political, and social bases for a concerted national economic strategy, Britain's economic fortunes came to depend heavily on the vagaries of finance-dominated accumulation and the wider world market and a low-skill, low-tech, low-wage, and even zero-hour service sector associated with a neoliberal race to the bottom. The combined impact of general macro-economic policies and specific micro-economic measures to restructure nationalized industries (which were over-represented in the 'north') plus government investment projects that have favoured London and the Rest of the South-East[2] have regional implications. It has benefitted the City of London, and rentier and producer service interests located in London and the South-East (Martin, 1988; Martin, Pike, Tyler & Gardiner, 2015; Peck & Tickell, 1992) plus mobile transnational capital, and high-tech industries. Marginal and poor localities in dynamic core cities, notably London, and regions have gained from their ties to the dynamic and internationalized core. Regions and third-tier cities and towns outside London and the Rest of the South East, especially where the decline or closure of traditional industries has not been countered by the rise of new sectors and where public services have suffered from withdrawn subsidies and other neoliberal austerity measures. Overall, this has generated far more job losses in manufacturing (both in absolute and relative terms) in the 'north' of England and the provinces than in the 'south'. The resulting divergent set of regional economies with marked differences in economic structure, sectoral composition and trade performance continues to constrain efforts to 'take back control' of the British economy.

These problems are aggravated by the historical weakness of the British state and its inability to pursue a serious economic strategy consistently and effectively. Post-war growth in other advanced economies had been secured with more or less good results in dirigiste regimes, corporatist regimes, and liberal regimes (Shonfield, 1965). However, the British state (understood in Gramscian terms as 'political society + civil society')[3] lacked the capacities to engage in statist intervention, effective corporatist coordination, or a consistently rigorous laissez-faire line. Its interventions therefore oscillated uneasily among the three strategies that all failed in their different ways in different conjunctures, thereby reproducing Britain's 'flawed Fordist' mode of growth (Jessop, 1980, 1992; Jessop, Bonnett, Bromley, & Ling, 1988). A weak state meant that efforts to promote re-industrialization, develop a competitive service sector, and modernize the wider society failed. In contrast, de facto or principled laissez-faire has enabled the City to thrive in a deregulated and international environment.

Indeed, while key aspects of the post-war social democratic and Conservative 'One Nation' post-war settlement have been rolled back, neoliberal policies have not provided the basis for a new national accumulation strategy or stable 'popular capitalist' social basis. Instead neoliberalization has promoted the deeper integration of (parts of) British economic space into the circuits of international financial capital and advantaged international profit-producing capital. The ever more visible polarization of wealth and income, the intensified pattern of uneven development, and the shift from a welfare to a workfare state are generating discontent (reflected most recently in the Brexit referendum). This in turn prompts measures to monitor the population, insulate government from popular demands for economic and social justice, encourage divide-and-rule tactics, and, whenever necessary, repress dissent.

Historical context and conjunctural shifts

While financialization in the UK has been boosted by neoliberalization, it has deep historical roots. This reflects the City of London's distinctive role as the leading international financial centre for international financial transactions. Financial capital (in the interconnected forms of money-dealing capital, stock-dealing capital, and interest-bearing capital) has long been dominant in the British power bloc (cf. Ingham, 1984). This is reflected in the dominance of neoliberal policy paradigms at different sites in the state apparatus and political regime. While the City of London has changed, with domestic banks and financial institutions ceding primacy to international financial institutions and with interest-bearing capital becoming more important than commercial capital, the City remains a key force in the power bloc and key factor in uneven development. It has gained influence due to financial innovation, increasing its leverage, and thanks to its massive internationalization. This weakens the ties between the interests of leading sections of the British power bloc (if, indeed, one can still talk of a *British* power bloc) and the development of British economic space as a whole. It has also weakened the ties between the power bloc and British working class, reinforced by the decline of traditional heavy industry, retail capital, and small and medium enterprises, all of which lack the capacity to challenge the hegemony of financial capital.

The growing split within the Establishment and wider society since the 1950s concerns the UK's relationship to Continental Europe and the EU and the alternatives such as Atlanticism, globalism, and protectionism. There is also a crisis of authority rooted in the decline of deference, loss of confidence among the ruling classes, and recurrent state failure. The recent legitimacy crisis results from the failure of successive neoliberal projects, pursued under Conservative, New Labour, and coalition governments alike, to deliver sustainable nationwide prosperity. The representational crisis is evident in a growing disconnection between the natural governing parties in Westminster, party members, and their voters. This created the space for the rise of left and right populism, for Corbynism as a social movement opposed to the Blairite rump of MPs who control the parliamentary party, and, of course, for the disaffection shown in the Brexit vote. The legitimacy and representational crises were exacerbated by the loss of control over public opinion, which is the hinge between political and civil society, over continued EU membership. This was due in part to the hostility of much of the British press. Finally, there is a wider organic crisis in the social order, reflected in contestation over

'British values', disputed national and regional identities, north–south and other regional divides, the metropolitan orientation of intellectual strata, and generational splits.

Overall, the combination of weak state capacities in the period of flawed post-war economic expansion and the subsequent pursuit of neoliberal strategies has produced a seriously weakened 'real economy' and hypertrophied rent-seeking financial sector. Thus, successive governments have failed to provide adequate technical and vocational training to address labour shortages, to protect worker and union rights to limit the race to the bottom and spur productivity-boosting capital investment, to encourage R&D to promote the knowledge-based economy, to overcome the housing crisis and reduce the unproductive 'housing sector borrowing requirement', to fund the National Health Service rather than sustain the military–industrial complex or reduce corporate and top-rate taxes, and to moderate uneven regional development. After the irruption of the NAFC, New Labour responded with measures to bail out the financial sector and, as a result, transformed a financial crisis into a fiscal crisis marked by rising public sector deficits, which were ruthlessly exploited by the Conservative Party, City of London, and right-wing press to discredit New Labour's hard-won reputation for economic competence. Cameron built on this economic, political, and intellectual failure to pursue a harder neoliberal line. And, despite her initial rhetorical critiques of the economic and social injustices of past policies, repeated on the steps of 10 Downing Street on becoming Prime Minister, the austerity state is surviving under Mrs May's premiership and the new Chancellor (Philip Hammond) is committed to further austerity to build reserves against possible economic and fisco-financial problems during the negotiations or following Brexit.

Financialization, Thatcherism, New Labour, and neoliberalism

A 1989 report in the Bank of England's *Quarterly Bulletin* questioned the benefits of London's role as an international financial centre. It noted:

> There may of course be disadvantages in hosting a major financial centre. Salaries and wages may be forced up, thus driving up rents and house prices, with undesirable social consequences. Regional disparities may be exacerbated and the congestion of local transport systems may be aggravated. The economy may face risks due to over-dependence on a single sector. The operation of monetary policy may become complicated by the need to nurture the financial sector. Regulation may need to be more complex than otherwise. Finally, it has sometimes been argued that the financial sector merely preys on the rest of the economy, adding to costs and distorting other markets – by, for instance, attracting able individuals who might be more socially productive in other areas such as manufacturing (Davis & Latter, 1989, p. 516).

Having noted this danger, the authors quickly responded that, 'on balance, the financial sector may be judged to offer substantial net benefits to the economy' (ibid.). Yet these worries were well-founded. Indeed, the feared tendencies have intensified in the last three decades and entrenched the UK economy's dependence on international finance. Uneven development has been reinforced to the benefit of London and the detriment of other regions. In short, the problems that became evident in the financial crisis in 2007–8 and continuing economic decline did not emerge out of the blue. The City of London has seen increasing internationalization and ever-closer integration into the global circuit of capital. Regulatory arbitrage played a key role here, when, following the 'Big Bang' that liberalized and deregulated financial capital, London could become the leading international centre for international financial capital. Indeed, it is noteworthy that many of the biggest financial scandals that have transpired in 2007–2018 were generated through activities in the City, regardless of the nationality or primary seat of the financial institutions involved.

Moreover, by privileging owner occupation in the hope of electoral benefit, successive governments boosted the financial services sector. This skewed investment towards sectors that serviced the consumption boom (retailing, distribution, personal financial services and credit, equity release) based on fictitious credit. This increased the mass and share of profits going to interest-bearing capital at the expense of profit-producing capital that creates internationally tradable commodities. In turn, this aggravated the crowding out effects of the housing sector borrowing requirement on productive investment, and discouraged regional labour mobility from areas of high unemployment to areas of labour shortage.

This illustrates on a national scale the more general observation of Martin and Gardiner about the multi-scalar effects of what I describe as neo-liberal finance-dominated accumulation:

> The financial crisis revealed the boom for what it was, a form of development that was highly *unbalanced*: on a global level, between creditor and debtor nations (especially China and the USA respectively); within the Eurozone, between the strong core members such as Germany and France, and the weaker peripheral members such as Spain, Italy and Portugal; and within countries, between consumption and investment, between services and production, between state revenues and spending, between rich and poor, and, spatially, between different cities and regions. For while the 'long boom' between the early 1990s and 2007 may have lifted most regions and cities, it lifted some much more than others. Indeed, in some instances (the UK is a particularly prominent case) it reinforced regional inequalities (Martin & Gardiner, 2018, p. 25).

Brexit

> [The Brexit vote] was a singular event that is but one symptom of a continuing organic crisis of the British state and society and a stimulus for further struggles over the future of the United Kingdom and its place in Europe and the wider world (Jessop, 2017, p. 133).

This claim illustrates Gramsci's observation that a crisis is 'a process and not an event (Gramsci, 1995, p. 219). Its course and outcomes depend on how crisis symptoms are construed and managed. Europe and the European Union have long been a neuralgic point of division inside the Conservative Party and within the establishment more widely. In this sense, the decision to run a referendum on Brexit and its result were symptoms of an organic crisis. The referendum result did not resolve this crisis but reproduced it in new guises.

This can be seen in the failure of the British state, the ruling party, business interests, or organized labour to develop a coherent negotiating position in the following two years. It was six months after the referendum vote, on 29 March 2017, that the official letter required under Article 50 of the Lisbon Treaty to formally notify the European Commission of the UK government's intention to withdraw from the European Union. The delay was not spent working out a negotiating position or preparing an exit strategy in the case of no deal. In contrast, the European Union prepared a tough negotiating position. Negotiations began on 19 June 2017, 11 days after the 2017 General Election, which, far from giving the Prime Minister, Theresa May, a strong mandate, saw her losing her majority and dependent for a majority on the support of Northern Ireland's hard-line Democratic Unionist Party MPs, which gave them a veto over decisions on the border issue and future relations with the Irish Republic. Negotiations focused first on the 'divorce' bill before post-Brexit arrangements could be discussed. After several unplanned delays, a fudged agreement on the conditions for discussing the final settlement and post-Brexit transition arrangements was reached in late December 2017. Some issues were agreed, others left ambiguous, and some postponed. The latter included the border arrangements between Northern Ireland and the Irish Republic. Discussions on this and other issues began on 19 March 2018. The Cabinet committee charged with preparing the UK's negotiating position failed to reach agreement in time for the June summit of the European Union. A negotiating position was eventually agreed at a full Cabinet meeting on 6 July 2018, based on fudging the government's redlines on sovereignty, trade, and free movement and 'cherry-picking' on customs arrangement for agricultural and manufactured goods while leaving services outside any future deal. Whether the negotiating position holds within the government and ruling party before negotiations begin was unclear as this article was finalized on 7 July 2018. It could well do so because time is short to secure a deal before the dead line and no deal would mean there is no transition period – only a cliff-edge exit for which the government has not prepared. Even before this, growing realization of the difficulties of exiting from a 45-year entanglement with the European Union led to a contested agreement on a 21-month-long 'transitional' arrangement during which little will change substantively. Accordingly, Brexit proper is due to happen eventually on 1 January 2021, which is four and a half years after the referendum.

The weakness of a neoliberalized state apparatus has much to do with these delays. The state, as argued above, has been unable to act in an effective dirigiste, corporatist, liberal (or, more recently, neo-liberal) manner. Muddling through on a week-by-week basis while trying different grand strategies is its modus operandi. The stark divisions within parliamentary parties, national parties, and the electorate on the issue of Brexit and its most suitable form have reinforced this. And, surprisingly, given how significant Brexit is for the prospects of business and finance, it has taken two years for major commercial, industrial, and financial interests to articulate their positions in public. In part this reflects the fact that the Balkanization of the UK economy means that there is no significant national or comprador bourgeoisie that could benefit from Brexit and that the multiple international linkages of capital also block a coherent stance. So, there is no collective voice of capital (apart from the plea for certainty) and it has taken almost two years for individual capitals, fractions, and sectors to begin to voice worries and begin special pleading. But this situation also reflects the toxic nature of pro-Brexit tabloid media reaction to any gain-saying of the 'will of the people', whether this gain-saying comes from the Supreme Court, the House of Lords, Cabinet members, Members of Parliament, respected think tanks, or other significant forces. This reflects the continuing hegemonic crisis in the power bloc, representational crises rooted in partisan dealignment, electoral volatility, and disaffection with politics, and crises of authority and legitimacy.

In addition, cumulative budget cuts and staff reductions in the civil service over 40 years have left the state without qualified staff to prepare serious impact reports on the implications of Brexit on specific sectors, regions, generations, and the wider society; likewise, it lacks sufficient personnel who understand the diplomatic, legal, financial and economic aspects of trade negotiations, which have long been delegated to the European Union, to present a clear Brexit strategy. These deficits matter because the European Union has a strong *rechtsstaatlich* (constitutional and legal) orientation such that negotiations occur within the framework of the Treaties, legal rules, and conventions and overseen by the Court of Justice of the European Union, which is charged with ensuring equal implementation and enforcement of the treaties, laws, and rules. Maintaining the legal integrity of the European Union, even as its range of activities expands in new directions following the Eurozone crisis, the rise of internal divisions on migration, and the Trump-induced, multi-faceted fractures in transatlantic unity, is crucial to its overall operation. The redlines set out in the government's initial negotiating position, notably regaining national sovereignty over laws, trade, and borders, threaten the legal identity of the European Union and limit possible Brexit outcomes. The British common law tradition has encouraged collective misapprehension on this point within parts of the British establishment and the pro-Brexit media, leading them to interpret Brussels' redlines as a rejection of compromise and attempt to 'punish' Britain for its temerity in voting to leave the European Union. Similar effects stem from the commitment to a nineteenth-century notion of national sovereignty in an increasingly integrated planet earth, world economy, and world of states that has recognized the need for – always contested – forms of governance to address supranational threats, challenges and crises.

> Much of what passes for 'negotiation' on the UK side ... has involved a desire to retain the benefits of EU membership while shrugging off the status and responsibilities of membership. But when Mrs May appeals for 'a comprehensive system of mutual recognition' she is going still further. She is not asking for something that applies within the EU. She is asking for something that even EU Member States do not expect of each other. A 'comprehensive system of mutual recognition' is *not* found within the EU. Mrs May is asking that the UK be treated *better* than a Member State of the EU (Weatherill, 2018).

Yet these complexities are ignored because, as Wren-Lewis notes, 'Brexiteers believed they owned the referendum victory, and so acted as if they had the right to decide what Brexit means' (2018). Following the referendum, the British public have been regularly informed that 'Brexit means Brexit', that the government is committed to securing the 'best Brexit for the whole of the United Kingdom' and that 'No deal would be better than a bad deal'. These anodyne assertions are a smokescreen for cluelessness on how to deliver Brexit and, even after agreement on the government's negotiating position in July 2018, there is no certainty that it will prove acceptable to the EU negotiators or the remaining member states. Some commentators are speculating that Brexiteers hope that they will reject it, so that a 'clean Brexit' on World Trade Organization terms would eventually ensue.

Apart from the Department for Exiting the European Union (DExEU), no department had Brexit as its top priority or a major priority in its Single Department Plan for 2017/18 financial year. This situation remains for 2018/19. Even departments whose briefs will be most impacted by Brexit have not integrated it into their priorities but mention it as a consideration relevant to their priorities (Lloyd, 2018; more generally on lack of preparation, see Owen, Lloyd, & Rutter, 2018). This is compounded by the paralysis of the Conservative Cabinet, parliamentary party, and grass-roots members, who are overwhelmingly elderly

Brexit supporters. As the deadline for an agreement approaches, the room for manoeuvre is shrinking (e.g. the issue of the Irish border, the problems of reconciling national autonomy with the complementary but different requirements of continued membership of the customs union (which bans internal tariffs) and single market (which includes freedom of movement as well as freedom in the flow of goods), the possibility of separate deals on goods and services, the special status of London as an international financial centre for international financial capital, fisheries and agriculture, and so on). There is also miscalculation about the speed and ease with which new free trade deals can be negotiated with other governments, each of which has its own negotiating agenda. A significant irony in the present situation is that, by and large, the advocates of hard Brexit lack expertise in many of these topics, thanks to a naïve understanding of national sovereignty that is inappropriate to a world of interdependent states and thanks also to a blind Ricardian faith in the virtues of free trade among nations premised on comparative advantage that is inappropriate to a world of just-in-time commodity chains and finance-dominated accumulation. Conversely, those who have expertise in these matters are largely opposed to Brexit in general and cannot, in any case, design a form of Brexit that is impossible in principle or, if it were feasible, cannot be delivered within the current time-frame (e.g. registration of aliens, customs software, trade negotiations). The point has been reached when there are not enough funds, staff, political clarity, or time to exit the EU on schedule, even on a 'clean Brexit', no deal basis, following World Trade Organization rules. This helps to explain the steady series of concessions to the EU negotiating redlines, such as the divorce bill, the granting of EU citizens full rights during the transition period, the 'backstop' plan for keeping Northern Ireland in the customs union and single market in the absence of any other arrangement acceptable to Ireland and the European Union more generally, no new trade deals to be implemented before 2020, and so on.

Ian Dunt's conclusions on the Brexit process shortly after the referendum remain valid:

> Britain's government is approaching Brexit ineptly, misjudging its opponent, underestimating the challenges and prioritising its short-term political interests over the long-term interests of the country. Our ministers have thrown away their leverage and failed to neutralise the advantages held by the EU. Through a mixture of ignorance and ideological frenzy, they are driving Britain towards a hard, chaotic Brexit (Dunt, 2016, pp. 154–50).

Uneven development after Brexit

Whatever the outcome of the Article 50 negotiations, Brexit will not reverse the historical legacies of uneven development. On the contrary, it is likely to worsen the situation for the Northern peripheral regions, where there was strong support for Brexit, relative to the City and the UK's southern core (Lavery, 2017, p. 39; see also Clarke, Goodwin, & Whitely, 2017). This can be seen in four areas: the trade effects of Brexit, the loss of EU structural funds and other regional support, and the regional economic impact of likely economic regress and falling government revenues. Overall this will damage Brexit-supporting regions and Brexit voters more than Remain-supporting regions.

First, the export base of London and the rest of the South East is far more internationalized than that of other UK regions and therefore less exposed to the impact of declining trade with the EU (Los, McCann, Springford, & Thissen, 2017). This reflects the economic and financial base of the South compared with the rest of the UK. Between 1993 and 2007, output in banking and finance increased by 180 per cent whilst manufacturing (upon which Northern economies remained more heavily reliant) saw increases of only 11 per cent (Martin, 2010, p. 37). London is the only city region to have exceeded pre-crisis levels of per capita output and is the only region to have increased employment in the financial sector since 2009 (Lavery, 2017). One consequence is that, whereas EU exports account for 7 per cent of London's gross product, other regions, notably in the North and South-West, depend far more heavily on EU markets and, indeed, the level of local dependence increased between 2000 and 2010 in 34 of the UK's Nuts-2 regions (Los et al., 2017, p. 789). In addition, as major manufacturing firms are now emphasizing publicly, their commodity chains are integrated with the EU and will be disrupted by tariffs, new customs frictions, and sterling devaluation. For example, the Society of Motor Manufacturers and Traders (SSMT) reports that 20–50 percent of components in the automotive sector are sourced from the EU (SSMT, 2014, p. 6). In contrast, London and the South East have seen decreasing reliance on EU demand in this period. The Brexiteers response that components could be sourced more cheaply from the world market and that competitive pressure would force EU suppliers to reduce prices ignores the complexities of trade deals and supply chains. Recognition of this risk seems to have informed the compromise negotiating position reached on 8 July 2018, which aims for a customs partnership in agricultural and manufactured goods.

Second, there will be a severe post-Brexit loss after of EU grants supporting UK institutions, cities and regions, and economic activities and replacing them through UK funding will diminish the much-vaunted 'Brexit dividend'. Regarding uneven development, EU structural funds have gone disproportionately to 'less developed' and 'transition' regions, such as the South West, Wales, Yorkshire and Humber, the North East, and North West.[4] For example, seven of the ten local economic partnerships that received the most structural funding were located in the North; the South was home to all of the ten partnerships that received the lowest level of funding (Hunt, Lavery, Vittery, & Berry, 2016, pp. 6–7).[5] Local authorities in rural areas also predict massive detriment as unaffordable homes, poor connectivity, skills gaps and health inequalities will threatening their future success and prosperity (Carroll, 2018).

Third, if there is no Brexit dividend, which is the most likely outcome according to calculations about the impact of all four possible Brexit scenarios from hard Brexit through a bespoke deal to the softest of Brexits (Global Future, 2018), this will limit the funds available to the UK government to cushion the impact in peripheral regions, cities, and towns and to assist their regeneration. The research by Jonathan Portes and associates for the Global Future think-tank found that even a bespoke deal, the government's preferred option, would have a net negative fiscal impact of about £40bn a year. Government reports indicate similar results.

Fourth, recent research by the Institute for Public Policy Research (Lloyd, 2018) and the Oliver Wyman consultancy (2018) have established that a hard Brexit would hit the cost of living for those outside London more because of their lower household incomes and the composition of their purchases of goods and services, which are more exposed to tariff increases (e.g. meat and dairy products) or prices increases due to devaluation (oil and gas). Overall, gains from importing 150 goods and services from agreeing free trade deals with all other countries in the world market will not compensate for the increased cost of imports from the European Union under any of the four Brexit scenarios (Oliver Wyman, 2018).

Conclusions

There is no pure case of neoliberalism, nor of the four types identified in my taxonomy. The British case is closest to a principled neoliberal regime shift and is an important case for the proposed periodization of such shifts into seven stages to date. Nonetheless, every case also has special features in general and in each stage. This is clearly so for the United Kingdom. The background to the post-war crisis is Britain's 'flawed Fordism', the dominance of finance capital economically and in the power bloc (Establishment) even during the heyday of Fordism, and a state that lacked the capacities to engage in effective corporatist, dirigiste, or liberal intervention in pursuit of a coherent accumulation strategy or state project. This provided the distinctive context for the principled neoliberal regime shift, pragmatically prefigured in the dying days of the 1975–79 Labour Government, that achieved its 'point of no return' or take-off moment in 1978. Subsequent stages of neoliberalization aggravated rather than reversing the flawed development of the British space economy, worsening its uneven development, and creating the conditions for the financial crisis. The latter in turn intensified the organic crisis of the state even as it provided an opportunity to strengthen the dominance of financial capital and extend neoliberalization. Yet austerity, uneven development, and disillusion also prepared the ground for the referendum vote for Brexit, the consequences of which include a continuation of the organic crisis of the British state, further uneven development, and Brexceptionalism. It seems as if the Brexit referendum was the hinge between 'a failed state' and 'a state intent on failure' (cf. Younge, 2016).[6] For an incapable government presiding over an ineffective state that has failed to plan for no deal and is more fearful of pro-Brexit media barons wielding power without responsibility than the *sotto voce* opposition of business and finance has sought to reclaim sovereignty without being able to able to exercise it effectively, let alone in the public good.

Notes

1. This taxonomy draws on Jessop (2016b, 2018).
2. Witness the 2012 Olympic Games, the Cross-Rail project in London, and the third Heathrow runway.
3. Cf. Gramsci (1971, p. 261).
4. Projects supported by the European Regional Development Fund created 44,331 jobs in Wales in the 2007–2013 funding round; other job creation figures were 20,149 (Yorkshire and Humberside), 20,602 (North East), and 29,795 (North West) (Hunt et al., 2016, p. 7).
5. There are 39 LEPS in total in England.
6. I owe the wonderful quotation from Gary Younge to MacLeod and Jones (2018). Younge actually described Britain as 'cutting the figure not so much of a failed state as a state intent on failure'. The quotation was too good not to use again but I amended the quotation and his extended coda to better reflect the argument developed in this article.

Acknowledgment

This article was written during tenure of fellowship at Cardiff University in the WISERD Civil Society Programme funded by the Economic and Social Research Council [award: ES/L009099/1]. My analysis benefitted from discussions with Martin Jones. I am also grateful to Phil Cooke for his patience as I finished the article and for his insightful feedback.

Disclosure Statement

No potential conflict of interest was reported by the author.

Funding

This article was written during tenure of fellowship at Cardiff University in the WISERD Civil Society Programme funded by the Economic and Social Research Council [grant number ES/L009099/1].

ORCID

Bob Jessop ⓘ http://orcid.org/0000-0001-8134-3926

References

Black, W. K. (2014, May 27). Posing as hyper-rationality: OMB's assault on effective regulation. *New Economic Perspectives.*

Brenner, N. (2004). *New state spaces.* Oxford: Oxford University Press.

Bruff, I. (2014). The rise of authoritarian neoliberalism. *Rethinking Marxism, 26*(11), 113–129. doi:10.1080/08935696.2013.843250

Carroll, L. (2018, July 4). Brexit to have greatest negative impact on regions outside London. *The Guardian.* Retrieved from https://www.theguardian.com/politics/2018/jul/04/brexit-greatest-negative-impact-regions-outside-london

Clarke, H., Goodwin, M., & Whitely, P. (2017). *Brexit: Why Britain voted to leave the European Union.* Cambridge: Cambridge University Press.

Davis, E. P., & Latter, A. R. (1989). London as an international financial centre. *Bank of England Quarterly Bulletin, 29*(11), 516–528.

Dunt, I. (2016). *Brexit. What the hell happens now?* London: Canbury Press.

Global Future. (2018). *Too high a price: The cost of Brexit, what the public thinks.* London: Global Future. Retrieved from https://ourglobalfuture.com/wp-content/ … /04/GlobalFuture-Too_high_a_price.pdf

Gramsci, A. (1971). *Selections from the prison notebooks.* London: Lawrence & Wishart.

Gramsci, A. (1995). *Further selections from the prison notebooks.* London: Lawrence & Wishart.

Hadjimichalis, C. (1987). *Uneven development and regionalism: State, territory and class in Southern Europe.* London: Croom Helm.

Hadjimichalis, C. (2018). *Crisis spaces: Structures, struggles and solidarity in Southern Europe.* London: Routledge.

Hudson, R. (2003). European integration and new forms of uneven development but not the end of territorially distinctive capitalisms in Europe. *European Urban and Regional Studies, 10*(1), 49–67. doi:10.1177/a032539

Hunt, T., Lavery, S., Vittery, W., & Berry, C. (2016). *UK regions and European structural and investment funds.* Sheffield, UK: Sheffield Political Economy Research Institute. *SPERI British Political Economy Brief No. 24.* Retrieved from http://speri.dept.shef.ac.uk/wp-content/uploads/2016/05/Brief24-UK-regions-and-European-structural-and-investment-funds.pdf

Ingham, G. (1984). *Capitalism divided? The City and industry in British social development.* Basingstoke: Macmillan.

Jessop, B. (1980). The transformation of the state in postwar Britain. In R. Scase (Ed.), *The state in Western Europe* (pp. 23–94). London: Croom Helm.

Jessop, B. (1992). From social democracy to Thatcherism: Twenty-five years of British politics. In N. Abercrombie, & A. Warde (Eds.), *Social change in contemporary Britain* (pp. 45–68). Cambridge: Polity.

Jessop, B. (2016a). Territory, politics, governance and multispatial metagovernance. *Territory, Politics, Governance, 4*(1), 8–32. doi:10.1080/21622671.2015.1123173

Jessop, B. (2016b). The heartlands of neoliberalism and the rise of the austerity state. In S. Springer, K. Birch & J. MacLeavy (Eds.), *The handbook of neoliberalism* (pp. 410–421). London: Routledge.

Jessop, B. (2017). The organic crisis of the British state: Putting Brexit in its place. *Globalizations, 14* (2), 133–141. doi:10.1080/14747731.2016.1228783

Jessop, B. (2018). Neoliberalism and workfare: Schumpeterian or Ricardian? In D. Cahill, M. Konings, M. Cooper & D. Primrose (Eds.), *SAGE handbook of neoliberalism* (pp. 347–358). London: SAGE.

Jessop, B., Bonnett, K., Bromley, S., & Ling, T. (1988). *Thatcherism: A tale of two nations*. Cambridge: Polity.

Lavery, S. (2017). Will Brexit deepen the UK's 'North-South' divide? In S. Lavery, L. Quaglia & C. Dannreuther (Eds.), *The political economy of Brexit and the UK's national business model*. Sheffield, UK: SPERI Paper No. 41. Retrieved from http://speri.dept.shef.ac.uk/wp-content/uploads/2017/05/SPERI-Paper-41-The-Political-Economy-of-Brexit-and-the-UK-s-National-Business-Model.pdf

Lloyd, L. (2018). *A missed chance to reassure that Whitehall has Brexit covered*. London: Institute for Government. Retrieved from https://www.instituteforgovernment.org.uk/blog/missed-chance-reassure-whitehall-has-brexit-covered

Los, B., McCann, P., Springford, J., & Thissen, M. (2017). The mismatch between local voting and the local economic consequences of Brexit. *Regional Studies, 51*(5), 786–799. doi:10.1080/00343404.2017.1287350

MacLeod, G., & Jones, M. (2018). Explaining 'Brexit Capital': Regional inequality and the austerity state. Unpublished paper.

Martin, R. (1988). The political economy of Britain's north-south divide. *Transactions of the Institute of British Geographers, 13*(4), 389–418. doi:10.2307/622738

Martin, R. (2010). Uneven regional growth: The geographies of boom and bust under new labour. In N. M. Coe & A. Jones (Eds.), *The economic geography of the UK* (pp. 29–46). London: Sage.

Martin, R., & Gardiner, B. (2018). Reviving the "northern powerhouse" and spatially rebalancing the British economy: The scale of the challenge. In C. Berry & A. Giovannini (Eds.), *Developing England's North: The political economy of the northern powerhouse* (pp. 23–58). Basingstoke: Palgrave-Macmillan.

Martin, R., Pike, A., Tyler, P., & Gardiner, B. (2015). *Spatially rebalancing the UK economy: Towards a new policy model?* Falmer, UK: Regional Studies Association.

Oliver Wyman (2018). *Costs up, prices up. Brexit's impact on consumer business and their customers*. London: Oliver Wyman. Retrieved from http://www.oliverwyman.com/our-expertise/insights/2018/jul/brexit-costsup--prices-up.html

Owen, J., Lloyd, L., & Rutter, J. (2018). *Preparing Brexit. How ready is Whitehall?* London: Institute for Government.

Peck, J., & Theodore, N. (2012). Reanimating neoliberalism: Process geographies of neoliberalization. *Social Anthropology, 20*(2), 177–185. doi:10.1111/j.1469-8676.2012.00194.x

Peck, J., & Tickell, A. (1992). Local modes of social regulation? Regulation theory, Thatcherism and uneven development. *Geoforum; Journal of Physical, Human, and Regional Geosciences, 23*(3), 347–363.

Piketty, T. (2014). *Capitalism in the 21st century*. Cambridge, MA: Harvard University Press.

Rasmus, J. (2010). *Epic recession*. London: Pluto Press.

Shonfield, A. (1965). *Modern capitalism: The changing balance between public and private power*. Oxford: Oxford University Press.

SSMT (2014). The UK automotive industry and the EU, *KPMG report*. Retrieved from https://www.smmt.co.uk/wp-content/uploads/sites/2/SMMT-KPMG-EU-Report.pdf

Weatherill, S. (2018). What mutual recognition really entails: analysis of the Prime Minister's Mansion House speech. Retrieved from http://eulawanalysis.blogspot.com/2018/03/what-mutual-recognition-really-entails.html

Weber, M. (2009) *General economic history*. Brunswick, NJ: Transaction Books <1923>

Wren-Lewis, S. (2018). The complete failure of the Brexit project. https://mainlymacro.blogspot.com/2018/04/the-complete-failure-of-brexit-project.html

Younge, G. (2016, June 30). Brexit: A disaster decades in the making. *The Guardian*. https://www.theguardian.com/politics/2016/jun/30/brexit-disaster-decades-in-the-making

Neoliberalism, urbanism and the education economy: producing Hyderabad as a 'global city'

Sangeeta Kamat

> This paper examines the emergence of Hyderabad as a hub of the global information technology economy, and in particular, the role of higher education in Hyderabad's transformation as the labor market for the new economy. The extensive network of professional education institutions that service the global economy illustrates the ways in which neoliberal globalization is produced through educational restructuring and new modes of urban development. Neoliberal globalization, however, is a variegated process wherein local social hierarchies articulate with state policies and global capital. This study shows how caste and class relations in the education sector in Andhra Pradesh are instrumental to forming Hyderabad's connection to the global economy. The contradictions of these regional realignments of education, geography and economy are manifest in the uneven development of the region and the rise of new socio-political struggles for the right to the city.

> Hyderabad is not just a city for hi-tech, it is a hi-tech city.
> (Mr. Chandrababu Naidu, Chief Minister of Andhra Pradesh in 2004)

> Only the state can take on the task of managing space on a grand scale.
> (Lefebvre [1978] quoted in Brenner, 2001, p. 793)

Hyderabad appears surreptitiously on the global map in the late 1990s. From among the major cities of India, Hyderabad was least expected to be the city with the potential to capitalize on the information technology (IT) boom and ascend to the status of a hi-tech city at the turn of the twenty-first century. Hyderabad's reputation until then was of an indolent ramshackle city that attracted mainly Indian tourists to the 'old city' (*purana shaher*) to view monuments such as the mosque with the four minarets (Charminar) and the Golconda fort built in the fifteenth century by Hyderabad's Muslim rulers. Dubbed the 'Silicon Valley of the East' by Bill Clinton during his visit to the country in 2000,[1] Hyderabad's new identity has been attributed to the visionary leadership of the state's then chief minister Chandrababu Naidu whose popular monikers were CEO Naidu and laptop CM. Chandrababu Naidu's Vision 2020 was the first official document that laid out an ambitious new plan to transform Hyderabad from a relatively obscure metropolis into a city that would be regarded as one of the nerve centers of the global economy within the decade.

Chief Minister Naidu's proposal was to create HITEC city (Hyderabad Information Technology Engineering Consultancy City) that would be a self-contained city within a city and provide IT businesses with built-in facilities for operations on a par with the best in the world. The state would provide high-speed connectivity, have its own power plant, a diesel-generating station for times of power outages, an earth station, satellite channels, its own water and sewage treatment plants, glare-free lighting, concealed copper wiring for piped music and paging systems in the common areas, and a four-lane super highway that would connect the city to a proposed new international airport. The plan was to create the most profitable and attractive conditions to lure companies that were leaders in technology and software development. Construction on 158 acres of land in the northwest suburbs of the city was initiated in 1997 and in less than four years many of the most prominent technology firms, foreign and domestic, had established their India offices in Hi-Tech city. Some of the big names include Satyam, Wipro, Infosys (Indian companies that are listed on the NASDAQ), followed by Oracle, Microsoft and Google–the last two especially were considered a historic coup of sorts for the state.[2] Hyderabad's reputation as Cyberabad has only become more firmly established since then, with the plan to make Hyderabad India's financial center and the technology hub of the country.

This narrative of Hyderabad's transformation is widely referenced but one that presents the transformation of the city at the level of real politik. History is represented through the lens of a charismatic leader as the protagonist who through his single-minded vision is able to fashion a wholly new economy and society, a kind of Weberian view of social change. The populist representation suppresses a more complex history that positions Hyderabad as a regional hub in the global economy. Available scholarship on the state of Andhra Pradesh (of which Hyderabad is the capital) illustrates the role of state development policies from the 1950s to the 1980s and their interplay with caste and class politics that established the conditions for the emergence of Hyderabad as a hi-tech city in the making. These studies show that the information technology revolution, economic globalization and the political leadership of Naidu were catalysts in a process that mobilized existing patterns of growth in the region for a major economic transition (Upadhya, 1988a, 1988b, 1997; Kamat, Hussain, & Mathew, 2004; Srinivasulu, 2002). In addition, recent anthropological and sociological research on the IT industry in Andhra Pradesh traverses the complex routes of migration of skilled labor from the region, the uneven manner in which the Andhra Pradesh IT industry is integrated into the global economy and the changing culture and identities of the new white-collar IT worker class (Biao, 2007; Upadhya & Vasavi, 2008). Recently, Hyderabad has been the subject of research by scholars of urban planning and governance who conclude that regional and city planning has been redirected to accommodate new globally mobile populations while neglecting the needs of established communities of Hyderabad (Kennedy, 2007; Ramachandraiah & Bawa, 2001).

My research is located in the intersections of these three strands of scholarship that trace the role of the state and the growth of the IT industry that produces a new geography and sociality of the city. Each of these studies is compelling in its own regard, but brought into conversation with one another and juxtaposed together these studies outline the peculiar shape and form of neoliberal globalization in India.

As such, these three strands of scholarship taken together provide insights into a particularly Indian version of neoliberal globalization which my research seeks to build upon. Through a focus on the education sector in Andhra Pradesh, my research explains the trajectory of educational development and policy that has enabled the growth of the IT sector in Andhra Pradesh. After all, the plan to establish HITEC city in Hyderabad may well have remained a pipe dream if it were not for the ready availability of skilled labor for the technology services sector. In other words, our understanding of neoliberal globalization in Andhra Pradesh (or India for that matter) remains partial and incomplete without an analysis of the education sector and its particular evolution in the region. Conversely, we cannot explain the specific nature of the education sector in Andhra Pradesh without locating it within the broader socio-economic transformations of the region and its ascendancy in the global economy.[3]

Accordingly, this paper is organized in two main parts. The first part traces the history of higher education in Andhra Pradesh in the decades preceding the take off of the IT industry in the region. This history illustrates the centrality of state policy and regional caste politics that results in a highly profitable and narrowly specialized professional education market in the region. These developments in the education sector eventually form the basis for the regional capture of global trends in the IT software industry. This historical backdrop to how Hyderabad appeared on the global map in the late 1990s identifies the continuities with state policy and regional politics rather than the banal representation of globalization as a break with the past, a representation that is typical among policy experts on Third World development. The second half of the paper provides an account of state planning in the post-1990s that builds on the existing politico-institutional relations and accelerates the process of global economic integration. Changes in education policy are once again a key ingredient in the restructuring of the region's economy singularly directed at attracting global capital and spurring economic growth. My research calls attention to two main issues that deserve further attention from education and globalization scholars. The first is that education policy and politics are imbricated in the new socio-spatial inequalities unleashed by neoliberalism and these relations need to be studied dialectically, and second, the transformation of the postcolonial state under conditions of neoliberal globalization is prompting new struggles for democracy and citizenship in the Third World that we need to engage with.

'Actually existing neoliberalism': a conceptual framework

My study of education and new urbanisms takes from the extensive literature on neoliberalism as a distinctive policy regime that drives the present phase of capitalist globalization (Brenner & Theodore, 2002; Harvey, 2005; Nef & Robles, 2000; Ong, 2006). Rooted in neoclassical economics, neoliberalism is an economic doctrine that provides both a policy roadmap and the intellectual justification for the expansion of the capitalist classes within the nation and globally. The fundamental premise of neoliberalism is that all societies, economies, institutions down to the level of the individual have to adapt, compete and abide by the objective laws of the market. Nef and Robles (2000) summarize the six-point program of neoliberalism: (1) re-establishing the rule of the market; (2) reducing public expenditure through cuts in subsidies, reduction in public services and dismantling welfare programs; (3) reorganizing the tax base by reducing direct taxes such as income and wealth tax and increasing indirect taxes on goods and services that benefit the investor class and reduce public revenue; (4) deregulating the private sector; (5) privatizing the public sector; and (6) doing away with the concept of the commons and the public good. The scholarship on globalization generally marks the 1970s as the period when neoliberalism made significant inroads into state policy in the advanced capitalist countries endorsed by influential political leaders such as Reagan and Thatcher (Harvey, 2005). In India, the definitive break from a welfare developmentalist regime to a neoliberal regime occurred in 1991 when the state undertook macro-economic reform that over a period of a decade would liberalize trade barriers, privatize public industries and deregulate markets to promote foreign investment.[4] The new orientation of the state indicates the historical movement of the Indian economy from an economy that is organized to meet national development goals and build internal capacity to an economy that is closely integrated with the world market.

While the policy prescriptions cited above form the fundamental core of the neoliberal policy regime, neoliberalism does not manifest itself in a uniform and identical manner the world over. The policy reforms interact with national, regional (subnational) and local contexts and histories to give a variegated character to neoliberalism in different places. Brenner and Theodore (2002) propose the analytical framework of 'actually existing neoliberalism' to account for the 'historically specific, ongoing and internally contradictory process of market driven socio-spatial transformation, rather than as a fully actualized policy regime, ideological form or regulatory framework' (p. 353). The concept of 'actually existing neoliberalism' therefore leads one to examine the *processes of neoliberalization* on the ground in specific places in their embedded form rather than refer to neoliberalism in its idealized universal form. This conceptual turn helps to shift the discourse on neoliberalism from abstract and decontextualized debates about state versus market or private versus public toward an analysis that reflects how neoliberal policy agendas evolve through 'their conflictual interaction with contextually specific political-economic conditions, regulatory arrangements and power geometrics' (p. 357).

'Actually existing neoliberalism' has proven to be a very productive framework to study the particular evolution of neoliberalism at the subnational and national level in India, and the contradictions generated therein for the postcolonial state. The analytical shift to neoliberalism as process helps to make sense of why and how certain neoliberal policies and programs are chosen over others, how these intersect with existing socio-political configurations at the provincial level, and the particular strategies that the postcolonial state deploys to mediate contradictions and conflicts. Quite simply put, for a country that claims to be the world's largest democracy the incorporation of a neoliberal market-based model in education and other social sectors is much more fraught, uneven and contradictory given its historical commitment to a welfare and developmentalist agenda. Certainly, the unfolding project of neoliberalism in Andhra Pradesh, with Hyderabad as the capital city at its epicenter, is well served by the analytics of 'actually existing neoliberalism' and helps to prise apart the multi-layered and socially dense character of neoliberalism in the region. As I detail in the following sections, the specific conjuncture of caste histories, class relations and postcolonial geographies that constitute Andhra Pradesh and its capital city offers a unique narrative of neoliberal globalization and resistances to it, at the same time that it represents an exemplary case of the neoliberal project.

Uneven geographies of development

Located in the southwestern part of India, Andhra Pradesh (AP) has a population of 76 million, with an estimated 7.6 million people residing in the metropolitan region of Hyderabad (the city and its suburbs). In the post-independence period, AP was the first state to be reorganized along linguistic lines, a policy that was subsequently adopted for other regions of the country. Though the language of the majority of the residents of the new state is Telugu, the three regions that were integrated were and remain remarkably distinct in their linguistic styles and cultures, social demographics and economic development, differences that remain a source of tension and conflict.

The three regions that were cobbled together to form the state of AP are: coastal Andhra in the eastern part of the state bordering the Bay of Bengal and part of the British Madras Presidency, Telangana to the northwest houses the state capital of Hyderabad and was part of the princely state of the Nizam, a Muslim ruler, and Rayalseema to the south was divided between the princely state of Mysore and Madras Presidency. In addition to distinct colonial legacies, the regions differ in their social composition of caste, tribal and religious groups. Coastal Andhra has a higher proportion of middle caste groups (also known as intermediate castes) who traditionally are peasant landowners, while the Telangana region has a significant representation of tribal groups (many of which are nomadic) and Other Backward Castes (OBCs) who are marginal farmers and landless laborers. Moreover, Hyderabad has a Muslim population of 41% but their representation in the economy and the state apparatus remains marginal.

Telangana is also a more drought-prone region with poorly developed irrigation systems and water shortage while coastal Andhra is lush and green with well-developed irrigation channels. The resource disparities are not an act of nature considering that Telangana has two major rivers, the Krishna and the Godavari, that flow from the west to the east towards coastal Andhra (in addition to several smaller rivers). While more than 70% of the catchment areas of these rivers are in Telangana, the construction of dams and canals has resulted in diversion of waters to coastal Andhra. This is one indicator of the political influence that peasant landowning middle castes of coastal Andhra[5] have historically been able to exercise *vis-à-vis* the state in terms of securing development investment and infrastructure for their region.[6] Coastal Andhra ranks significantly higher than Telangana and Rayalseema on socio-economic indicators. Nine of the ten districts of Telangana are identified as 'Backward' by the Indian government. The exception is Hyderabad district in which the capital city of Hyderabad is located (see Figure 1 for a map of the three distinct regions of AP).

The Commission set up by the Indian government in 1955 to examine the formation of AP recognized the potential for deepening inequalities between Telangana and coastal Andhra and foresaw a disastrous future for Telangana in the new state reorganization. To quote from their report:

Figure 1. Map of Andhra Pradesh illustrating the three regions: Telangana, coastal Andhra, and Rayalseema.

> One of the principal causes of opposition to Vishalandhra also seems to be the apprehension felt by the educationally-backward people of Telangana that they may be swamped and exploited by the more advanced people of the coastal area. In the Telangana district outside the city of Hyderabad education is woefully backward ... the real fear of the people of Telangana is that if they join Andhra they will be unequally placed in relation to the people of Andhra and in this partnership the major partner will derive all the advantages immediately while Telangana itself may be converted into a colony by the enterprising coastal Andhra. (State Reorganisation Commission cited in the Sri Krishna Committee Report, Government of India, 2010, p. 6)

The narrative of AP as the poster child for globalization needs to be understood in relation to this historical backdrop of uneven geographies of development that have exacerbated in the ensuing decades. More significantly, socio-economic inequalities between native residents of Telangana and those of coastal Andhra have deepened in the period that coincides with the state's IT boom and economic growth of the past two and half decades. The education gap highlighted in the above quote as a crucial factor in structuring inequalities between the two regions have persisted and intensified in the subsequent decades, owing in no small part to state policy that benefited powerful social groups from coastal Andhra. In the following section, I elaborate on developments in the education sector that reflect precisely the fears expressed in the Commission's report and that generate the context for a more systematic unfolding of the neoliberal project.

Caste politics, the postcolonial state and education policy

The Indian state's development approach in the post-independence period has been formative in accentuating these regional disparities. One of the priorities of the newly independent state was to become self-sufficient in food production and the Green Revolution that was expected to increase grain production was adopted as a national program. With the help of scientific expertise and aid from the USA and the former Soviet Union, high-yielding seeds and mechanization of farming were introduced, farmers were trained and the Green Revolution was hailed a resounding success when India was able to declare food self-sufficiency in the 1960s (Chibber, 2003).[7] Coastal Andhra farmers were in an optimal situation to benefit from the Green Revolution given their sizable land ownership, access to irrigation and ease of securing credit to purchase pesticides and fertilizers. Carol Upadhya's insightful research of the Kamma and Reddy caste groups in coastal Andhra explains how their caste affiliations and networks were important sources of social and symbolic capital that enable their political and economic dominance in the state from the early post-independence years through the Green Revolution period and after. Her richly detailed research of the intermediate peasant castes of coastal Andhra illustrates how in this particular case caste identity and networks were mobilized toward class mobility that transformed an agrarian class into an urbanized professional and bureaucratically powerful class primarily through accessing higher education (Upadhya, 1988a, 1988b, 1997).[8]

Following the success of the Green Revolution, the peasant caste groups from coastal Andhra use their agricultural surplus to establish engineering and medical colleges with considerable support from the Indian state. Private engineering colleges were first established in coastal Andhra districts of East Godavari, Guntur and Krishna in the late 1960s and early 1970s (Kamat et al., 2004; Upadhya, 1997). Affluent rural caste groups that were disadvantaged in a public education sector that was both small in scale and highly selective founded their own degree-granting institutions that were subsidized by the state. Over a period of a decade, an extensive network of 'aided' colleges that were financed with agricultural surplus by wealthy peasant caste groups offered science, engineering and medical degrees.[9] Demand for professional degrees only grew and by the 1980s this sector of aided private higher education in engineering and the sciences rapidly expanded. Caste-based investment in higher education was thus a primary mode through which economic mobility occurred and set the stage for the development of an extensive private higher education sector funded by coastal Andhra capital.[10]

Coastal Andhra caste groups organized themselves into charitable education trusts, charged high fees, but provided special scholarships to students from their particular social groups. The state aided the formation of these colleges generally through heavily subsidized land grants and other infrastructural support. The state also instituted an accreditation mechanism (AITCE) and a standardized state-wide exam that standardized the curriculum and also gave credibility to these institutions.[11] The state was responsive to the political aspirations of powerful coastal Andhra caste groups that were further enriched by an expanding private sector, while the public sector was allowed to stagnate. The casualties of this dual system, a private sector on the rise and a public sector in decline, were students from economically disadvantaged backgrounds, lower castes, Dalits[12] and tribal youth whereas students from affluent rural middle caste and from English-speaking urban middle-class families were able to access education and employment that prepared them for jobs in the emerging technology economy. In other words, a social compact was in place for nearly three decades between the state and the affluent middle castes that allowed the state to contain class and caste conflict, albeit at the expense of a significant majority who remained excluded from higher education.

Education and socio-spatial reform in the making of a 'global city'

The emergence of a strong professional education sector in AP represents the articulation of the postcolonial state's modernization project that privileged science and technology with caste aspirations for political and economic dominance in the urban economy. The remarkable growth of this sector, however, was during the period of neoliberal reform and the information technology boom. From 37 engineering colleges in 1996, the number grew to 540 colleges in 2009 (Government of India, 2010, p. 146). With the unexpected growth of the IT-related economy in the developed world and the trend toward outsourcing, these private institutions were able to step in as the supply chain for technical labor for the global service industry. The improbable conjuncture of regional politics and global economic shifts explains why AP is today one the main suppliers of Indian software engineers to the global economy (Biao, 2007). Relevant to my argument here is that the investment in private education is overwhelmingly from coastal Andhra and so is the skilled labor in the new economy.

In addition to the social (i.e. caste) character of the class divide, a second most significant manifestation of the class divide is the uneven spatial development of the region. While the bulk of the investment in education has originated from coastal Andhra, a majority of the private colleges, universities and allied education services are concentrated in the metropolitan region of Hyderabad. On the other hand, if one takes Hyderabad out of the equation in terms of educational infrastructure and access, the Telangana region does extremely poorly. The education infrastructure in Hyderabad is closely integrated with the IT and Information Technology Education Services (ITES) economy that has constituted nearly 99% of the exports of the state for the past five years (Government of India, 2010). While there are regional investors in the IT and ITES industry (here too the important local players hail from coastal Andhra), the majority are foreign firms.

Education and economic growth in AP is therefore geographically constituted resulting in stark differences between the capital city of Hyderabad and the rest of Telangana. Hyderabad has become well integrated into the global economy while districts surrounding Hyderabad remain severely underdeveloped and disconnected from the triumphal narrative of AP as a global economic hub.[13] The disproportionately high number of suicides by artisans and farmers in Telangana is just one of the tragic indicators of the systematic deprivation and loss of hope faced by those who have no place in Hyderabad's new economy.[14]

The synergy between education–economy that have configured Hyderabad as an island of growth amidst a region of immiseration and underdevelopment exemplifies the relations between capital and the state in a period of neoliberal economic reform. The AP state is a crucial agent in regulating, facilitating and augmenting the conditions for capital investment and growth in the education and IT manufacturing and services economy. Most importantly, the state through special directives, parastatal agencies, rezoning strategies, and infrastructural investment is involved in creating the 'built environment' to promote the productive capacities of specific localized places. In his study of state reorganization in western Europe Brenner summarizes the changes in state functions in the neoliberal context:

> In contrast to the Keynesian welfare national states of the post-war era, which attempted to equalize the distribution of population, industry and infrastructure across the national territory, the hallmark of glocalizing states is the project of *reconcentrating* the capacities for economic development within strategic subnational sites such as cities, city-regions and industrial districts, which are in turn to be positioned strategically within global and European economic flows. (2003, p. 198, emphasis in the original)

The AP state has engaged in a similar reorganization of space to consolidate and expand the IT and ITES economy and the labor market that this economy depends upon. Special economic zones (SEZs), 'software parks' (HITEC city being one of them) ringed by superfast highways, posh high rises, international schools, private hospitals, and shopping malls has created a city with a globally connected population proximate to the old city but socially and economically far removed from it. Urban restructuring related to housing, transportation and entertainment interlock with education and business activities to constitute a zone of production that is hitched to global economic trends and bypasses the local economy. The state has encouraged real-estate speculation in the peri-urban and rural areas surrounding the software parks through land auctions that attract national and foreign investors. Vast tracts of agricultural land have been sold to private developers at discounted rates near HITEC city that are free of zoning regulations related to the commercial, residential or industrial use of land. In addition to exemptions from labor laws, environmental clearances, and other special incentives, companies setting up their offices in these locations are also given additional land at reduced rates based on the number of employees they hire. To avail of the rebate, a minimum number of 100 employees must be hired. Many of these clearances, special rebates and incentives are automatically granted in an effort to minimize bureaucratic procedures. To meet specific skill demands in the ITES market, the AP state also set up a subsidized training facility in the area (Kennedy, 2007). Quite clearly, the state does not simply depend upon 'market forces' to unleash the productive capacities of the region, but is actively propelling and commanding the development of the economy in particular directions (Kennedy, 2007).

Further, in its efforts to attract global investment and business into the 'global city-region', the state leverages existing socio-political alliances to agglomerate capital and labor for the global city region, the prime source for which is coastal Andhra. For example, three of the most prominent real-estate and construction firms that are involved in building extensive office and residential complexes, and highways and transportation infrastructure are associated with members of parliament from coastal Andhra. This has also resulted in increased migration from coastal Andhra into Hyderabad and its peri-urban districts (Government of India, 2010). In 2008,

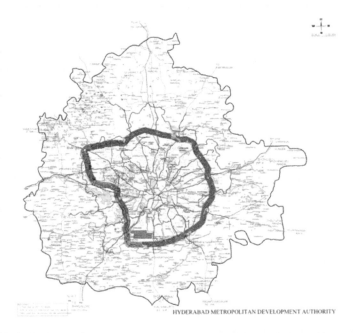

Figure 2. The map of Greater Hyderabad that includes districts outside Hyderabad city, reorganized as Greater Hyderabad governed by the Hyderabad Metropolitan Development Authority.

the state redrew the boundaries of Hyderabad city to encompass peri-urban districts of Telangana into the city to form Greater Hyderabad governed by a new parastatal body, the Hyderabad Metropolitan Development Authority (see Figure 2).[15]

Responsible for 'planning, co-ordination, supervising, promoting and securing the planned development of the metropolitan region', the authority of the new agency supersedes institutions of democratic governance such as municipal corporations, district-level state bodies and elected village councils (www.hmda.gov.in). Important here is that older administrative bodies are not dissolved but are repositioned within new institutional arrangements governed by conditionalities and incentives. Through state rescaling and reterritorialization of space the state is not simply adapting to a changing economy but is a strategic actor in determining the economic geography of the region (Brenner, 2003, 2004; Kennedy, 2007; Scott, Agnew, Soja, & Storper, 2001).

In the education sector, the shift toward a competition state is evident in the policy changes and new governance frameworks adopted by the state. For one, the state has pursued policies that blur the boundaries and differences between public and private institutions by cutting public expenditure, eliminating caps on tuition fees and requiring state institutions to augment their income through fee increases, 'flexible' hiring policies, and leasing university land to private companies.[16] The objective here is to foster entrepreneurship among public institutions and integrate public education with market demands. Consultative processes with faculty are circumvented and administrators have appropriated greater authority. The changes, some *de jure* and others *de facto*, undermine the broader educational mission of these institutions by introducing a corporate culture in the public sector and a closer alignment with market demands. Thus without officially privatizing public universities, the state nevertheless is compelling public universities to function as per market demand, a significant departure from the mission of public universities in postcolonial India.[17] The profitability of the extensive network of private engineering colleges and training institutes are offered as justification for the state's initiatives in the public sector.

Hyderabad illustrates the socio-political and historical context that transitions the developmental state into a 'competition state' in which the state subordinates the welfare and developmental needs of its citizens in favor of the profitability of the corporate sector and political elites (Cerny, 1997). Ultimately, as the sovereign legal authority, the state is the most privileged institution to regulate, channel and coordinate capital and organize the economic geography of the region. Consequently, the neoliberal state becomes an agent for the commodification of social relations situated in a wider market-dominated field.

Neoliberal urbanism and struggle for the city

The inauguration of a 'global city region' has visibly created two vastly different socio-economic regions and deepened class and other social contradictions in Telangana. Educational and other social infrastructure, economic investment and employment opportunities in areas outside of the global city region have deteriorated and have fomented tensions and unrest in the region. These contradictions and antagonisms have coalesced into a battle for Telangana that has gained significant momentum in the past one year. Important to note here is that students from the two state universities in Telangana, Osmania University and Kakatiya University, were the first to mobilize and reclaim the struggle for separate statehood for Telangana (Hyderabad Forum for Telangana, 2009; Janyala, 2009; 'Student JAC', 2010). The demand for a separate Telangana is a historic one and was first launched in 1969, a little over a decade after regional boundaries were redrawn to form the state of Andhra Pradesh. However, it is the state's project of neoliberal urbanism that has refocused discontent and opened old wounds about coastal Andhra's 'colonization' of Telangana.

The militant student protests shut down colleges and universities in the region for several months at a stretch, periodically shut down the city and have led to an alarming number of student suicides. According to media reports, between November 2009 and February 2010, there were 60 suicides by young people in Telangana, many of them self-immolations (Government of India, 2010, p. 387).[18] The student deaths and continuing student protests have galvanized diverse cross-sections of society including farmers, unorganized workers, unions, school teachers and university faculty, and political parties to join the movement and bring the issue to the national stage. While the fundamental issues of the movement are access to quality and affordable education, jobs, livelihood security and basic amenities, the diverse constituencies of the movement have united on a common resolution of autonomy for Telangana as the only way to address the historical and ongoing educational and economic marginalization of the people of Telangana (Hyderabad

Forum for Telangana, 2010; Kannabiran, Ramdas, Madhusudhan, Ashalatha, & Pavan Kumar, 2010; Venugopal, 2009). The struggle for a separate Telangana has been framed as usurpation of the region and its resources by 'outsiders' that has effectively excluded established residents of the region from participating in the economy or gaining access to the benefits of Hyderabad's economic growth. The movement redefines citizenship and entitlements on the basis of '*mulki*' (native or resident in Hyderabadi Deccani language) that is not based on an identitarian politics of ethnicity, religion, caste or language but is a broad category that refers to the distinctive socio-cultural identity and economic history of Telangana that existed prior to the formation of AP (Kannabiran et al., 2010; Rajamani, 2009).

The struggle for a separate Telangana is a clear and provocative challenge to the dynamics of socio-spatial restructuring that characterizes neoliberal reform in many urban regions of the world. As yet the movement has not explicitly framed their opposition as a resistance to neoliberalism; the term neoliberalism as such remains absent from the English-language publications of the movement and media presentations of the leadership. However, some segments of the student and political leadership explain that issues highlighted by the struggle are inextricably linked to the neoliberal model of development that the Indian state and regional elites have embraced, and the movement is a people's rejection of this model of development. Articulating the marginalization of Telangana not only in terms of social relations at the regional level (i.e. coastal Andhra elites) but understanding their systematic relation to global economic forces and neoliberal ideology is the task at hand, at least for some segments of the movement.[19]

The focus on inequities in education and the sustained participation of students in the Telangana struggle reflect the far-reaching impact of neoliberal restructuring in the education sector. The case of AP also shows that the decline of traditional economies and the rise of post-industrial information-based economies are having a significant impact on erstwhile developing regions of the world where agriculture has been the primary sector of the economy. Higher education, one that is narrowly specialized in the professional sciences and technology fields becomes the only foreseeable route to jobs and economic security. Educational institutions being largely controlled by coastal Andhra entrepreneurs, the struggle for independence from coastal Andhra resonates with the students from Telangana. However, the movement has yet to develop a critique that goes beyond caste politics to understand the interconnections between the education sector in AP and neoliberal globalization (Maringanti, 2010). The rudiments of such a critical analysis are present in the discourse of the student movement. The caste critique is deeply inflected with a class critique as students object to the commodification and corporatization of education that has not only enriched coastal Andhra and its investor class but promotes an education system that is disengaged from the interests and realities of most communities and classes in the region.

The contest at the moment has centered on Hyderabad as the hub of the 'knowledge economy' and has become the focal point for a regional/provincial struggle for resources, rights and entitlements that at its heart raises questions about democracy, development and equity in a globalized world.[20] While the movement is a prospective challenge to dominant neoliberal logic, it also portends contradictions of its own. In 1969, the identity of '*mulki*' or resident was perhaps less problematic and easier to negotiate than it is today. A cultural politics of 'nativism' poses challenges for an interconnected world that is premised on the circulation, however unevenly, of people and resources across local, regional, national and international borders. A nativist movement also has reactionary tendencies as seen in the recent upsurge in anti-immigrant politics in western Europe and the USA and poses a challenge for progressive democratic movements. The struggle is ongoing and the outcomes are uncertain. That said, as an exemplar of 'actually existing neoliberalism', scholars and activists have much to gain from paying close attention to the evolving conflict around education and the constitution of Hyderabad as a 'global city'.

Notes

1. 'March 24th, 2000 will forever remain a red letter day in the 400 years history of Hyderabad as it is for the first time that an American President is on a visit to South India and Hyderabad has got the rare honor to have been considered in the itinerary of the American President' (http://www.reachouthyderabad.com/clinton4.htm). In 2002, Bill Gates' decision to visit Hyderabad and bypass Bangalore city, the other hub of the software industry, was also noted as Hyderabad's ascendant position in the global economy.
2. As a commentator on a technology web blog phrased it, 'The decision of Microsoft Corp to set up a software development centre, the first out of the USA has put the industry in euphoria' (see http://www.microsoft.com/india/msidc/life/hyderabad.aspx).
3. In this paper I limit my focus to developments in the higher education sector that have been most vital to the region's capture of the IT sector, though state and elite discourse on schools have also been significant to constituting neoliberal globalization as the new policy regime in Andhra Pradesh.
4. The structural adjustment program (SAP) of the World Bank and the International Monetary Fund imposed neoliberal policies on borrower nations as conditionalities in exchange for loans. Countries in Africa and Latin America were subject to structural adjustment in the 1980s, much earlier than India. Highly indebted countries had much less negotiating power than for instance India and the deleterious effects of neoliberal policies or SAP were apparent much earlier in these countries.
5. Kamma, Reddy and Raju are the three main middle caste (non-Brahmin) peasant groups dominant in coastal Andhra.
6. Rayalseema that lies to the south of the state is also disadvantaged and impoverished similar to Telangana and lags behind coastal Andhra in economic and educational infrastructure. For purposes of this paper, I shall focus on the conflict between coastal Andhra and Telangana that are more relevant to this research.
7. One of the earliest critiques of the Green Revolution and the harm it has done to the environment and to small farmers and cultivators can be found in Shiva (1989).
8. There are several studies of intermediate peasant caste groups in other parts of India that illustrate the articulation of caste and class. Well-known cases of class mobility using caste as a specific resource are the Patidars of Gujarat and the Jats of Punjab (see Breman, 1994; Jeffrey, Jeffery, & Jeffery, 2008). What distinguishes the coastal Andhra intermediate caste group is their purposeful shift into an urban professional and bureaucratic class rather than a business and trading class or investing in more land to become powerful feudal landlords. Instead securing professional education for their children and their community, largely a preserve of the Brahmins (upper caste), was an early strategy of the coastal Andhra peasant caste groups.
9. State policy allowed for three types of educational institutions at all levels: wholly public institutions that were state owned, aided institutions that received subsidies from the state and were established as non-profits, and wholly self-financed privately owned institutions that were also required to be non-profit. In the past three decades, the private sector has grown exponentially in comparison to aided institutions while the number of state institutions has been stagnant; 10% of professional colleges in AP are government or

government-aided colleges. In the last two years, the national government has been trying to rapidly expand the public sector to be globally competitive.

10. Upadhya (1988a) notes that well-off rural families from coastal Andhra would invariably invest in at least one family member's professional education in a nearby town or in the capital city. As a result, coastal Andhra families typically had more exposure to urban culture and the modern economy that also gave them cultural and political capital in the villages. Their social networks were also much more diverse and influential as a result of the rural–urban connection. See Upadhya (1988a) for a sociological history of coastal Andhra groups using Bourdieu's framework.

11. Accreditation also allowed these institutions to charge higher fees.

12. Dalit is a term for downtrodden, in the Hindu caste hierarchy the group that is designated as the lowest order of the caste hierarchy and therefore were regarded as 'untouchable'. Untouchability is illegal under the Indian constitution but atrocities and discrimination against dalits even within modern urban sectors of India remains a serious issue. An analogous comparison would be the persistence of institutional and other forms of racism against African Americans in the USA.

13. The neoliberal thesis that educational investment follows the job market and that Hyderabad is merely a case in point is untrue if one examines the education sector in coastal Andhra. Although primarily a rural economy with traditional industries of fishing, manufacturing and trade, coastal Andhra has very favorable indices on educational infrastructure, quality and achievement, on a par with and in certain instances even better than the capital region of Hyderabad. The state aid budget for education is significantly higher for coastal Andhra than for Telangana and government schools are far more desirable compared to those in the capital region of Hyderabad (Government of India, 2010; Save the Children, 2007).

14. From 2004 to 2005, there were 663 suicides by farmers and weavers in Telangana, 231 in Rayalseema and 174 in coastal Andhra (Government of India, 2010, p. 366). From 1997 to 2007, the period of neoliberal economic reform, farmer suicides reached epidemic proportions in several states in India, the highest numbers have been in Maharashtra followed by AP, Karnataka, Punjab and Kerala (Patel, 2007; Sainath, 2010).

15. Hyderabad metropolitan region is 7,100 km^2. For a sense of the size and scope of the expansion of the city, the new metropolitan region of Greater Hyderabad is now the size of Goa, a state famous for its beaches that attracts foreign tourists. Greater Hyderabad now is larger than Mumbai, Bangalore and Chennai put together (Government of India, 2010).

16. There were recent protests by faculty and students against the Vice Chancellor of Hyderabad Central University on the proposed lease of university land to multinationals ('Staff, Students Protest', 2010).

17. In the postcolonial context, the explicit mission of state universities was to equalize educational opportunities, contribute to national development and strengthen participatory citizenship, all of which were considered fundamental elements for a robust democracy.

18. Estimates of total number of suicides for a separate Telangana are 313, of which 60 were between the ages of 18 and 25. See the Sri Krishna Report (Government of India, 2010, p. 387).

19. Author's interview with Professor Kodandram Rao, President of the Telangana Political Joint Action Committee, Hyderabad, 27 December 2010. Also author interview with two members of the Student Joint Action Committee, Osmania University, Hyderabad, 5 January 2011. The decentralized nature of the movement in its current phase where different groups are self-organizing as Joint Action Committees that are non-party political action groups across diverse ideological lines and that are autonomous from the political party for an independent Telangana suggests that there may be diverse tendencies in the movement. It is too soon therefore to say whether a unified challenge to neoliberalism will emerge as a focal point of the movement, though the possibility cannot be dismissed.

20. In response to the growing political movement for a separate Telangana, the national government instituted a special committee chaired by retired Justice Sri Krishna to

examine the claims of uneven development, discrimination and distinct culture, and provide its recommendations. The special committee released a detailed and exhaustive report on 5 January 2011 but did not propose any definite resolution to the demand for state autonomy. While the movement continues, the government of Andhra Pradesh has yet to yield a considered response to the report or the issues raised by the movement.

References

Biao, X. (2007). *Global 'body shopping': An Indian labor system in the information technology industry*. Princeton, NJ: Princeton University Press.

Breman, J. (1994). *Beyond patronage and exploitation: Changing agrarian relations in south Gujarat*. New York: Oxford University Press.

Brenner, N. (2001). State theory in the political conjuncture: Henri Lefebvre's comments on a new state form. *Antipode, 33*, 783–808.

Brenner, N. (2003). 'Glocalization' as a state spatial strategy: Urban entrepreneurialism and the new politics of uneven development in western Europe. In J. Peck and H. Wai-Chung, Yeung (Eds.), *Remaking the global economy: Economic–geographical perspectives* (pp. 197–215). New York: Sage.

Brenner, N. (2004). *New state spaces: Urban governance and the rescaling of statehood*. New York: Oxford University Press.

Brenner, N., & Theodore, N. (2002). Cities and the geographies of 'actually existing neoliberalism'. *Antipode, 34*, 349–379.

Cerny, P. (1997). Paradoxes of the competition state: dynamics of political globalization. *Government and Opposition, 32*, 251–274.

Chibber, V. (2003). *Locked in place: State building and late industrialization in India*. Princeton, NJ: Princeton University Press.

Government of India. (2010). *Report of the Committee for Consultations on the Situation of Andhra Pradesh*. Chairperson, Justice Sri Krishna. New Delhi: Ministry of Home Affairs, Government of India. Retrieved from http://mha.nic.in/

Harvey, D. (2005). *A brief history of neoliberalism*. New York: Oxford University Press.

Hyderabad Forum for Telangana. (2009). *Appeal to political parties on people's demand for a separate Telangana*. Secunderabad, India: Author.

Hyderabad Forum for Telangana. (2010). *Whose Telangana is it? Myths, facts and realities*. Secunderabad, India: Author.

Janyala, S. (2009, December 7). Student agitation adds force to Telangana movement. *Indian Express*, p. 2.

Jeffrey, C., Jeffery, P., & Jeffery, R. (2008). *Degrees without freedom: Education, masculinities and unemployment in north India*. Stanford, CA: Stanford University Press.

Kamat, S., Hussain, M.A., & Mathew, B. (2004). Producing hi-tech: Globalization, the state and migrant subjects. *Globalization, Societies and Education, 2*(1), 5–23.

Kannabiran, K., Ramdas, S., Madhusudhan, N., Ashalatha, S., & Pavan Kumar, M. (2010). *On the Telangana trail*. Secunderabad, India: Chityala Ailamma Centre for Interdisciplinary Research.

Kennedy, L. (2007). Regional industrial policies driving peri-urban dynamics in Hyderabad, India. *Cities, 24*, 95–109.

Maringanti, A. (2010). Telangana: Righting historical wrongs or getting the future right? *Economic and Political Weekly of India, 45*(4), 33–38.

Nef, J., & Robles, W. (2000). Globalization, neoliberalism and the state of underdevelopment in the new periphery. *Journal of Developing Societies, 16*(1), 27–48.

Ong, A. (2006). *Neoliberalism as exception: Mutations in citizenship and sovereignty*. Durham, NC: Duke University Press.

Patel, R. (2007). *Stuffed and starved: The hidden battle for the world food system*. Brooklyn, NY: Melville House Publishing.

Rajamani, R. (2009). Nativity and narrative themes in Telangana art. In B. Bhushan & N. Venugopal (Eds.), *Telangana: The state of affairs* (pp. 147–151). Hyderabad, India: Deccan Press.

Ramachandraiah, C., & Bawa, V.K. (2001). Hyderabad in the changing political economy. *Journal of Contemporary Asia, 30*, 562–574.

Sainath, P. (2010, December 27). Of luxury cars and lowly tractors. *The Hindu*, OpEd, p. 9.

Save the Children. (2007). *Where are schools going? Setting minimum standards for quality education in schools in Andhra Pradesh*. Hyderabad, India: Save the Children.

Scott, A.J., Agnew, J., Soja, E., & Storper, M. (2001). Global city-regions. In A.J. Scott (Ed.), *Global city-regions: Trends, theory, policy* (pp. 11–30). New York: Oxford University Press.

Shiva, V. (1989). *Staying alive: Women, ecology and development*. London: Zed Books.

Srinivasulu, K. (2002). *Caste, class and social articulation in Andhra Pradesh: Mapping differential regional trajectories*. ODI Working Paper 179. London: Overseas Development Institute.

Staff, students protest at HCU. (2010, February 9). *The Hindu*, p. 3.

Student JAC calls for Telangana Bandh. (2010, January 20). *Business Standard*, p. 3.

Upadhya, C. (1988a). The farmer-capitalists of Coastal Andhra Pradesh. *Economic and Political Weekly of India, 28*, 1433–1442.

Upadhya, C. (1988b). The farmer-capitalists of Coastal Andhra Pradesh. *Economic and Political Weekly of India, 27*, 1376–1382.

Upadhya, C. (1997). Social and cultural strategies of class formation in Coastal Andhra. *Contributions to Indian Sociology, 31*(2), 169–193.

Upadhya, C., & Vasavi, A.R. (2008). *In an outpost of the global economy: Work and workers in India's information technology industry*. New York: Routledge.

Venugopal, N. (2009). Demand for separate Telangana: Towards understanding the core issues. In B. Bhushan & N. Venugopal (Eds.), *Telangana: The state of affairs* (pp. 33–54). Hyderabad, India: Deccan Press.

Neoliberalism and the demise of public education: the corporatization of schools of education

Marta Baltodano

Neoliberalism has brought fundamental changes to the way schools of education prepare professional educators; among them is the pressure for schools of education to produce fast-track teacher preparation programs that bypass traditional requirements. Due to the privatization of public education, a new market has emerged to train educators and administrators for charter schools. The No Child Left Behind Act has made the old multipurpose PhD in education obsolete and has led to fast-track EdDs to train school administrators to raise test scores. In this era of corporate schooling, colleges of education are competing with online and for-profit colleges to increase student enrollment. Academic capitalism has entered into the classroom and it has redefined the academic premises upon which the entire higher education system was instituted. This article asks, what are the implications of this new educational arrangement for the purpose of education and the development of a critically informed mass of democratic citizens? This article proposes a critical dialog among educators, parents, labor groups, and grassroots organizations and an action plan to stop the dismantling of public education.

Introduction

Neoliberalism in the US has transcended the realm of economic policies to become a political rationale that is undermining the major structures, processes, and institutions of American liberal democracy, particularly public education.

This study documents how the tenets of American liberal teacher education represented in a vision of rigorous content knowledge, democratic schooling, and social justice have been distorted and appropriated by the corporate goals of education. This article illustrates how schools of education have been affected by neoliberal reforms including a drastic transformation in the preparation of teachers, the intensification of the business of accreditation, the appropriation of multicultural education, and the formation of a new managerial and professional middle class to support the privatization of education.

This article particularly examines how professional organizations and accrediting institutions, such as NCATE and AACTE,[1] along with other powerful players of neoliberalism, like Teach For America, and a handful of foundations, have shaped the current state of teacher preparation and contributed to the destruction of public schooling.

I examine the political and economic policies that have altered the structures, pedagogical practices, and intended democratic goals of teacher education. I reflect on schools as "little democracies" that are supposed to prepare citizens for active civic participation (Dewey 2004).

Inspired by the work of Maxine Greene, John Dewey, Martha Nussbaum, and others, I propose a new imaginative engagement with the conception of the "public good" to counteract 30 years of neoliberal hegemonic attacks against public education.

This article is a much-needed reflection on the compromised state of teacher education and its gradual deterioration as a result of neoliberal policies. It offers a framework for starting a critical dialog among the many constituencies of public schooling to reclaim education as a public good.

Methodology

This research study is part of a larger inquiry that uses critical policy analysis to examine the discursive relations that have naturalized the corporate agenda of schools of education. While the larger study involves interviews and additional fieldwork, the research for this article is based on critical textual analysis of documents. They include: (1) review of legislation approved during the civil rights movement, among them the Elementary and Secondary Act, the Higher Education Act, the Immigration and Naturalization Act, the Civil Rights Act, the Voting Rights Act, and the Education for All Handicapped Children Act; (2) critical textual analysis of public policy documents, like the affirmative action executive order, the No Child Left Behind Act (NCLB) and Race to the Top; (3) analysis of university records that provide information about the financial restructuring of three universities that are part of this study; (4) examination of NCATE policy documents, reports, and accreditation criteria; (5) critical analysis of the Obama administration speeches, including the president's statements on education and particularly, some of his secretary of education's speeches and press reports; (6) textual analysis of newspaper and digital media describing events related to the reconstitution of public schools and the attacks against teachers and their unions; and (7) fieldnotes of institutional and community practices in my workplace and the city where I live that has the second highest concentration of charter schools in the nation. This research is also informed by the everyday performances in the university in which I work that have been shaped and exacerbated by the current climate of educational accountability.

Critical policy analysis has evolved from the field of critical discourse analysis (Luke 1995–1996) and it is centered on the application of discourse theories to policy studies (Taylor 1997). Discourse theories encompass a broad application of Foucault's theories of discourse, Gramsci's theory of hegemony, and Fairclough's focus on language as a social practice, to critically scrutinize public policy (Codd 1988; Taylor 1997).

The application of these theoretical frameworks to the analysis of policy has resulted in a methodology that offers a more sophisticated examination of the intent, meaning, and discourse of public policy (Taylor 1997). Critical policy analysis focuses on three fundamental aspects: "contexts, texts, and consequences" of policies (Taylor 1997, 33), but always attending to the issues of meaning and interpretation.

It is important to note that *critical policy analysis* widely differs from the narrow, linguistic approach to policy statements (McHoul 1984), because the fine-grained analyses have to be juxtaposed with the larger political and economic context in which these policies have emerged. As Codd (1988) argues, "policy documents … are ideological texts that have been constructed within a particular context. The task of deconstruction begins with the recognition of that context" (Codd 1988, 243–4; Taylor 1997).

Therefore, critical policy analysis unmasks the "workings" of the discourses, defined by Foucault as "power-infused systems of knowledge" (Muetzenfeldt 1992, 4). These discourses are formed and sustained by the construction of "trusts" about the social and natural world, trusts that become the taken-for-granted definitions and categories by which governments rule and monitor their populations and by which members of communities define themselves and others (Luke 1995–1996, 9).

I sought to reveal the master narratives that have been constructed around the dismantling of public education and the preparation of teachers in the US. What follows is a review of the principles of the American tradition of liberal public education as articulated by founding and contemporary philosophers of education.

Public education and the *common good*

As Maxine Greene (1982) asserted a long time ago, "there is little talk today about the connection between public education and freedom" (4). More than in any other period of American history, teachers hava been stripped of their most precious role: the duty to educate a generation of fully informed democratic citizens. Neoliberalism has taken away the joy of learning, the creativity of teaching, and the formation of strong public intellectuals. Public education is gradually fading and is being replaced by new privatized forms of schooling. The results are the lack of an articulate public and the reduction of public spheres to contest the dominant neoliberal vision of society. The humanities and the arts are being eliminated from the curriculum of public schools (Nussbaum 1998, 2010). As a result, the newer generation of students is losing: "the ability to think critically; the ability to transcend local loyalties and to approach world problems as a 'citizen of the world;' and, finally, the ability to imagine sympathetically the predicament of another person" (Nussbaum 2010, 7).

The realization that something has gone awry in education has gradually begun to sink in. As Ravitch (2010) reflects:

> At the present time, public education is in peril. Efforts to reform public education are, ironically, diminishing its quality and endangering its very survival. (242)

> As a nation, we need a strong and vibrant public education system [… which] is a fundamental element of our democratic society. Our public schools have been the pathway to opportunity and a better life for generations of America … To the extent that we strengthen them, we strengthen our democracy. (241–2)

The tradition of liberal public education, although not without failures and contradictions, was an ongoing project grounded in the philosophical tenets of John Dewey. His vision of schooling was based on the fundamental principle that schools were indispensable for the establishment of a civil society that could enact and sustain a democracy. Dewey (1916, 1956, 2004) believed that if schools were "little democracies" they could prepare citizens for active civic participation. He assigned teachers with the responsibility to play a leading role in preparing American citizens for active engagement in a democratic society. Dewey visualized education as the "wellspring of democracy itself" (Dewey 1916; Wirth 1966). He believed the values of American democracy, such as equal opportunity and social justice[2] were the backbone of the school curriculum.

Dewey strongly opposed the assumption that schools were places for drills, discipline, and dull exercises. He visualized "teachers as scholars and as students of the psychology of the learning process" (Wirth 1966, 53), and he could not accept the widespread belief that children could be taught by someone who did not problematize the psychological and philosophical implications of teaching. His major contributions were a theory of learning based on experiential teaching in a social-cultural context; the incorporation of students' experience into the curriculum; the vision of students as full citizens; and the retreat from the false dichotomy between theory and practice (Dewey 2004).

Vital to that tradition of American liberal education have been the incorporation of Socratic teaching to resolve real life problems, the practice of public debate and role playing in the classroom to develop critical voice, and a strong integration of the arts and literature to release the imagination and develop empathy for the Other (Greene 1991, 1995; Nussbaum 2010). These components are fundamental to forming, "a certain type of citizen: active, critical, curious, capable of resisting authority and peer pressure" (Nussbaum 2010, 72).

In contrast to this educational model is the rote learning and teaching to the test of neoliberal education that negates the possibility of even fantasizing about achieving the values of equal opportunity, justice, and social mobility. The banking concept of education (Freire 1970) sanctioned by neoliberalism is training students to become docile citizens.

The rise of neoliberalism in the US

The decline of the American economy in the 1970s and 1980s, caused by an international restructuring of labor and capital, was the backdrop to the economic policies carried out during the Reagan presidency (Torres and Schugurensky 2002). Reaganomics was the popular term given to the implementation of the first neoliberal policies in the US, which were grounded on the work of Friedrich von Hayek and Milton Friedman of the Chicago School of Economics[3] (Brown 2003; Symcox 2009). This economic school of thought fully opposed the previous Keynesian policies that advocated strong regulation of the economy and had created the welfare state of the previous decades.

"Capitalism with a human face" (Brittan 1995) developed in the US after the stock market crashed in 1929. President Franklin Delano Roosevelt, who took power at the depths of the Great Depression, retreated from the previous *laissez faire* capitalism of Adam Smith and instituted the New Deal, which sought protection for American workers through the establishment of minimum wages, collective bargaining, and social security.

In the following years, John F. Kennedy's and Lyndon Johnson's presidencies advanced this welfare economy through the New Frontier and Great Society programs. Additional social legislation was enacted to protect the poor, the elderly, those with special needs, and other marginalized groups. Medicaid and Medicare were instituted, and funds for low-income students, childhood education, and bilingual instruction were allocated through the Elementary & Secondary Act, the Higher Education Act, and the Bilingual Education Act (Baltodano 2009; Symcox 2009). This was a time when the welfare society was consolidated to protect the civil and economic rights of US citizens.

However, by the late 1970s, the postwar economic accumulation had been exhausted (Compton and Weiner 2008, 14) and capitalism appeared to be arriving at the "point of no return" (Balibar 1995, 64). A world recession emerged and American corporations began complaining about the plunging of their profits due to labor demands to increase wages for workers, and the international competition to keep prices down. They demanded special protection from the government, as the international economic crisis was threatening their survival. These corporations called for a return to the unregulated market of the pre-Great Depression as the only way to continue being viable (profitable).

This time, "as the economy slowed, state revenues failed to keep pace with social expenditures, and taxpayers began to express resentment towards those who benefited the most from state revenues" (Torres and Schugurensky 2002, 431): the largely disenfranchised social groups that had benefited from the social gains of the civil rights movement. This precipitated the end of the social contract that Americans had established with the government to become a mediator of the economy (Torres and Schugurensky 2002).

The end of the welfare state led to a radically free market where maximized competition, free trade, elimination of tariffs, and government protection for business replaced social assistance for the poor. Many of the regulations that the government had imposed on the financial and manufacturing industries to protect the American worker were abandoned (e.g. NAFTA, CAFTA, outsourcing of jobs through maquiladoras). Gradually the US, along with other leading world economies, intensified the implementation of post-Fordist production and trade and formally entered into a new global market.

Unlike Fordism, "that involves mass production based on moving assembly-line techniques operated with semi-skilled labour, that is, a mass worker" (Amin 1994, 9; Jessop 1995), post-Fordism operates a highly hierarchical and specialized division of labor where labor protections are diminished. Post-Fordism is characterized by: "new methods of production based on microelectronics, by flexible working practices, a much reduced role for trade unions in society, a new individualism, a reduction of state intervention, and a new relation between production and consumption" (Bonefeld and Holloway 1991, 1).

The post-Fordist model is also called "Toyotism," which was inspired by the management and production system implemented by the automobile maker Toyota in Japan in the late twentieth century. One of the most important features of Post-Fordism or "Toyotism" is that it has created a new kind of division of labor in which a small, highly skilled, highly paid management oversees a disposable mass of very poor, immigrant, part-time alienated workers with no job security, union protection, or vested relationship to the work site.

Vanished is the social protection of previous generations of workers, as neoliberalism powerfully encouraged the deregulation of labor laws and targeted labor unions and public schools as the greatest obstacles to the "freedom" of the market (Torres and Schugurensky 2002, 432).

The development of neoliberalism as political rationality

The welfare society that preceded the rise of neoliberalism in the US was not only characterized by comprehensive economic reforms to protect the American worker and the poor; it also included significant legislation that reinterpreted the dimension of civil liberties recognized in the Constitution and the Bill of Rights. Some of these laws were: (1) the Immigration and Naturalization Act of 1965, which prohibits the use of racial quotas; (2) the ratification of the Civil Rights Act (1964) and the Voting Rights Act (1965) prohibiting racial discrimination; (3) the executive orders 10925 (1961) and 11246 (1965) demanding affirmative action; and (4) the passage of the Education for All Handicapped Children Act (1975) creating inclusive education. These policies were the result of the civil rights movement and the cultural revolution of the 1960s that brought to the forefront of America's consciousness the early liberal values of equal opportunity and social justice. The multicultural education movement later advanced these social reforms by developing awareness of the difficult experiences of the marginalized groups that were protected by these regulations and advocated for more inclusive policies.

However, a group of neo-conservative scholars (Crozier, Huntington, and Watanuki 1975) perceived these democratic events as clear attacks on American democracy. They argued that the participation of marginal groups that were previously politically apathetic (Kaase and Newton 1995, 25) risked the: "danger of 'overloading' the political system with demands which extended its functions and undermined its authority" (Huntington 1976, 37). The essential goal of the Report on the Governability of Democracies (Crozier, Huntington, and Watanuki 1975) was to create awareness about the need to make democracies and their citizens "more able to service capital" (Davies and Bansel 2007, 250), rather than creating additional needs for a government already overwhelmed with meeting the needs of all its emergent and diverse citizens:

> At the present time, a significant challenge comes from the intellectuals and related groups who assert their disgust with the corruption, materialism, and inefficiency of democracy and with the subservience of democratic government to "monopoly capitalism." The development of an "adversary culture" among intellectuals has affected students, scholars, and the media [...] In an age of widespread secondary school and university education, the pervasiveness of the mass media, and the displacement of manual labor by clerical and professional employees, this development constitutes a challenge to democratic government. (Crozier, Huntington, and Watanuki 1975, 6–7)

This facet of neoliberalism – to make democracies and people more governable – has rarely been examined. However, back in the late 1970s Foucault (1978/1979) addressed neoliberalism as a form of governmentality[4] when he was lecturing at the College de France. He discussed the implementation of Ordo-liberalism[5] in Europe and the Chicago School of Economics arising in the mid-twentieth century in the US (Brown 2003, 5).

Foucault's discussion did not focus on the economic policies of neoliberalism but on the ways that it becomes a "mode of governance." He contended that neoliberalism as political rationale morphs into a large ideological apparatus that transforms the nature of the state, the notion of citizenship, and produces new subjectivities, moralities, behaviors, and desires. The shifting of what was considered common sense becomes "a new organization of the social" (Brown 2003, 2).

What follows is a description of the characteristics of neoliberalism as a political rationale and as a form of governmentality, grounded in the work of Foucault (1978/1979), Brown (2003), and Davies and Bansel (2007):

- Neoliberalism takes control of the political sphere and subsumes it entirely to the needs of the market. The individual citizen becomes a *homo oeconomicus* and every single area of social, cultural, and political life is reduced to the simple economic principles of cost-benefit, production, and efficiency (Brown 2003, 9).
- Neoliberalism develops new discourses, institutional practices, rewards, norms, and new common-sense values to engulf every single aspect of human life into this form of governmentality. "Neo-liberalism involves a normative rather than ontological claim about the pervasiveness of economic rationality and advocates the institution building, policies, and discourse development appropriate to such a claim. Neo-liberalism is a constructivist project" (Brown 2003, 9).
- Neoliberalism as a political rationale does not mean *laissez faire* capitalism. In this form of governmentality, there is always active political intervention and manipulation of all the social institutions, from the media, the law, the arts, schools, and universities, to the most important protagonist of all, the state (Brown 2003, 9).
- Under neoliberalism the state acquires a new identity. It becomes the protector of capital and its role is reduced to the enactment of monetary, fiscal, social, and educational policies to nourish and protect the market. The legitimacy of the state is based on its ability to be true to this function (Brown 2003, 10).
- Under neoliberalism, government practices are reduced to the same calculating equations of profitability and cost-efficiency benefits. Gone are the commitments to equality and social justice grounded on the traditional liberalism of the founding fathers (Brown 2003, 10).
- Under neoliberalism the individual citizen becomes one of the most important targets. This is not related to the individualism of Adam Smith but it is a redefinition of the role of citizens as "entrepreneurial actors in every sphere of life" (Brown 2003, 15). In this form of governmentality, individuals become rational subjects whose goal in life is to be self-sufficient. They blame themselves for their own failures regardless of the structural constraints they may face. "A 'mismanaged life' becomes a new mode of depoliticizing social and economic powers and at the same time reduces political citizenship to an unprecedented degree of passivity and political complacency" (Brown 2003, 15). Nevertheless, the neo-liberal citizen defines herself as having the power of freedom, represented in the many choices that the free market offers.

As Davies and Bansel (2007) claim:

Neoliberalism functions at the level of the subject, producing *docile subjects* who are tightly governed, and who, at the same time define themselves as free. Individuals, we suggest, have been seduced by their own perceived powers of freedom and have, at the same time, let go significant collective power, through, for example, allowing the erosion of union power. (249)

- Under liberalism the public-minded individual is replaced by the *homo oeco-nomicus* and the body politics is replaced by a group of entrepreneurs and consumers. "Civil society is reduced to a domain for exercising this entrepreneurship" (Brown 2003, 38). It is important to remember how Margaret Thatcher, the leader of neoliberalism in Europe summarized this concept: "There is no such thing as a society" (cited in Hursh 2005, 12).
- As a form of governmentality, neoliberalism corrodes the institutions, values, and processes of liberal democracies (Brown 2003). It seeks to eliminate the notion of education as "a common and public good in the public interest" (Luke 2005, 161).

The privatization of state institutions, particularly the defunding of public education, appears to have serious implications for the future of American democracy.

Neoliberalism and the demise of education as a public good

The assaults against public education during the 1980s responded to the allegations of neoliberalism that schools were not responding to the needs of the economy or supporting US efforts to consolidate its leadership in the emergent global market. The publication of several state and commission reports[6] convinced American society that something was wrong with public education. The alarming cries for educational reform centered on teacher education. Schools were accused of failing students and universities were blamed for the lack of preparation of teachers. Accreditation institutions assumed a greater role by assuring that the curriculum and pedagogical practices of teacher preparation were aligned to the goals of neoliberalism. Gradually the goal of public education was changed from forming critical citizens for a healthy democracy to focusing on their development of functional skills to be economically productive (Hursh 2005, 5).

The rhetoric of neoliberalism – the shifting of common sense – was displayed in the campaign to discredit public education.[7] Americans lost confidence in the revered institution of public schooling. Neoliberalism blamed schools for the inequalities created by the unregulated market while increasing stratification and exclusion through a militant standardization movement that relied on testing, publication of test scores, and ranking of public schools.

Simultaneously, neoliberalism instilled fear in the public that the decline of American economic power was imminent if schools were not fixed. Neoliberalism became associated with democracy, economic stability, accountability, and more importantly, school choice. Schools, teachers, and their unions were portrayed as institutions that were compromising the success of the American economy. This was the case in Wisconsin when in 2010 Governor Walker proposed a controversial bill to substantially diminish the collective-bargaining rights of thousands of public school teachers while increasing their contributions to their pensions and health benefits under the excuse that those cuts were essential to reduce the state deficit. The bill, which also included a provision limiting the percentage of property taxes that the state could raise to offset its debt, and would end enrollment caps for charter schools, was approved in the midst of one of the most powerful protests at the national level. This was a very symbolic piece of legislation as it signaled the path that other states might follow to continue undermining public school teachers and their unions.

The NCLB represents the culmination of 20 years of rampant attacks against public education and one of the most important achievements of neoliberalism. Through NCLB the federal government was able to enact legislation that erased the tradition of local control of schools, with the only exception being Indian reservations (McCarty 2008). Schools became at once standardized in the name of accountability. Under NCLB, schools are required to publish disaggregated data on students' test scores and use specific scientific curricula to make improvements on students' achievement. Teachers continue receiving permanent training on how to teach to the test and they are penalized if their students' test scores are not raised. Because test scores reflect a myriad of influences, including the students' family income (Hursh 2004), schools in these working class communities are being shut down, reconstituted, or offered "for sale" because they could not meet the intended academic improvements. As a result, they become charter schools managed by non-profit charter management organizations or for-profit businesses.

This is part of the reconstitution of public services under the new neoliberal state. Education is no longer a public good offered and protected by the government; it has become a commodity that can be traded in the market. "Neoliberalism, unlike liberalism, withdraws value from the social good. Economic productivity is seen to come not from government investments in education, but from transforming education into a product that can be bought and sold like anything else" (Davies and Bansel 2007, 254). Forgotten are the intended democratic goals of public education.

The appropriation of universities as cultural spaces

Universities, where the institution of tenure protects academic freedom, have been one of the few remaining public spheres where face-to-face communities have articulated the connection between education and freedom (Greene 1982). However, as educational institutions, they have also fallen prey to the expansion of neoliberal policies. Since the late 1970s, neoliberalism began introducing fundamental changes to the way universities operate, using the strategy of "piecemeal functionalism."[8]

University restructuring began in, "1978 when the US Business-Higher Education Forum was established to create partnership between corporations and universities to support science, math, and technology" (Torres and Schugurensky 2002, 436). However, it soon became clear later that the intention of this group was to align higher education institutions to the goals of neoliberalism. According to Torres and Schugurensky (2002, 436), since its inception the Forum was, "interested in influencing policy formation and creating ideological hegemony, aligning higher education with the business and corporate sector." Similar interest groups proliferated later, including a Canadian version, the Canadian Corporate-Higher Education Forum, launched in 1983 (Torres and Schugurensky 2002), and the Business Roundtable consisting of the top 300 CEOs in the nation, which focused on education from 1989 on (Kumashiro 2010).

Michael Useem (1984) argues that these changes in higher education respond to the implementation of what he describes as "institutional capitalism"[9] that seeks to intensify the alliances between corporations and cultural institutions (Torres and Schugurensky 2002, 435). The increasing presence of corporate executives in boards of regents and boards of trustees of universities aims to influence the direction of their academic and non-academic work to support the expansion of globalization (Torres and Schugurensky 2002, 435). As such, these reconstituted governing boards have diligently embraced the discourse of accountability and standardization initiated in the 1980s and supported the demands, "for a permanent assessment of the outcomes of the higher education system" (Torres and Schugurensky 2002, 443).

The power brokers of neoliberalism

The Business Roundtable, formed in 1972 and dedicated to influencing education since 1989, was responsible for organizing a powerful group of billionaires, philanthropists, and foundations with the purpose of implementing neoliberal reforms in public education. Part of this original group were the: "Annenberg Center, the Broad Foundation [from Los Angeles real estate magnate Eli Broad], Education Trust, Harvard Graduate School, and the editorial boards of major newspapers" (Kumashiro 2010, 59).

Later on, other powerful players joined this effort, among them: the Bill and Melinda Gates Foundation, the Walton Family Foundation, the Michael and Susan Dell Foundation, the Lilly Endowment, the David and Lucile Packard Foundation, the W.K. Kellogg Foundation, and the Doris and Donald Fisher Fund (Kumashiro 2010; Ravitch 2010). However, the three most powerful donors controlling the direction of public education are Eli Broad, the Walton Family Foundation from the founder of Wal-Mart, and Bill and Melinda Gates (Ravitch 2010).

The city of Chicago is one example of the changes that these powerful business groups are able to make by pouring millions of dollars into initiatives and groups that are dismantling liberal public education. Renaissance 2010 was the program initiated by Mayor Richard Daley and envisioned intellectually by the Commercial Club of Chicago to restructure Chicago Public Schools (Kumashiro 2010, 58). Arne Duncan, a non-educator and the CEO of Chicago Public Schools, was chosen as Obama's secretary of education because he pioneered the reconstitution of public schools under Renaissance 2010, and was responsible for implementing the goal of closing 60 low-performing public schools and opening 100 new ones as small schools, charter, or contract schools by 2010.

To date, 75 inner city schools have opened with mixed results and Chicago is one of the cities with the highest numbers of alternative certification programs and reconstituted schools because of the strong monetary support of philanthrocapitalists (Ravitch 2010) for educational initiatives that promote the privatization of public schooling (Kumashiro 2010; Lipman 2003).

Not coincidentally, another powerful player in the campaign to restructure teacher preparation is Teach for America, which has emerged as one of the most overlooked groups that has coalesced with neoliberalism to dismiss the notion that teachers need formal teacher education before stepping in a classroom.

Teach for America has an authoritative presence in Washington, DC,[10] Chicago, and other major metropolises across the nation. According to Miner (2010):

> TFA spends significant organizational time, energy, and money on its alumni, who are arguably the source of the organization's true political power. The most famous alumni are Michelle Rhee, former chancellor of the Washington, DC public schools, and Mike Feinberg and David Levin, founders of the KIPP Schools. (28)

It was in Chicago where Teach for America started and where Michelle Rhee ran the New Teachers Project, which created the Chicago Teaching Fellows Program, another replica of the Teach For America (TFA) alternative certification program.

TFA's permanent lobbying of major school districts has made their members authoritative participants in all the reform efforts to dismantle public education. For example, in the districts that are undergoing severe budget cuts, senior teachers are laid off and replaced by TFA corps. "More recently, in Washington, DC, former TFA corps member and current Schools Chancellor Michelle Rhee laid off 229 teachers in October, but only six of the 170 TFA teachers in the system, according to the *Washington Post*" (Miner 2010, 29). Miner, citing Peter Downs, president of the St Louis elected school board, says, "that the district pays $2000 a year to TFA for each of its recruits" (Miner 2010, 27–8).

TFA's major donors are the: "Broad Foundation, the Michael and Susan Dell Fundation, the Doris and Donald Fisher Fund, the Rainwater Charitable Funds, and the federal government via AmeriCorps and the US Department of Education" (Kumashiro 2010, 58). In 2008, TFA listed: "Wachovia as one of five corporations donating more than $1 million at the national level. The others are Goldman Sachs, Visa, the biotechnology firm Amgen, and the golfing tournament Quail Hollow Championship" (Miner 2010, 30). Included in this list are some of the corporations responsible for the financial debacle of the past few years. In addition the Walton Family Foundation, created by Sam Walton, founder of Wal-Mart, contributed $9 million to TFA, which is the single largest contribution to the organization (Miner 2010, 32).

In 2008, TFA spent more than 500,000 dollars[11] lobbying state and federal legislatures to pass legislation to approve alternative teacher certification and other pro-business educational initiatives (Miner 2010, 32).

These are certainly major concerns about an organization that plays such a powerful and authoritative role in the demise of public education and actively benefits from the restructuring of teacher preparation.

The commodification of schools of education

Schools of education are the most affected by these whirlwinds of neoliberal reforms.[12] Among the major changes are drastic transformations in the preparation of teachers, the intensification of the business of accreditation, the appropriation of multicultural education, and the formation of a new managerial and professional middle class to support the privatization of education.

Teacher education has been systematically degraded since the 1980s with the publication of dozens of reports attacking public schools, teachers, and the universities that prepare them. One of the most intense targets has been to dismantle traditional teacher preparation programs that have an extended residency component and a coaching model to prepare and induct pre-service teachers. For example, Teach for America, and Secretary of Education, Arne Duncan, have strongly criticized long-term teacher preparation because they deem it lengthy, expensive, and unnecessary.

The commanding forces of neoliberalism, among them the federal government, local states, business groups, and accrediting institutions, are urging the creation of fast-track teacher preparation programs. This happens in spite of the fact that abundant research links student achievement to traditional teacher credentialing (Cochran

Smith 2001; Darling-Hammond 2000, 2001; Darling-Hammond, Berry, and Thoreson 2001; Darling-Hammond and Young 2002; Weiner 2007, 275; Wilson, Floden, and Ferrini-Mundy 2002; Zeichner 2006).

As Kumashiro (2010) argues, the excuse that alternative routes to teacher certification challenge the monopoly of the universities has resulted in a proliferation of alternative teacher certification outside higher education institutions. These short-lived teacher preparation programs are reproducing at a fast pace while universities are also creating alternative teacher credentialing programs to remain competitive in that market.

Arne Duncan, Obama's secretary of education and one of the most recognized czars of neoliberalism, has spent most of his tenure encouraging the creation of alternative certification models and attacking schools of education, evinced by the speeches at Columbia Teachers College and at the AACTE conference. What follows is an excerpt from Duncan's (2009) speech at Teachers College:

> Now I am all in favor of expanding high-quality alternative certificate routes, like High Tech High, the New Teacher Project, Teach for America, and teacher residency programs. But these promising alternative programs produce fewer than 10,000 teachers per year. The predominance of education schools in preparing teachers is not the only reason this is a national priority and a critical concern for higher education ... America's taxpayers already generously support teacher preparation programs. And it is only right that this investment should be well spent.[13] (http://www.ed.gov/news/speeches/teacher-preparation-reforming-uncertain-profession)

This is an excerpt from Duncan's talk at AACTE (2010):

> In my talk last fall at the Teachers College at Columbia I called for a sea-change in our schools of education. I challenged schools of education for failing to teach aspiring teachers how to use data to differentiate and improve instruction, and boost student learning. Great teacher after great teacher I've talked with around the country told me that they learned those skills on the job, not in school. I criticized some ed schools for a lack of rigorous and relevant research, and for failing to provide sufficient high-quality, hands-on practical training about managing the classroom, especially for high-needs students. And I said that colleges of education had to do a much better job of gathering data on the effectiveness of their graduates in the classroom and their impact on student achievement. At present, most colleges of education know little to nothing about the impact of their graduates on student learning.[14] (http://www.ed.gov/news/speeches/preparing-teachers-and-school-leaders-tomorrow-secretary-arne-duncans-remarks-american)

These remarks are part of a campaign to prepare the public for new incoming changes to teacher certification. Duncan proposed a new national exam for all teacher candidates that would measure their teaching competence and the quality of their teacher preparation programs. Those schools of education that rank highest will be rewarded with money from the Race to the Top initiative (Berlak 2010).

In California, there are already several entrance and exit exams, among them the CBEST (California Basic Educational Skill Test), CSET (California Subject Examination for Teaching), RICA (Reading Instruction Competence Assessment), CalTPA (California Teacher Performance Assessment), and the additional evaluations of the NCATE and other credentialing commissions. Thus, Duncan's proposal to require PACT (Performance Assessment for California Teachers) as a national exit exam (which is being used as an alternative to CalTPA) would add another layer of federal control of what teachers need to learn in order to teach.

According to a teacher educator (Berlak 2010) whose department uses PACT to assess credential candidates: "teaching patterns valued by PACT are primarily aspects of explicit, systematic, direct instruction that will instill in students knowledge specified by the state-mandated standards and measured by standardized tests" (43–4). The creation of signature assignments in Live-Text and other commercial software paid for by the students is already interfering with the academic freedom of faculty to determine their own assessment methods.

The tactics of neoliberalism are multiple and concurrent. Alternative certification creates competition and deprofessionalizes teaching, while NCLB, Race to the Top, and accrediting institutions force schools of education to align their curriculum and pedagogical practices to the formation of the *homo oeconomicus*.

Marketing, accreditation, and diversity

As the "cash cows" of most universities, schools of education are also pressured to increase student enrollment and to compete with all the purveyors of public and private education, which in this era of corporate schooling includes online universities, for-profit higher education institutions, and private educational corporations. Therefore, schools of education are seeking accreditation at higher rates to become more marketable because what sells well is the promise of accountability and excellence.[15] Institutions like NCATE currently accredit 657 colleges of education and 100 more are in the process of being accredited nationwide. Arne Duncan highlighted the significance of national accreditation as part of his mission to align education to the needs of the market:

> As you know, the accreditation of schools of education is a voluntary process, and historically coursework had been given greater priority than clinical training for students in accreditation. But there also are encouraging signs that colleges of education want to make self-policing more meaningful, with clinical experience driving coursework. Both NCATE, the National Council for Accreditation of Teacher Education, and AACTE, the American Association of Colleges for Teacher Education, are firmly behind the new drive to link teacher preparation programs to better student outcomes. (Duncan 2009)

It is expected that the imminent establishment of a national exam for credentialing teacher candidates that will convey quantitative data on students' competence and quality of their program, will be used by national accrediting institutions to grant or refuse accreditation of teacher preparation programs.

National accreditation has also contributed to the reification of diversity. Schools of education in their quest to seek NCATE accreditation have developed mission statements and conceptual frameworks that articulate NCATE's commercial notion of diversity and social justice that attracts aspiring teachers. Nonetheless, the tendency of schools of education to link NCATE with the concept of social justice triggered an alarming response from conservative groups that support neoliberal policies. As a result, in 2007, NCATE withdrew the term social justice from its accreditation training documents in response to concerns that the council was emphasizing too much diversity:

NCATE has never required a "social justice" disposition; NCATE expects institutions to select professional dispositions they would like to see in the teachers they prepare. The term "social justice," though well understood by NCATE's institutions, was widely and wildly misinterpreted by commentators not familiar with the workings of NCATE. NCATE has never had a "social justice" standard and thus did not enforce such a standard. (NCATE 2007)

If there was any hope that NCATE would reaffirm its original role of advocating for the inclusion of social justice, diversity, and equity as it did in 1977 when it required the inclusion of multicultural education in teacher education, this statement leaves no doubts about its political orientation. Accrediting institutions, particularly NCATE, play an essential role as regulators of the educational market.

New degrees for the neoliberal society

Another change in schools of education has arisen as a result of the rapidly emerging and powerful managerial middle class that provides support to the policies of neoliberalism. According to Apple (2001), these are people with backgrounds in management and efficiency techniques who provide the technical and: "professional support for accountability, measurement, product control, and assessment that is required by the proponents of neoliberal policies [...] and tighter central control in education" (57).

Thus, neoliberalism has generated a new market to train teachers and administrators for charter schools, and leaders with expertise in management techniques. Schools of education are creating new academic programs and degrees with specialization in charter schools and leadership in urban education. In addition, because NCLB made the old multipurpose PhD in education obsolete (Guthrie 2009), schools of education are creating fast-track doctorates (EdD) in educational leadership[16] to train school administrators, with the ultimate goal of improving academic achievement as measured by student test scores.

This new market has proven so popular and profitable that schools of education have entirely reorganized their academic units to accommodate the large number of students who seek to obtain a doctorate in three years without the intensity of its research-oriented counterpart (Goldring and Schuermann 2009; Guthrie 2009; Levine 2005a, 2005b).

Public relations, national rankings, and managerialism

Another important development is related to the reconfiguration of schools of education as powerful players in the educational marketplace. Traditionally, the US News & World Report rankings have driven the academic and administrative decisions of schools of education, however, at present neoliberalism has exacerbated those demands. Deans of schools of education are forced to increase their standing as a basic marketing strategy to increase student enrollment. As a result, more often they devote an unprecedented amount of time to networking with the constituencies that provide feedback on the rankings,[17] in addition to their expanding fundraising activities.

Public relations have become so fundamental for schools of education that new positions have been created for communication managers, public relations officials, directors of development offices, and media coordinators within these academic units. The work of these new staff members has become crucial to make schools of education and their leaders significant players in the educational market.

Lastly, one of the most visible changes in schools of education can be observed in how these academic units are being financially administered. *Managerialism* has taken over the administration of universities (Apple 2001) and particularly schools of education. The corporate practices of performance-based assessments, recruiting, marketing, bottom lines, business reports, standardization, work norms, and tuition-based revenues have gradually penetrated the daily life of these academic institutions.

Academic capitalism has entered American universities and it is redefining the academic premises upon which the entire higher education system was instituted. Universities, which are the last public space protected by academic freedom to promote the development of public intellectuals, are losing ground to the globalization of higher education.

Reclaiming public education as a common good

Nussbaum (2010) proposes a *human development paradigm* to counteract the *education for profit* that is replacing American liberal education. This model emphasizes the dignity of all citizens and focuses on broadening the basic spectrum of human and political rights to include social and economic rights (e.g. education and health), which have not yet been ratified by the US government. This *human development* model seeks to inspire in its citizens:

- The ability to think well about political issues affecting the nation, to examine, reflect, argue, and debate, deferring to neither tradition nor authority.
- The ability to recognize fellow citizens as people with equal rights [...] to look at them with respect, as ends, not just as tools to be manipulated for one's own profit.
- The ability to have concern for the lives of others, to grasp what policies of many types mean for the opportunities and experiences of one's fellow citizens, of many types, and for people outside one's own nation.
- The ability to see one's own nation, in turn, as a part of a complicated world order in which issues of many kinds require intelligent transnational deliberation for their resolution. (Nussbaum 2010, 26)

These concepts should be taught through the integration of literature, arts, math, and science; the discussion of economic history, political geography, and global citizenship; and the examination of theories of social and global justice from a political theory perspective (Dewey 2004; Greene 1995; Nussbaum 2010, 91–2).

Fundamental to the teaching of this human development approach are the pedagogical model of Socratic teaching (or problem-posing pedagogy as Freire calls it), the teaching of debate, the integration of role-playing, the use of experiential teaching, and the practice of the arts. Among the important goals of this kind of education is the capacity to inculcate in students empathy for their fellow citizens. This has been one of the most significant components of traditional liberal education and a key concept for the preservation of the common good.

In addition, Andrzejewski, Baltodano, and Symcox (2009) propose a collective vision for social justice that includes transformative principles for protecting teachers and their work, transforming the curriculum of public schools and universities, and transforming the preparation of teachers beyond NCATE (281–5). Among some of these guidelines and declarations of rights for teachers and students are the following:

- Teachers must have the protection to form and join labor unions of their choice, and initiate grievance processes against those (union leaders as well as school leaders) who are not protecting the rights of teachers or are involved in corruption.
- Teachers must have protection to exercise academic freedom for research, creative activity, and dissemination of knowledge.
- Teachers must be able to teach human rights, social and environmental justice and peace.
- Teachers must be able to create their own curriculum as long as it meets the benchmarks for grade level. No teacher should be forced to follow teacher-proof curricula, or be threatened, harassed, or demoted for not implementing pre-package curriculum. (282)

- Teacher candidates must have the freedom to learn pedagogical skills and global political knowledge that will make them competent teachers and transformative intellectuals in the classroom.
- Teacher candidates must have the freedom to experience modeling of pedagogical models such as problem posing pedagogy, Socratic dialogues, questioning, feedback, authentic pre- and post-assessment, experiential learning, heterogeneous grouping, peer grouping, and so forth.
- Teacher candidates must have the freedom to experience student-teaching before being formally inducted into the classroom. (284)

These two frameworks (Andrzejewski, Baltodano, and Symcox 2009; Nussbaum 2010) are not driven by a utopian vision of education. They closely resemble the constitution of many industrial countries, including the US, are inspired by the work of recognized educators worldwide, and are based on human rights conventions ratified by the majority of the world's nations. These visions may be used as an initial platform to initiate a conversation and launch a movement to reclaim education as a public good.

Michael Apple (2001) remembered Paulo Freire saying that "education must begin in critical dialogue," (218) and this is the conversation that this article seeks to inspire. It proposes the immediate task of organizing a grassroots movement comprised of teachers, students, community activists, union leaders, and faculty at colleges of education and liberal arts who are concerned with the demise of education as a *public good*.

This organic process is essential to create historical blocs (Gramsci 1971) and counter hegemonic alliances to reclaim the public spheres that have been offered for sale (Apple 2001). This organizing effort may take the forms of teachers' study groups, student councils, neighborhood councils, faculty support groups, community meetings, teacher union convocations, and so forth. The most important thing is that Americans begin to have a conversation about what kind of education and what kind of democracy they seek to sustain.

Among some of the most pressing issues to consider for these constituencies may be the following:

- Reexamine, evaluate, and support the reconfigured role of unions in public schools.
- Reclaim local control of public schools and reconfigure local school boards where parents and teachers are the majority.

- Create strong and authentic partnerships between local schools, local unions, and universities' teacher education programs.
- Conceptualize and implement teacher preparation models that reflect the best practices and the best interest of students.
- Encourage greater involvement of educators and members of this movement in public office to enact legislation to protect education as a public good.
- Seek judicial protection to stop the federal government from interfering in the local control of schools.
- Create new teacher accreditation organizations that truly respond to a professional and civic vision of public schooling.
- Organize faculty groups to create awareness in departments and colleges about the advancement of neoliberalism in higher education.
- Reimagine teacher education in terms of professional identity, democratic goals, and structural arrangements with the larger society (Wilkinson 2007).

The issues to consider are far broader and deeper than what is suggested here, but a critical dialog about the state of education in the US would be a starting point in the quest to protect the most important of the social institutions of American liberal democracy, public education.

Notes

1. NCATE is the National Council for Accreditation of Teacher Education; AACTE is the American Association of Colleges for Teacher Education.
2. Dewey's beliefs in the intrinsic relationship between theory and practice were fundamental for his conception of teachers as transformative intellectuals who were morally attentive to larger social reforms. Dewey believed that schools were public spaces to critically assess the excesses of the industrial movement and to advocate for those who were being silenced.
3. Friedrich von Hayek and Milton Friedman were recipients of the Nobel Memorial Prize in Economics in 1974 and 1976, respectively.
4. Foucault's 1978 and 1979 College of France lectures had been recorded in audiocassettes and were unpublished and untranscribed until 2004, when the first edition of this work was published in French. In 2008, these lectures were translated and published in English.
5. Ordoliberalism is the term given to the neoliberal governmentality conceptualized by members of the Freiburg School after WWI in Germany and implemented in West Germany after WWII. In spite of the fact that this school had existed in parallel to the Frankfurt School of Critical Theory, it had opposite views on many of the key issues. Ordoliberalism impacted the development of the Chicago School of Economics in the US; however, the latter became more radical (Lemke 2001). Unlike Adam Smith's assumptions about the natural forces of the market, Ordoliberalism proposed that the market is not innate, and therefore, the government has to intervene in order to protect it. The state has to create competition, and encourage demand to keep the market alive. In this view, capitalism is a social construct, created and maintained by the government (Brown 2003; Lemke 2001). There is no such thing as the "logic of the market." It is the state that defines the life and direction of the economy.
6. Among these reports were: *A Nation at Risk: The Imperative for Educational Reform* (National Commission on Excellence in Education 1983); *A Nation Prepared: Teachers for the 21st Century: The Report of the Task Force on Teaching as a Profession* (Carnegie Forum on Education and the Economy 1986); *Tomorrow's Teachers* (Holmes Group 1986); *Time for Results: The Governors' 1991 Report on Education* (National Governors' Association 1991), and *Goals 2000* (United States Department of Education 1985).

7. See for example popular films like "Waiting for Superman" (2010).
8. This technique is defined as the way norms and changes are introduced gradually, "lessening the chance people will grasp the overall scheme and organize resistance" (Sklar 1980, 21, cited in Davies and Bansel 2007, 251). "Piecemeal functionalism" has been one of the most successful methods that neoliberalism has used to render itself invisible and gradually consolidate its platform of governmentality (Davies and Bansel 2007). The invisibility of neoliberalism makes it difficult to challenge the depth of the social reorganization carried out by this ideology.
9. Useem uses the term "institutional capitalism" to differentiate it from the *family* and *managerial* capitalism of previous eras (Torres and Schugurensky 2002, 435).
10. TFA is so influential in the White House that it successfully orchestrated a campaign against Linda Darling-Hammond, one of its most vociferous critics, when she was considered for a key position in the Obama administration (Miner 2010).
11. This is the maximum amount allowed for political lobbying for a 501(c)3 organization.
12. For example, during spring 2010, a graduate school of education in a public Tier-1, research university in the Southwest was "de-established" and collapsed into a teachers college because the university board of regents and the state legislature considered it more profitable to focus on teacher preparation than subsidizing an entire academic unit devoted to research. Tenure and non-tenure faculty were told they were "free agents" and were instructed to search for jobs somewhere else.
13. Arne Duncan's 2009 address at Columbia Teachers College, "Teacher Preparation: Reforming the Uncertain Profession."
14. Arne Duncan's 2010 address at the American Association of Colleges for Teacher Education Conference, "Preparing the Teachers and School Leaders of Tomorrow."
15. According to the NCATE's mission (2010), "Applicants to an NCATE accredited institution will have the assurance that the institution's educator program has met national standards and received the profession's 'seal of approval'" (3).
16. See for example the EdD programs in educational leadership at Vanderbilt University, University of Southern California, Pepperdine University, Arizona State University, and St Louis University among many others.
17. Some of the people who provide feedback on the quality of schools of education are alumni, superintendents, principals, and other deans of schools of education. The names of participants cannot be revealed because their participation was confidential according to the protection offered by the Institutional Review Board (IRB) that approved this research.

References

Amin, A. 1994. *Post-Fordism: A reader*. Oxford: Blackwell.
Andrzejewski, J., M. Baltodano, and L. Symcox, eds. 2009. *Social justice, peace and environmental education. Transformative standards*. New York, NY: Routledge.
Apple, M.W. 2001. *Educating the right way. Market, standards, God, and inequality*. New York, NY: Routledge.
Balibar, E. 1995. *The philosophy of Marx*. London: Verso.
Baltodano, M. 2009. The pursuit of social justice in the United States. In *Social justice, peace and environmental education. Transformative standards*, ed. J. Andrzejewski, M. Baltodano, and L. Symcox, 273–87. New York, NY: Routledge.

Berlak, A. 2010. Coming soon to your favorite credential program: National exit exams. *Rethinking Schools* 24, no. 4: 41–5.

Bonefeld, W., and J. Holloway. 1991. *Post-Fordism and social form*. London: Macmillan.

Brittan, S. 1995. *Capitalism with a human face*. Cambridge, MA: Harvard University Press.

Brown, W. 2003. Neoliberalism and the end of democracy. *Theory & Event* 7, no. 1. DOI: 10.1353/tae.2003.0020.

Carnegie Forum on Education and the Economy. 1986. *A nation prepared: Teachers for the 21st century. The report of the task force on teaching as a profession*. New York: Carnegie Forum on Education and the Economy.

Cochran Smith, M. 2001. Reforming teacher education. *Journal of Teacher Education* 52, no. 4: 263–5.

Codd, J. 1988. The construction and deconstruction of educational policy documents. *Journal of Education Policy* 3, no. 3: 235–47.

Compton, M., and L. Weiner, eds. 2008. *The global assault on teaching, teachers, and their unions*. New York, NY: Palgrave Macmillan.

Crozier, M., S.P. Huntington, and J. Watanuki. 1975. *The crisis of democracy: Report on the governability of democracies to the trilateral commission*. New York, NY: New York University Press.

Darling-Hammond, L. 2000. Teacher quality and student achievement: A review of state policy evidence. *Education Policy Analysis Archives* 8, no. 1. http://epaa.asu.edu/ojs/article/view/392.

Darling-Hammond, L. 2001. *The research and rhetoric on teacher certification: A response to "teacher certification reconsidered"*. National Commission on Teaching and America's Future. Palo Alto, CA: Stanford University.

Darling-Hammond, L., B. Berry, and A. Thoreson. 2001. Does teacher certification matter? Evaluating the evidence. *Educational Evaluation and Policy Analysis* 23, no. 1: 57–77.

Darling-Hammond, L., and P. Young. 2002. Defining "highly qualified teachers": What does "scientifically-based research" actually tell us? *Educational Researcher* 31, no. 9: 13–25.

Davies, B., and P. Bansel. 2007. Neoliberalism and education. *International Journal of Qualitative Studies in Education* 20, no. 3: 247–59.

Dewey, J. 1916. *Democracy and education*. New York, NY: Macmillan.

Dewey, J. 1956. *The child and the curriculum; and the school and society*. Chicago, IL: University of Chicago Press.

Dewey, J. 2004. *Democracy and education. An introduction to the philosophy of education*. Mineola, NY: Dover.

Duncan, A. 2009. *Teacher preparation: Reforming the uncertain profession*. New York, NY: Columbia University Teachers College. http://www.ed.gov/news/speeches/teacher-preparation-reforming-uncertain-profession.

Duncan, A. 2010. Preparing the teachers and school leaders of tomorrow. Speech given at the American Association of Colleges for Teacher Education Conference, February 19, in Atlanta, GA. http://www.ed.gov/news/speeches/preparing-teachers-and-school-leaders-tomorrow-secretary-arne-duncans-remarks-american.

Foucault, M. 1978/1979. *The birth of biopolitics. Lectures at the College de France*. Trans. G. Burcher and ed. A. Davidson. New York, NY: Palgrave Macmillan. (Original work published in 2004 in French by Editions du Seuil/Gallimard).

Freire, P. 1970. *Pedagogy of the oppressed*. New York, NY: Seabury Press.

Goldring, E., and P. Schuermann. 2009. The changing context of K-12 education administration: Consequences for Ed.D. program design and delivery. *Peabody Journal of Education* 84, no. 1: 9–43.

Gramsci, A. 1971. *Selections from the prison notebooks*. Trans. and ed. Q. Hoare and G. Smith. New York, NY: International Publishers.

Greene, M. 1982. Public education and the public space. *Educational Researcher* 11, no. 4: 4–9.

Greene, M. 1991. Values education in the contemporary moment. *Clearing House* 64, no. 5: 301–4.

Greene, M. 1995. *Releasing the imagination: Essays on education, the arts, and social change*. San Francisco, CA: Jossey-Bass.

Guthrie, J.W. 2009. The case for a modern doctor of education degree (Ed.D.): Multipurpose education doctorates no longer appropriate. *Peabody Journal of Education* 84, no. 1: 3–8.

Holmes Group. 1986. *Tomorrow's teachers*. East Lansing, MI: The Holmes Group.

Huntington, S.P. 1976. The democratic distemper. In *The American Commonwealth*, ed. N. Gazer and I. Kristol, 9–38. New York, NY: Basic Books.

Hursh, D. 2004. Undermining democratic education in the USA: The consequences of global capitalism and neo-liberal policies for education policies at the local, state, and federal levels. *Policy Futures in Education* 2, nos. 3–4: 607–20.

Hursh, D. 2005. Neoliberalism, markets and accountability: Transforming education and undermining democracy in the United States and England. *Policy Futures in Education* 3, no. 1: 3–15.

Jessop, B. 1995. The regulation approach, governance and post-Fordism: Alternative perspectives on economic and political change? *Economy and Society* 24, no. 3: 307–33.

Kaase, M., and K. Newton. 1995. *Beliefs in government*. Vol. 5. Oxford: Oxford University Press.

Kumashiro, K.K. 2010. Seeing the bigger picture: Troubling movements to end teacher education. *Journal of Teacher Education* 6, nos. 1–2: 56–65.

Lemke, T. 2001. The birth of biopolitics: Michel Foucault's lecture at the College de France on neo-liberal governmentality. *Economy and Society* 30, no. 2: 190–207.

Levine, A. 2005a. *Educating researchers: The education schools project*. Washington, DC: The Education Schools Project. http://www.edschools.org/EducatingResearchers/educating_researchers.pdf.

Levine, A. 2005b. *Educating school leaders: The education schools project*. Washington, DC: The Education Schools Project. http://www.edschools.org/pdf/Final313.pdf.

Lipman, P. 2003. Beyond accountability: Toward schools that create new people for a new way of life. In *High stakes education: Inequality, globalization, and urban school reform*, ed. P. Lipman, 169–92. New York, NY: Routledge.

Luke, A. 1995–1996. Text and discourse in education: An introduction to critical discourse analysis. *Review of Research in Education* 21, no. 1: 3–48.

Luke, C. 2005. Capital and knowledge flows: Global higher education markets. *Asia Pacific Journal of Education* 25, no. 2: 159–74.

McCarty, T. 2008. The impact of high-stakes accountability policies on Native American learners: Evidence from research. Queensland Study Authority. http://www.qsa.qld.edu.au/6322.html.

McHoul, A.W. 1984. Writing, sexism and schooling: A discourse analytic investigation of some recent documents on sexism and education in Queensland. *Discourse* 4, no. 2: 1–17.

Miner, B. 2010. Looking past the spin. *Rethinking Schools* 24, no. 3: 24–33.

Muetzenfeldt, M., ed. 1992. *Society, state and politics in Australia*. Sydney: Pluto Press.

National Commission on Excellence in Education. 1983. *A nation at risk: The imperative for educational reform*. Washington, DC: US Department of Education.

National Council for Accreditation of Teacher Education (NCATE). 2007. NCATE issues call for action; defines professional dispositions as used in teacher education. http://www.ncate.org/public/102407.asp?ch=148.

National Council for Accreditation of Teacher Education (NCATE). 2010. NCATE's mission. http://ncate.org/Public/AboutNCATE/tabid/179/Default.aspx.

National Governors' Association. 1991. *Time for results: The governors' 1991 report on education*. Washington, DC: National Governors' Association.

Nussbaum, M. 1998. *Cultivating humanity: A classical defense of reform in liberal education*. Cambridge, MA: Harvard University Press.

Nussbaum, M. 2010. *Not for profit: Why democracy needs the humanities*. Princeton, NJ: Princeton University Press.

Ravitch, D. 2010. *The death and life of the great American school system: How testing and choice are undermining education*. Philadelphia, PA: Basic Books.

Sklar, H. 1980. *Trilateralism: The trilateral commission and elite planning for world management*. Montreal: Black Rose Books.

Symcox, L. 2009. From a Nation at Risk to No Child Left Behind: 25 years of neoliberal reform in education. In *Social justice, peace and environmental education. Transformative standards*, ed. J. Andrzejewski, M. Baltodano, and L. Symcox, 53–65. New York, NY: Routledge.

Taylor, S. 1997. Critical policy analysis: Exploring contexts, texts, and consequences. *Discourse: Studies in the Cultural Politics of Education* 18, no. 1: 23–35.

Torres, C.A., and D. Schugurensky. 2002. The political economy of higher education in the era of neoliberal globalization: Latin America in comparative perspective. *Higher Education* 43, no. 4: 429–55.

United States Department of Education. 1985. *Goals 2000*. Washington, DC: Author.

Useem, M. 1984. *The inner circle: Large corporations and the rise of business political activity in the US and UK*. Oxford: Oxford University Press.

Waiting for Superman. Directed by Davis Guggenheim. Hollywood, CA: Paramount Vintage, 2010.

Weiner, L. 2007. A lethal threat to US teacher education. *Journal of Teacher Education* 58, no. 4: 274–86.

Wilkinson, G. 2007. Civic professionalism: Teacher education and professional ideals and values in a commercialized education world. *Journal of Education for Teaching* 33, no. 3: 379–95.

Wilson, S., R. Floden, and J. Ferrini-Mundy. 2002. Teacher preparation research: An insider's view from the outside. *Journal of Teacher Education* 53, no. 3: 190–204.

Wirth, A.G. 1966. *John Dewey as educator: His design for work in education (1894–1904)*. New York, NY: Wiley.

Zeichner, K. 2006. Reflections of a university-based teacher educator on the future of college- and university-based teacher education. *Journal of Teacher Education* 7, no. 3: 326–40.

Fixing contradictions of education commercialisation: Pearson plc and the construction of its efficacy brand

Curtis B. Riep

ABSTRACT

This paper explores some of the fundamental contradictions related to the commercialisation of education and how Pearson plc – 'the world's leading multinational education company' – is trying to overcome these challenges through discourse and semiotics. Pearson's *Efficacy Framework* is a semiotic-calculative device created to measure the impact of educational products and services sold by the company. This paper examines the ways in which the efficacy programme and tools developed by Pearson represent a type of 'social fix' intended to resolve contradictions linked to education commercialisation by demonstrating the 'measurable impact' and 'outcomes' resulting from its educational products and services and communicating that to customers, shareholders, policymakers, state managers and partners. Efficacy will be analysed as it relates to a hegemonic 'knowledge brand' in the making in education that is being actively promoted and appropriated by Pearson. Pearson, therefore, aims to construct a corporate brand and reputation around *efficacy* based on legible measures of performance, which this paper argues is in response to risks and contradictions associated with the commercialisation of education.

Introduction

Education has increasingly been rendered as a commodity that is produced, consumed and exchanged through market mechanisms. In turn, a global education industry has emerged, constituted by systems of rules, policies, processes and social forces that interact dialectically to influence education commercialisation (Ball, 2012; Robertson & Dale, 2015; Verger, Lubienski, & Steiner-Khamsi, 2016). For instance, economic globalisation has increased the demand and cross-border supply of educational services and products; international trends in education policy and governance reforms have advanced the logic of decentralisation, standardisation, austerity and evidence-based policy paradigms that involve increased private-sector participation and market-oriented restructuring; the growth of information technologies (IT) in relationship to learning has also created new market opportunities, and hence; the commodification and financialisation of education has undergone considerable expansion and intensification across all levels from pre-primary schooling to higher education and lifelong learning (Verger et al., 2016). In 2014, Bank of America-Merrill Lynch estimated that the global education industry was worth US$4.5–5 trillion and expected to grow to US$6–8 trillion by 2017 (Hartnett, Leung, & Marcus, 2014, p. 6).

This paper explores some of the contradictions of education commercialisation and ways in which global edu-businesses try to overcome such contradictions through discourse and semiotics in order to secure capital accumulation.

Pearson plc, the self-adorned 'world's leading learning company' is a paradigmatic case to study the growth of the global education industry and edu-businesses that seek to profit from it. Pearson is an influential, yet largely unaccountable, actor, partner, contractor and enabler of shifting political logics and processes connected to neoliberal globalisation that is transforming education into a sector guided by market principles, financial logics and capital accumulation strategies. And while Pearson is the focus of this paper, this analysis is concerned with a much broader phenomenon that relates to how edu-businesses attempt to legitimate and secure their profit-making activities in education.

Pearson's commercial activities in education span pre-primary to post-secondary levels and language to lifelong learning sectors in more than 70 countries around the globe. It has an extensive business portfolio in education with products and services related to assessment, publishing, curricula, data management/processing, administration and learning and technology as well as the Pearson Affordable Learning Fund that provides 'low-cost' private schooling in the global-South and the operation of private colleges in the global-North such as Pearson College London. In 2015, Pearson's sales dropped by 5% but remained substantial at £4.5 billion.

John Fallon, the Chief Executive Officer of Pearson, states: 'We think education will turn out to be the great growth industry of the 21st century' (Pearson plc, 2012, p. 8). This belief stems from socio-economic trends taking place on a global scale:

> As rapid advances in technology continue to disrupt the world of work, the economic value of education and skills will continue
> to increase. Governments spend trillions of dollars per year on education and training; and, each year, the still rapidly growing middle class invests more of its own increasing wealth in the education of themselves and their children. And yet, the world fails to meet the learning needs of far too many of our fellow citizens (Pearson plc, 2013, p. 9).

For more than a decade, Pearson has gone about restructuring the company into a globally integrated education conglomerate in order to capitalise on 'the sustained and growing global demand for greater affordability, access, and achievement in education' (Pearson plc, 2014, p. 17). As the company claims:

> ...the bigger Pearson's social impact – in improving access to good quality education and ensuring that translates into meaningful learning outcomes for far more people – the more we can create a faster growing and more profitable company, and do so in a sustainable manner (Pearson plc, 2015, p. 6).

Therefore, the company's 'commercial goals and social purpose are mutually reinforcing' (Pearson plc, 2012, p. 34). For Pearson then, demonstrating 'social impact' is 'a form of justification of the company's commercial activities, or a form of legitimation for profit' (Junemann & Ball, 2015, p. 6).

In turn, Pearson aims to generate data that makes legible and visible the 'outcomes' and/or 'performance' of its educational commodities. It is part of a corporate strategy whereby Pearson intends to rebrand and reinvent itself as the 'efficacy company' in education that can deliver social impact in the form of effective and efficient outcomes for learners. As Marjorie Scardino, the former CEO of Pearson (1996–2012), announced in 2012: 'We're setting out to become the efficacy company…we need to define ourselves by how effective we are, by the impact we make'. John Fallon, the current CEO of Pearson, has maintained that: 'We want to be able to demonstrate that everything we do as a company delivers an improved learning outcome'. Hence, the goal of Pearson is to construct a corporate brand and reputation around efficacy that builds trust with customers and legitimates its for-profit activities in education.

This paper aims to contribute to the growing body of literature on the global education industry by focusing on particular discourse, ideas, meanings, brands, desires and symbols used by education corporations like Pearson to advance capitalist restructuring in education. Scholarly attention that deconstructs the discourse and semiotics mobilised by transnational corporate actors for the purpose of commodifying more and more of the education sector is necessary for understanding the expansion and intensification of the global education industry and opening it up to critique. Therefore, this paper examines the discursive and semiotic techniques of Pearson that aim to construct a corporate brand and reputation around 'efficacy' in order to overcome contradictions related to education commercialisation.

This paper adopts a 'cultural political economy' approach (Best & Paterson, 2010; Jessop, 2004; Jessop & Sum, 2006; Robertson & Dale, 2015; Sum, 2010; Sum & Jessop, 2013) to examine the cultural (or discursive) aspects of capitalist restructuring associated with the political economy of education. In the first section, I outline four fundamental contradictions related to education as a commodity. In the next section, I examine how Pearson is trying to 'fix' such contradictions through its *Efficacy Framework*: a semiotic-calculative device created to measure the performance of educational products and services sold by the company. Methodologically, the semiotic and discursive techniques and practices for collecting, measuring and disseminating data contrived from Pearson's *Efficacy Framework* will be analysed using an approach based on critical semiotic analysis and critical political economy (Jessop, 2004, 2010). It will be argued that Pearson's *Efficacy Framework* is meant to fix contradictions linked to education commercialisation by ensuring consumers, clients, shareholders, policymakers, state managers and partners the efficacy of its products and services. By constructing a corporate brand and reputation around efficacy based on legible, measurable and auditable techniques, Pearson aims to secure capital accumulation in the global education industry despite risks and contradictions that exist. The notion of efficacy will also be discussed as it relates to a hegemonic 'knowledge brand' in the making in education which is being actively promoted and appropriated by Pearson. In the conclusion, a brief overview of insights gleaned from this paper will be discussed.

Education as a commodity: contradictions and crises-tendencies

The liberal propensity to treat education as an economic commodity involves contradictions and crisis-tendencies in *at least* four fundamental ways. Yet, it is important to note that not all forms of education as a commodity are contradictory. Typically, tutoring and some types of professional/corporate learning have been delivered as commodities that are bought and sold privately. Hence, the following discussion is concerned with broader conceptions of education including those forms generally regarded as a 'common good' and/or constitutionalised as a 'human right' such as primary, secondary and tertiary education. Here, contradictions are referred to as the 'various ruptures and inconsistencies both among and within the established social arrangements' (Seo & Creed, 2002, p. 225).

First, education in its commodity form is a contradiction given that learning and the transmission of knowledge that takes place can be secured otherwise than through market exchange. For example, reciprocity and/or redistribution via state or communal patronage can provide educational services without user fees. Many countries around the globe provide free, high-quality public education to their citizens. Yet, this is the exception not the norm. It is a matter of political will and priorities.

Education is essential to human activity, survival and growth, intrinsically linked to life itself. Indeed, the 'ability to acquire knowledge and culture, is one of the fundamental purposes of civilization' (Piketty, 2014, p. 308). Yet, under conditions of political and economic liberalism it has been rendered as something that is increasingly bought and sold – representing a 'fictitious commodity' (Polanyi, 2001). Like knowledge, education 'acquires a commodity form insofar as it is *made artificially scarce*' (Jessop, 2007, p. 120; emphasis added). Education is 'made artificially scare' as a result of political choices, interactions, tactics, financial outflows and structures of power and influence through which the supply and provision of quality education is 'rationed' (Gillborn & Youdell, 2000). As state provision and supply of education is systematically reduced in relation to demand, the participation of private (foreign) actors has increased in the sector along with cross-border supplies of education (Verger et al., 2016). In spaces of state retrenchment, new commercial opportunities have emerged for corporate actors to help fill the 'governance gap' in the form of outsourcing arrangements, public–private partnerships and the direct provision of for-profit education (Bhanji, 2008). In the global North, market opportunities have mostly come in the form of curriculum and assessment services, traded as commodities, as governments 'open up' the sector to requests for tender that are assumed to be the most cost-effective and efficient mode of delivery. Charter school programmes and higher education institutes privately owned and operated as businesses also occupy education markets in the global North. In the global South, for-profit actors increasingly sell schooling as commodities where the political and economic determination to deliver quality education for all is lacking (Macpherson, Robertson, & Walford, 2014). Education commercialisation, therefore, is a social and political construction, and contradiction, given that learning can take place in non-commodity forms including reciprocity and/or redistribution via state or communal patronage.

The second contradiction linked to education commercialisation concerns the 'use-value' and 'exchange-value' aspects of educational commodities. 'Exchange-value refers to a commodity's market-mediated monetary value for the seller; use-value refers to its material and/or symbolic usefulness to the purchaser. Without exchange-value, commodities would not be produced for sale; without use-value, they would not be purchased' (Sum & Jessop, 2013, p. 243). A contradiction exists insofar as educational commodities are sold at prices that are not congruent with their symbolic and/or economic utility. As David Harvey points out:

> All the commodities we buy in a capitalist society have a use value and an exchange value. The difference between the two forms of value is significant. To the degree they are often at odds with each other they constitute a contradiction, which can, on occasion, give rise to a crisis (2014, p. 15).

In education, this type of contradiction and crisis-tendency can take many forms. For example, governments purchase mass-produced and standardised examinations from corporations such as Pearson that shape the design and meaning of education, yet the focus on data-based scores and results produced by commodities for testing can often be at odds with notions of 'quality' in learning. Educational consumers of higher education accumulate mass debt investing in credentials and degrees in order to enhance their human capital and economic outlook, yet may still end up un(der)-employed. And in low-income countries, the aspirational poor expends significant proportions of family income on for-profit schooling delivered by multinational corporations, yet rather than alleviating poverty, often entrenches it.

Contemporary capitalism is largely considered to be a knowledge-based economy in which 'knowledge has become the most important factor of production and the key to economic competitiveness' (Jessop, 2007, p. 115). Under such conditions, education has become dominated by an instrumentalist view in which education is valued insofar as it develops human capital and economic competitiveness, referring to the skills, information and knowledge acquired from education that enhance the productivity of the human being as an economic factor of production (Robeyns, 2006). Learning, as an investment in the production of human capital within knowledge-based economies, also remakes consumers of education into economic factors of production that become integrated into capitalist structures of subjugation (Simons, 2006). This brings us to the third contradiction.

Education commercialisation both expands and intensifies private control and influences over the learning and transmission of knowledge and socialisation that takes place within systems of education, which is even more salient in knowledge-based economies given that it also increases private (oftentimes corporate) control in the social relations of production. This dilemma can be linked to what has been called the 'fundamental contradiction of capitalism' (Jessop & Sum, 2006):

> This exists between the increasing socialization of productive forces and continuing private control in the social relations of production. Networked knowledge-based economies heighten this contradiction from both sides. On the one hand, the socialization of productive forces is accelerated in a knowledge-based economy by the increased importance of the 'general intellect' (or accumulated knowledge in the form of an intellectual commons) and the increased scope for 'economies of networks' that are generated in and through multi-actor, polycentric and multiscalar networks ... In particular we can discern a growing tension between the logic of an information society (based on the collective appropriation of the use value generated by the general intellect and network economies)

and the logic of an information economy (based on the private appropriation of the exchange values generated by the fictitious commodification of knowledge and the capacity to capture networks for private benefit) (p. 343).

The augmentation of private control and influence in systems of education resulting from commercialisation enable private actors to exercise increased authority over social relations of production since they structure that which disseminates and transfers the 'general intellect' deemed useful and employable in knowledge-based economies. In turn, at the same time as private economic actors increasingly influence, and profit from, the distribution of knowledge via market exchange, those who purchase it also become socialised as productive forces in knowledge-based capitalist economies – reflecting a fundamental contradiction.

An example of this 'fundamental contradiction of capitalism' is demonstrated by Pearson's edu-business activities in the Philippines. In 2013, Pearson partnered with Ayala Corporation to establish a for-profit chain of 'low-fee' private high schools in the Philippines known as Affordable Private Education Centers (APEC). In addition to selling schooling as a commodity, APEC delivers a 'reverse-engineered' curriculum oriented to meet the labour needs of industry (Riep, 2015). For instance, APEC aims to produce a repository of cheap and semi-skilled workers employable as call centre agents in the emerging business process outsourcing (BPO) sector in the Philippines. Not by coincidence, Ayala is a business leader in the BPO sector in the Philippines. In turn, this reflects the ways in which private authority exercised by corporations in education also influences the social relations of production.

The fourth contradiction, or rather crisis-tendency, linked to education commercialisation is a culmination of the preceding three contradictions already outlined: that is, the (re)distribution of education through market mechanisms has produced and exacerbated social inequality, inequity and segregation (Ball, 1993; Apple, 2001; Ball, 2003; Gewirtz, Ball, & Bowe, 1995; Lauder et al., 1999; Marginson, 1997). Marketised and commercialised education increases inequality by restricting and/or organising access according to levels of payment (or rather, privilege). And while Pearson claims 'market-based approaches can accelerate access to quality education' (http://www.pearson.com), this approach intends to commodify the exact inequality it implicates – which is as much a contradiction, as it is an impending social crisis.

Fixing contradictions through discourse and semiotics

Contradictions and crisis-tendencies linked to education commercialisation can be resolved (if only temporarily) through 'social fixes' ('where social is understood in terms of social practices with discursive and extra-discursive moments') (Sum & Jessop, 2013, p. 246). Social fixes reflect contested and compromised, repeated and varied processes including a range of social, political and economic forces and projects that 'secure a relatively durable pattern of structural coherence in the handling of the contradictions and dilemmas inherent in the capital relation' (Jessop & Sum, 2006, p. 321). Fixes can be studied in relation to their semantic, institutional and spatio-temporal dimensions: insofar as particular *institutions*, embedded in the contradictions of capital, make strategic use of structural and *discursive selectivities* that favour some actors, alliances, interests, projects, visions and so on, which include *spatial* and *temporal boundaries* within which modes and phases of continued capital accumulation become normalised (Sum & Jessop, 2013). This paper focuses on the semiotic (or discursive) formations put in place by Pearson that aim to fix contradictions and crisis-tendencies related to education commercialisation.

Semantically, a social fix 'limits what can be seen, imagined, communicated and understood, and, through specific discursive fields (orders of discourse) they provide the categories that connect to particular fields of social relations' (Sum & Jessop, 2013, p. 247). Pearson has created an *Efficacy Framework* to categorise and delimit 'what can be seen, imagined, communicated and understood' about the company by measuring, calibrating and communicating the 'efficacy' of its educational commodities. Pearson claims 'an education product has efficacy if it has a measurable impact on improving people's lives through learning' (Barber & Rizvi, 2013, p. 12). By focusing on the 'measurable impact' that an educational commodity can have on the life of a consumer/learner, Pearson intends to reconfigure the parameters by which its edu-business activities are judged and perceived in order to shape the social perceptions of consumers and how they come to know, or what they know, about Pearson and its products. It is a semiotic social fix designed to maintain business growth and profitability in a context of risk and contradiction.

Pearson's Efficacy Framework

The *Efficacy Framework* developed by Pearson is designed to calculate the 'measurable, proven impact on learners' lives' (Pearson plc, 2014) resulting from the consumption of educational commodities sold by the company. It is a standardised review process that assigns a particular rating to Pearson's products and services, based on a four-point colour-coded scale, measured in relation to four criteria areas: outcomes, evidence, planning and implementation, and capacity to deliver. Evaluating and calculating product efficacy is done to ensure 'that all Pearson products and programmes address the factors that could affect the learning outcomes that they are ultimately able to produce, in a consistent way' (Pearson plc, 2013, p. 16). If it is determined that a product is demonstrating positive results in line with the *Efficacy Framework*, then the 'product is likely either already demonstrating efficacy, or at least on the path to efficacy' (Barber & Rizvi, 2013, p. 17). Pearson's *Efficacy Framework*, therefore, is a meaning-making apparatus designed to calculatedly attach the notion of 'efficacy' and its associated meanings to the products and operations of the company through visible and legible performance metrics.

Yet, what is crucially missing from Pearson's *Efficacy Framework* is a clear way to measure product efficacy that connects inputs to outputs. Although this auditing tool emphasises 'outcomes' there are no clear measures to account for the inputs that make the outcomes of learning possible. As is the case with Pearson and its *Efficacy Framework*:

> ...when organizations do not have clear measures of productivity which relate their inputs to their outputs, the *audit* of efficiency and effectiveness is in fact a process of *defining* and

operationalizing measures of performance for the audited entity. In short the efficiency and effectiveness of organizations is not so much verified as constructed around the audit process itself (Power, 1997, p. 51).

Hence, the *Efficacy Framework* is a process for naming and defining performance outcomes rather than verifying them. Pearson claims that:

Fundamentally, efficacy is about defining what outcomes we need to achieve for our learners and building in the capabilities to measure and improve those outcomes. Starting with outcomes requires a shift in the way education companies build and market their products and services (Barber & Kumar, 2015, p. 10).

In turn, Pearson is attempting to grow its global edu-business by focusing on the auditability, deliverability, and hence, marketability of outcomes.

This renewed focus on outcomes is part of Pearson's organisational shift from a business that provides education inputs (e.g. selling textbooks) to one that provides education outputs (e.g. measurable and 'certifiable' learning outcomes) as pointed out by Hogan, Sellar, and Lingard (2016a). By focusing on the outcomes of its educational products and programmes, Pearson intends to modify the way in which the company and its edu-business activities are seen and judged by consumers.

Pearson claims its products and services deliver four types of outcomes related to efficacy: (1) *access*, which refers to the degree that learners can access a product (e.g. in terms of technology and socio-economic access); (2) *completion*, which refers to the tasks and courses completed by learners; (3) *achievement*, which refers to the standards of competencies, skills and qualifications achieved and (4) *progression*, which refers to the learners ability to progress onto further education, training or employment (Barber & Kumar, 2015, p. 21). Pearson also makes the distinction between learn*ing* and learn*er* outcomes in which the former are 'statements about what has been learned' and the latter refers to the 'way a human life is transformed by an educational experience' (Barber & Kumar, 2015, p. 20). By marketing learn*er* outcomes as the more expansive ways in which 'a human life is transformed by an educational experience', Pearson intends to show the ways in which the acquisition of products and services sold by the company results in a set of instrumental outcomes that improve the lives of consumers.

To date, Pearson has completed over 200 'efficacy reviews' and by 2018 the company plans to report publicly on the efficacy of its entire global product portfolio with the same rigor and consistency as its financial reporting.[1] As Pearson claims:

This new and transparent approach to efficacy is central to our purpose and also makes good business sense. We hope that by demonstrating the evidence base that supports our products we will encourage a deeper engagement with learning outcomes across the education sector and at the same time clearly demonstrate the benefits of using those products (Pearson plc, 2013, p. 14).

So far Pearson has released more than a dozen 'efficacy reports'. One of which was a review of CTI Education Group – a private higher education institute that serves approximately 10,000 students across 12 campuses in South Africa.

Pearson has been the 100% owner of CTI since 2013. On the company's website it claims that 'Pearson's strong brand, educational resources and global reach will help leverage CTI's strengths and transform the higher education landscape in southern

Africa' (http://www.cti.ac.za/about-us/). At CTI, the focus is on 'arming students with real-life career skills and training them to succeed as employable graduates in a competitive 21st century economy' (CTI Education Group, 2016, p. 3). In turn, an 'intended outcome' advertised by CTI is employment or further education and training which students should achieve if they successfully complete tasks, modules, pass exams and attain the qualification they enrolled in to do at CTI. Sixty-eight per cent of CTI graduates find full-time, part-time or voluntary work or move onto further education or training, according to Pearson. However, Pearson also admits there are 'limitations to this data because responses are self-reported and the survey only had a 25 percent response rate' (http://www.pearson.com/efficacy-and-research/efficacy-reports.html). Therefore, correlations that lead to extrapolation are oftentimes oversimplified causing an impression of (in)efficacy that is misrepresented. The 'efficacy report' on CTI claims that:

> Pearson is continuing to investigate the efficacy of CTI and is establishing mechanisms to make efficacy research easier and more accurate to conduct. Students this year will receive a unique student identifier, allowing CTI to track student progression through the institute longitudinally. The unique student identifiers, paired with a redeveloped data infrastructure, will help Pearson conduct research around how successfully students engage with the course, achieve their qualifications, complete their module tasks, and progress after they've graduated (http://www.pearson.com/efficacy-and-research/efficacy-reports.html).

Putting in place efficacy mechanisms that show the impact of CTI, therefore, is a semiotic/discursive strategy meant to secure business operations.

Pearson has also released an efficacy report for its product aimswebPlus, which is a data-intensive assessment and reporting tool that helps educators track student progress in subjects such as reading and mathematics at each grade level from kindergarten to Grade 8. The United States and Canada are its key markets, and it currently reaches 3.8 million learners. Pearson has conducted evaluations that suggest testing results derived from aimsweb correlate with results scored by students on state tests in reading in math, 'which is one way to demonstrate the product's validity' (http://efficacy.pearson.com/product-progress/aimswebplus.html):

> In a study of roughly 1,000 students at each grade level from grades 3 to 8, Pearson found correlations ranging from 0.60 to 0.72 between scores on aimsweb reading assessments and scores on state reading tests in North Carolina and Illinois. Another study of about 700 students at each grade level from grades 3 to 8 found correlations ranging from 0.57 to 0.78 between scores on aimsweb math assessments and state math tests in North Carolina and Illinois. Pearson has also demonstrated that students who do poorly on their aimsweb assessments are unlikely to do well on their state math and reading tests – up to 85 percent of grades 3–8 students who failed their state math tests and up to 80 percent of students who failed their state reading tests were correctly flagged by aimsweb as at-risk. This sort of predictive accuracy allows teachers to develop and implement the proper educational interventions for those students who are at-risk of failing state exams.

By their very nature, tests produce calculable results and scores. Pearson's efficacy review of aimsweb, therefore, is a type of double audit. Since it aims to assess the validity of a product, yet, the product under review is itself a test that evaluates the ability of a student. It is a test of tests. However, what is lost in this fixation over results is the inputs (curricula, teachers, pedagogy, etc.) that make the outcomes of education possible.

Vital to the *Efficacy Framework* and review process is the collection of 'efficacy evidence' that enables Pearson to 'generate valid and reliable claims about the products' impact on learner outcomes' (http://www.pearson.com/efficacy-and-research.html). Evidence of efficacy can be 'as simple as user surveys and as complex as randomized-controlled trials or longitudinal research' (Barber & Kumar, 2015, p. 24). It differs for each product based on the targets of learning outcomes and where a product is within its lifecycle. For example, Pearson states that if it were:

> ...to study whether our universities in South Africa are adequately preparing graduates for careers, we might plan to do a longitudinal analysis to measure career outcomes over time. On the other hand, to study whether those graduates felt satisfied with their education, we may conduct a simple online survey before they graduate (Barber & Kumar, 2015, p. 24).

Standards of evidence collected by Pearson vary in complexity: from surveys that determine levels of customer satisfaction, to pre- and post-tests that indicate a correlation between products and the attainment of certain outcomes, to controlled studies that isolate the impact of products and thereby provide evidence of practical and/or statistical significance.

Pearson's efficacy evidence is meant to resolve the uncertain relationship that exists between the exchange-value and use-value of educational commodities by demonstrating the 'measurable impact' its products and services have 'on improving people's lives through learning' (Barber & Rizvi, 2013, p. 12). Yet, these calculations are highly reductionist and can misleadingly attribute certain outcomes to products or services rather than intake variables. Isolating and measuring the correlational effect that a particular educational commodity has on the life outcomes of a learner is abundantly complex given the confluence of background variables that effect learning and its ability to 'improve' the life of a learner. Pearson intends to perform longitudinal and systematic analysis over long periods of time to collect explanatory evidence that shows the 'measurable impact' its products and services have on learner outcomes. However, in the interim, the company plans to continue to 'depend on test and exam results, graduation rates and other measures as proxies' (Barber & Rizvi, 2013, p. 13). Yet, a potential conflict may arise from using standardised exam results to measure the efficacy of Pearson's products, which is particularly problematic in the United States where Pearson is the largest provider of education assessments. Pearson has multi-year contracts with the federal government and more than 25 states to administer and score examinations. By linking efficacy evidence to standardised tests, also prepared and scored by Pearson, this system can be manipulated so that Pearson products are framed and seen as the correlative factor that produces certain desired results. Indeed, the *Efficacy Framework* is designed to define and operationalise measures of performance for products and services sold by Pearson.

Efficacy as a hegemonic 'knowledge brand' in the making in education

Pearson claims it 'adopted the term "efficacy" from the pharmaceutical industry, where demonstrating the efficacy of medical interventions through systematic trials is essential' (Barber & Rizvi, 2013, p. 12). In the education industry, the recontextualisation of efficacy involves demonstrating the ways in which education interventions (i.e. products, services, programmes) deliver efficient and effective outcomes. For over a century, education administrators have been concerned with the operational efficiencies of industrialised systems of education. However, since the 1990s neoliberal rationality and practices of government have intensified demands for national systems and various programmes of education to produce *cost-effective results*. A hegemonic discourse related to efficiency, (cost-)effectiveness, usefulness, productivity and performance (i.e. efficacy) – constructed by the dialectical interaction of ideas, institutions and material power – now governs education, globally. For Pearson, advertising effective and efficient outcomes to customers is a cleverly devised strategy to align the company's commercial activities with a 'neoliberal imaginary' (conceived as the semiotic aspects that give meaning and shape to politics and economics) which has become hegemonic in education policy, practice and discourse.

New public management (NPM) is the dominant mode of governance aligned with neoliberal rationality. It 'consists of a cluster of ideas borrowed from the conceptual framework of private sector administrative practice' (Power, 1997, p. 43) that involves the inculcation of market values and principles for governing public services (Lynch, 2015). A politics of cost-control, outsourcing, contractualisation and the creation of market and quasi-market mechanisms represent the organising principles and methods of service delivery according to NPM (Power, 1997). This involves 'the reconstitution of the state from that of service delivery provider to a combination of regulation, performance monitoring, contracting and the facilitation of new providers of public services' (Ball, 2012, p. 36). Yet, this 'hollowing out of the state' brought on by NPM also 'generates a demand for audit and other forms of evaluation and inspection to fill the hole' which is said to enhance 'accountability to customers for the quality of service via the creation of performance indicators' (Power, 1997, p. 43). In turn, the spread of NPM is believed to be:

> …the success of political discourses which have demanded improved accountability of public services…in terms of performance. It has been argued that taxpayers have rights to know that their money is being spent economically, efficiently, and effectively – the three E's – and that citizens as consumers of public services are entitled to monitor and demand certain minimum standards of performance (Power, 1997, p. 44).

With greater demands for improved accountability in public services, Pearson is appropriating a discourse of efficacy to stabilise concerns and anxieties related to neoliberal restructuring and education commercialisation.

As citizens are remade into consumers of 'public' services while governments increasingly outsource their responsibilities to new private providers, 'value for money' (VFM) evaluations have become increasingly important. VFM refers to assessments that determine whether or not a buyer, given their available resources, has obtained maximum value for the products they purchase. Pearson explains: 'As governments – and individuals – invest more in education, they are demanding better value for money. They expect better teaching, better outcomes and more accurate ways of measuring progress' (Pearson plc, n.d., p. 3). VFM is listed on Pearson's *Efficacy Framework* as a key outcome by which its products and services are evaluated. VFM auditing is concerned with defining and judging *accountability* in terms of efficiency and effectiveness: '*efficiency* as accountability for ensuring that maximum output is obtained from the resources employed or that minimum resources are used to achieve a given level of output/service' and '*effectiveness* as accountability for ensuring that outcomes conform to intentions, as defined in programmes' (Power, 1997, p. 50). In education, accountability is monitored through the 'increasingly intrusive surveillance of staff in the name of efficiency and performance management' (Connell, 2013, p.102) which includes mass-produced and standardised examinations that test both student and teacher effectiveness in relation to desired programmatic outcomes. Auditing performance in education for accountability purposes based on efficiency and effectiveness also restructures programmes and systems of education to conform with calculable outcomes and performance indicators. As Lynch (2015) points out 'because auditing is about inspection, control and regulation (Lingard, 2011; Power, 1994; Shore & Wright, 1999), its introduction into the education lexicon signifies the development of a whole new system of disciplinary regulation through measurable accountability, quality assurance and performance' (p. 194). Hence, the discursive and disciplinary power of efficacy resides in its ability to render systems of education as something auditable, and hence, measurable via performance monitoring. In turn, this forms the basis of a new mode of accountability between education consumers and private providers like Pearson based on VFM propositions.

A 'discursive formation' (Foucault, 1970) related to patterns and concerns for efficacy in education is becoming increasingly dominant; augmented by extra-discursive formations connected to institutions, neoliberal politics and economic restructuring. A globalised testing regime represents this discursive pattern towards efficacy in education based on measurable performance. The Programme for International Student Assessment (PISA), Teaching and Learning International Survey (TALIS) and Indicators of National Education Systems (INES), all of which are administered by the Organisation for Economic Co-operation and Development (OECD), represent some of the most prominent examples of the globalised testing establishment. In 2014 Pearson won a competitive tender by the OECD to develop the frameworks for PISA 2018 to define which educational outcomes will be measured and how. In addition to international testing regimes like those administered by the OECD and Pearson, there are multitudinous examples of governmental and non-governmental actors that reverberate neoliberal discourses related to efficacy as the art of how best to govern education (see Table 1).

Circulating transnationally within policy networks the discourse of efficiency and effectiveness has become hegemonic: normalised, institutionalised, packaged, marketed, branded and consumed in various policy settings and sold by consultancy firms and private enterprise. Diverse and complimentary institutions interlinked by a familiar economic imaginary conduct their operations in line with this dominant managerialist knowledge. As a result, networks and hegemonic blocs have formed that administer and prescribe, at various levels, a market-disciplinary project in education based on performance and efficiency. The re-contextualisation of performative discourses are (re) appropriated and relocated in ways that both fit and reaffirm existing social relations (Bernstein, 1996). The development of pre-packaged and ready-made models (such as measures of performance, outcomes, standards, curriculum, modules, manuals and methods of delivery) associated with 'intellectual expertise' and leadership (including

Table 1. Examples of different institutions and discourses related to efficacy in education across different scales.

Scales	Institutions	Efficacy discourse, documents and/or instruments	Description
International	UNESCO	*General Educational Quality Analysis/Diagnosis Framework (GEQAF)*	Analytical tool for member states to diagnose and analyse cost-efficiencies/inefficiencies of education systems
	World Economic Forum	*New Vision for Education – Unlocking the Potential of Technology 2015*	Advocates that educational technology can be aligned with learning objectives to efficiently deliver instruction and learning
Regional	Inter-American Development Bank	*Education: Sector Policies 2015*	Efficiency of investments in education by the bank is a main of objective in order to achieve cost-effective results
	World Bank, Africa Region	*Index of efficiency*	Measures the amount of public resources 'wasted' on children who drop out before finishing primary education or on repetition years
National	UK Government, Department for Education	*Review of efficiency in the schools system 2013*	Policy paper that reviews the relationship between how schools allocate their budget and the results they achieve
	Bill & Melinda Gates Foundations, United States	*Intensive Partnerships for Effective Teaching*	An initiative in the United States that measures teacher efficacy to produce learning outcomes and to improve overall teaching effectiveness
Local	Ontario Ministry of Education	*School Effectiveness Framework: A support for school improvement and student success*	A guide for school boards to improve school effectiveness and student outcomes
	Chelsea Public Schools, Massachusetts	*District Improvement Plan 2011–2016*	A district goal is to evaluate the cost-effectiveness and efficacy of policies and procedures that are standards-based and driven by student achievement data

Source: Personal compilation based on website information and online policy documents from different institutions, accessed on 5–7 January 2016.

government officials, academics, consultants, firms, technocrats, etc.) form an assemblage of knowledge and experts that have given rise to a hegemonic 'knowledge brand' of efficacy in education. Sum and Jessop (2013) define a 'knowledge brand' as:

> ...a resonant hegemonic meaning-making device advanced in various ways by 'world-class' gurus–academics–consultants who claim unique knowledge of a relevant strategic or policy field and pragmatically translate this into (trans-)national policy symbols, recipes and toolkits that address policy problems and dilemmas and also appeal to pride, threats and anxieties about socio-economic restructuring and changes. In this regard, a knowledge brand is a trans-national manifestation and condensation of institutional, organizational and discursive power in the knowledge–consultancy–policy circuit. After all, not all forms of knowledge are equal; some are more prominent and 'brandized' than others. Thus knowledge is at the same time diffused and condensed along specific nodal points, the location of which is extra-discursively as well as discursively conditioned (p. 305)

Efficacy, therefore, is a hegemonic 'knowledge brand' in the making in education, by which programmes and systems of education are discursively and extra-discursively governed in order to yield cost-effective 'results' and productivity.

Imagined reputation

Pearson's efficacy programme and tools are meant to construct a corporate image and reputation around the 'knowledge brand' of efficacy and its associated meanings related to performance, effectiveness and usefulness. As the company claims: 'We know what's really important – commercially, strategically, ethically – is that every product we make and sell can be measured and judged by the outcomes it helps to achieve' (Pearson plc, 2014, para. 1). 'Measurable impact' and 'outcomes' calculated by Pearson's *Efficacy Framework* represent the data from which the company intends to establish a 'cognitive frame' (Beckert, 2010) for consumers to understand, evaluate and judge the edu-business practices and products of Pearson. It is a semiotic social fix that 'limits what can be seen, imagined, communicated and understood' (Sum & Jessop, 2013, p. 247) about Pearson and its products – which is largely in response to the crisis of reputation that has afflicted the company's brand and image in recent years.

As Pearson claims: 'our business depends on a strong brand, and any failure to maintain, protect and enhance our brand would hurt our ability to retain or expand our business' (Pearson plc, 2013, p. 43). Yet, a number of indicators show fractures in the Pearson brand: the company's stock declined by 40% in 2015; the company lost multimillion dollar contracts to deliver tests in New York and Texas; protests against its standardised examinations and data management products and practices have increased throughout the United States including boycotts, demonstrations and student walkouts and refusal to write Pearson-made tests; an ongoing FBI investigation into collusion between Pearson, Apple and the Los Angeles Unified School District regarding a US$1.3 billion project to equip all K-12 students with a personal iPad has gone public; teacher union activism, particularly by the global federation of teacher unions, Education International, along with civil society organisations around the globe have made Pearson the object of resistance; a webpage has emerged in which disgruntled consumers of Pearson can voice their complaints (http://pearson-education.pissedconsumer.com), and a growing body of articles and blogs condemning Pearson such as *Forbes* article 'Everybody hates Pearson' all indicate that the social perception of the company is problematic. In turn, Pearson's efficacy programme is designed to shape (or reshape) how consumers perceive, rationalise, value and think about its products in order to manage contradictions and crisis-tendencies related to its edu-business activities.

Constructing a corporate brand and reputation around efficacy relies on demonstrable outcomes. Pearson's global programme of efficacy, therefore, is meant to make visible and legible the impact of its products. As part of this project, Pearson has announced an 'ambitious vision' known as the 'Efficacy Growth & Impact Goals' by which the company 'commits to impacting the lives of 200 million learners by 2025 in critical ways' that includes providing access to primary, secondary and post-secondary education, enhancing literacy and numeracy, and improving student employability (http://www.pearson.com/about-us/growth-and-impact.html). Quantifiable metrics that show proof of impact are produced by standardised test results, graduation rates, customer surveys and other proxies that are meant to give the impression of efficacy. As Michael Power points out, the reputation of different organisations can be socially constructed through auditing practices and techniques that conjure up perceptions of effectiveness, productivity, value, etc. (Power, 1997, 2007). By generating evidence-based calculations that 'prove' the efficacy of its products, Pearson intends 'to construct and manage social perceptions' (Power, 2007, p. 129) and forge a corporate reputation around the calculability and auditability of efficacy. In doing so, the company claims measurable impact goals 'will serve as a driver of Pearson's future growth and profitability' (http://www.pearson.com/about-us/growth-and-impact.html).

For Pearson the aim is to develop a reputation in which its educational commodities are seen and 'shown to deliver meaningful, measurable outcomes' (Barber & Kumar, 2015, p. 4). Hence, Pearson is marketing a type of 'neo-social mode of accountability' connected to education commercialisation, bound by market rationality (Hogan et al., 2016a; Hogan, Sellar, & Lingard, 2016b; Vogelmann, 2012). The 'term "neo-social" refers to the economisation of social responsibilities produced by demands that market actors assume social responsibilities that complement, or enhance, their focus on profit and market capitalisation' (Hogan et al., 2016a, p. 244). This is part of Pearson's new corporate social responsibility strategy that emphasises accountability to consumers in the form of outcomes that demonstrate product efficacy, which has also been highlighted in the works of Hogan et al. (2016a, 2016b)). Indeed:

> Pearson have embraced performative accountability as a way to conjure a moral dimension to its operations, presenting itself as a corporation focused on a double bottom line of profitability for its shareholders and social responsibility for improving people's lives through learning (Hogan, Sellar, & Lingard, 2015, p. 6).

Pearson, for example, states:

> We believe in the concept of shared value: that long-term financial success is a direct result of delivering social outcomes. So for us, efficacy makes perfect business sense. If our products deliver what our customers and learners need, we will be commercially successful (Barber & Kumar, 2015, p. 15).

Hence, by mobilising the discourse and practices of efficacy and efficacy auditing, Pearson aims to construct a particular reputation – imagined or real – to overcome contradictions related to its edu-business activities.

As part of this restructuring and rebranding process around efficacy, Pearson recruited 'education expert' Sir Michael Barber in 2011. Appointed as Pearson's Chief Education Advisor, Barber is 'leading Pearson's worldwide programme of efficacy and research ensuring the impact of the programme on the learner outcomes of Pearson and its customers' (http://www.pearson.com/michael-barber/bio.html). Prior to Pearson, Barber was the Head of global education practice for McKinsey & Company. He also served the UK government (from 1997–2005) under Tony Blair's regime as both the Head of the Prime Minister's Delivery Unit and as Chief Adviser to the Secretary of State for Education on School Standards. Barber has also worked as a global consultant with governments in Australia, Punjab, the United States and Ontario. By recruiting Barber, Pearson also gains his connections, status, reputation and influence in high-profile policy networks. As Hogan et al. (2015) point out:

...Barber, as 'a leading authority on education systems and education reform' (Pearson plc, 2011) with connections to a range of government and academic actors in education policy globally, is able to help constitute an assemblage in which Pearson might become seen as a morally authoritative agency in educational matters ... For example, Barber, as a former bureaucrat, can help to communicate the relevance and currency of Pearson's activities to government officials, and this likely serves to promote the perceived legitimacy and authority of using Pearson for government contracts and services (p. 49).

For Pearson the goal is to develop the reputation of a moral authority in education. However, in November 2016, Pearson announced that Barber decided he will leave the company and his position as Chief Education Advisor in late 2017, instead to continue working with governments.

Conclusion

Education commercialisation involves fundamental contradictions and crisis-tendencies which Pearson is attempting to overcome through discourse and semiotic techniques. This paper explores the ways in which Pearson aims to make visible, legible and calculable the effectiveness and usefulness of its products through practices and apparatuses connected to its *Efficacy Framework*. Yet, it is not only Pearson that markets 'impact' and 'outcomes'. Other education companies like Laureate Education, Inc., the largest for-profit higher education company in the world, advertises 'strong student outcomes' and a 'proven quality and reputation' while Bridge International Academies, Ltd., the largest for-profit provider of low-cost schooling in the world, claims it has a social mission to school 10,000,000 children in low-income countries while demonstrating 'impact evaluation results'. Claims such as these are meant to legitimate commercial activities in the education sector. In response, critical students, educators, administrators and citizens must be conscious of, and act upon, instances when they are being sold illusory outcomes, symbols and results that lose sight of the self-determining, humanistic and emancipatory elements of education.

Current social arrangements related to the global education industry demonstrate that those who have the most to gain from education commercialisation are the global edu-businesses and edu-preneurs selling products, services, policies and programmes (Verger et al., 2016). Consequently, the goal of Pearson's *Efficacy Framework* is to show that purchasing and consuming its educational products is a 'win-win' for vendors and customers alike – a double bottom line based on profitability for shareholders and social outcomes for learners. However, not is all as it might seem. As this paper demonstrates, the *Efficacy Framework* is a 'meaning-making device' (Sum & Jessop, 2013, 305) that intends to delimit what can be seen, imagined, communicated and understood about Pearson and its products. This semiotic-calculative device is designed to shape the social perceptions of customers, policymakers, state managers and shareholders by defining and operationalising the measurable impact and outcomes that are said to result from Pearson's educational commodities – and thus, constructing an imagined reputation around performance and effectiveness. By focusing on the discourse and devices mobilised by 'the world's leading education company' that aims to uphold the capital relation in education despite contradictions and crisis-tendencies that exist, this paper contributes to our understanding of the global education industry and the ways in which it might be (temporarily) stabilised or expanded. Ultimately, it is hoped that contradictions related to education commercialisation, rather than be normalised and institutionalised by the efforts of those who benefit from them, 'can be a fecund source of both personal and social change from which people emerge far better off then before' (Harvey, 2014, p. 3) by opening them to critique, to action and transformation.

Acknowledgements

I am most grateful to Rob Aitken from the Department of Political Science and Jerry Kachur from the Department of Educational Policy Studies both at the University of Alberta for their mentorship and guidance during the course of writing this paper. Review and comments from Sam Sellar at the Manchester Metropolitan University are also gratefully acknowledged as is the feedback received from two anonymous reviewers. This work was supported by the Social Sciences and Humanities Research Council of Canada (SSHRC).

Note

1. Pearson claims its efficacy reports 'will be audited by an external firm, which will validate [its] approach, data, and conclusions' (Barber & Kumar, 2015, p. 5). The multinational auditing firm, PricewaterhouseCoopers (PwC), has been chosen as the external partner to 'validate' Pearson's efficacy findings. However, PwC has its own history of corruption, fraud, tax evasions and negligent auditing practices. For example, as part of the *Luxembourg Leaks* it was made public in 2014 that PwC negotiated 548 tax avoidance schemes with 343 multinational corporations in Luxembourg. In another case, PwC was found to be unethically favoured by the World Bank in a bid to privatise the water distribution system in Delhi, India.

Disclosure statement

No potential conflict of interest was reported by the author.

Funding

This work was supported by the Social Sciences and Humanities Research Council of Canada [Joseph-Armand Bombardier Canada Graduate Doctoral Award].

References

Apple, M. W. (2001). Comparing neo-liberal projects and inequality in education. *Comparative Education, 37*(4), 409–423. doi:10.1080/03050060120091229

Ball, S. J. (1993). Education markets, choice and social class: The market as a class strategy in the UK and the USA. *British Journal of Sociology of Education, 14*(1), 3–19. doi:10.1080/0142569930140101

Ball, S. J. (2003). *Class strategies and the education market: The middle classes and social advantage*. New York: RoutledgeFalmer.

Ball, S. J. (2012). *Global Education Inc: New policy networks and the neo-liberal imaginary*. New York, NY: Routledge.

Barber, M., & Kumar, A. (2015). *On the road…to delivering learning outcomes.* Pearson: Always Learning. Retrieved October 1, 2015 from: https://efficacy.pearson.com/content/dam/corporate/global/efficacy/files/Pearson_OntheRoad_150330.pdf

Barber, M., & Rizvi, S. (2013). *The incomplete guide to delivering outcomes.* Pearson: Always Learning. Retrieved September 29, 2015 from: https://efficacy.pearson.com/content/dam/corporate/global/efficacy/files/the-incomplete-guide-to-delivering-learning-outcomes.pdf

Beckert, J. (2010). How do fields change? The interrelations of institutions, networks, and cognition in the dynamics of markets. *Organization Studies, 31,* 605–627. doi:10.1177/0170840610372184

Bernstein, B. (1996). *Pedagogy, symbolic control and identity: Theory, research, critique.* London: Taylor & Francis.

Best, J., & Paterson, M. (2010). *Cultural political economy.* London: Routledge.

Bhanji, Z. (2008). Transnational corporations in education: filling the governance gap through new social norms and market multilateralism?. 6(1), 55-73. doi:10.1080/14767720701855618

Connell, R. (2013). The neoliberal cascade and education: An essay on the market agenda and its consequences. *Critical Studies in Education, 54*(2), 99–112. doi:10.1080/17508487.2013.776990

CTI Education Group. (2016, March 23). *Efficacy report.* Retrieved March 28, 2016 from: https://efficacy.pearson.com/content/dam/corporate/global/efficacy/samples/CTIMGI/CTI%20MGI%20Research%20Report.pdf

Foucault, M. (1970). *The order of things: An archaeology of the the human sciences.* United Kingdom: Tavistock Publications.

Gewirtz, S., Ball, S., & Bowe, R. (1995). *Markets, choice and equity in education.* Buckingham: Open University Press.

Gillborn, D., & Youdell, D. (2000). *Rationing education: Policy, practice, reform and equity.* Buckingham: Open University Press.

Hartnett, M., Leung, B., & Marcus, J. (2014, April 30). *The thundering word: Investment strategy.* Bank of America-Merrill Lynch. Retrieved September 22, 2016 from: https://mlaem.fs.ml.com/content/dam/ML/Articles/pdf/ATW-The-Thundering-Word.pdf

Harvey, D. (2014). *Seventeen contradictions and the end of capitalism.* New York, NY: Oxford University Press.

Hogan, A., Sellar, S., & Lingard, B. (2016a). Commercialising comparison: Pearson puts the TLC in soft capitalism. *Journal of Education Policy, 31*(3), 243–258. doi:10.1080/02680939.2015.1112922

Hogan, A., Sellar, S., & Lingard, B. (2015). Network restructuring of global edu-business: The case of pearson's Efficacy Framework. In W. Au & J. Ferrare (Eds), *Mapping corporate education reform: Power and policy networks in the neoliberal state.* New York, NY: Routledge.

Hogan, A., Sellar, S., & Lingard, B. (2016b). Corporate Social Responsibility and Neo-Social Accountability in Education: The Case of Pearson plc. In A. Verger, C. Lubienski, & G. Steiner-Khamsi (Eds), *World Yearbook of Education 2016: The global education industry.* New York, NY: Routledge.

Jessop, B. (2004). Critical semiotic analysis and cultural political economy. *Critical Discourse Studies, 1*(2), 159–174. doi:10.1080/17405900410001674506

Jessop, B. (2010). Cultural political economy and critical policy studies. *Critical Policy Studies, 3* (3–4), 336–356. doi:10.1080/19460171003619741

Jessop, B. (2007). Knowledge as a Fictitious Commodity: Insights and Limits of a Polanyian Analysis. In A. Buğra & K. Ağartan (Eds), *Reading Karl Polanyi for the 21st century: Market economy as a political project.* Basingstoke: Palgrave Macmillan.

Jessop, B., & Sum, N. L. (2006). *Beyond the regulation approach: Putting capitalist economies in their place.* Cheltenham: Edward Elgar.

Junemann, C., & Ball, S. J. (2015, June). *Pearson and PALF: The mutating giant.* Brussels: Education International.

Lauder, H., Hughes, D., Watson, S., Waslauder, S., Thrupp, M., Strathdee, R., Hamlin, J. (1999). *Trading in futures: Why markets in education don't work.* Buckingham: Open University Press.

Lingard, B. (2011). Policy as numbers: ac/counting for educational research. *The Australian Educational Researcher, 38,* 355–382. doi:10.1007/s13384-011-0041-9

Lynch, K. (2015). Control by numbers: New managerialism and ranking in higher education. *Critical Studies in Education, 56*(2), 190–207. doi:10.1080/17508487.2014.949811

Macpherson, I., Robertson, S., & Walford, G. (Eds). (2014). *Education, privatisation and social justice: Case studies from Africa, South Asia and South East Asia.* Oxford: Symposium.

Marginson, S. (1997). *Markets in education.* St. Leonards: Allen & Unwin.

Pearson plc. (2011). Annual report and accounts 2011. Retrieved October 14, 2015 from http://ar2011.pearson.com/ar2011.pearson.com/media/99381/full_report2011.pdf.

Pearson plc. (2012). Annual report and accounts 2012. Retrieved October 16, 2015 from: http://ar2012.pearson.com/assets/downloads/15939_PearsonAR12.pdf.

Pearson plc. (2013). Annual report and accounts 2013. Retrieved October 27, 2015 from: https://www.pearson.com/content/dam/corporate/global/pearson-dot-com/files/annual-reports/ar2013/2013–annual-report-accounts.pdf

Pearson plc. (2014). Annual report and accounts 2014. Retrieved November 3, 2015 from: https://www.pearson.com/content/dam/corporate/global/pearson-dot-com/files/annual-reports/ar2014/01%20PearsonAR_FULL.pdf

Pearson plc. (2015). Pearson 2015 interim results. Retrieved October 27, 2015 from: https://www.pearson.com/content/dam/one-dot-com/one-dot-com/global/Files/news/news-annoucements/2015/2015-half-year-full-press-release_Final.pdf

Piketty, T. (2014). *Capital in the twenty-first century.* Cambridge, MA: The Belknap Press of Harvard University Press.

Polanyi, K. (2001). *The great transformation: The political and economic origins of our time* (2nd ed.). Boston, MA: Beacon Press.

Power, M. (1994). *The audit explosion.* London: Demos.

Power, M. (1997). *The audit society: Rituals of verification.* New York, NY: Oxford University Press.

Power, M. (2007). *Organized uncertainty: Designing a world of risk management.* New York, NY: Oxford University Press.

Riep, C. B. (2015). *Corporatised education in the Philippines: Pearson, Ayala Corporation and emergence of Affordable Private Education Centers (APEC).* Brussels: Education International.

Robertson, S. L., & Dale, R. (2015). Towards a "critical cultural political economy" account of the globalising of education. *Globalisation, Societies and Education, 13*(1), 149–170. doi:10.1080/14767724.2014.967502

Robeyns, I. (2006). Three models of education: Rights, capabilities and human capital. *Theory and Research in Education, 4*(1), 69–84. doi:10.1177/1477878506060683

Seo, M. G., & Creed, W. E. (2002). Institutional contradictions, praxis, and institutional change: A dialectical perspective. *Academy of Management Review, 27*(2), 222–247.

Shore, C, & Wright, S. (1999). Audit culture and anthropology: neo-liberalism in british higher education. *5*(4), 557–575. doi:10.2307/2661148

Simons, M. (2006). Learning as investment: Notes on governmentality and biopolitics. *Educational Philosophy and Theory, 38*(4), 523–540. doi:10.1111/j.1469-5812.2006.00209.x

Sum, N. L. (2010). A cultural political economy of transnational knowledge brands: Porterian "competitiveness" discourse and its recontextualization in Hong Kong/Pearl River Delta. *Journal of Language and Politics, 9*(4), 546–573. doi:10.1075/jlp.9.4.05sum

Sum, N. L., & Jessop, B. (2013). *Towards a cultural political economy: Putting culture in its place in political economy.* Cheltenham: Edward Elgar.

Verger, A., Lubienski, C., & Steiner-Khamsi, G. (2016). *World Yearbook of Education 2016: The global education industry.* London: Routledge.

Vogelmann, F. (2012). Neosocial market economy. *Foucault Studies, 14,* 115–137. doi:10.22439/fs.v0i14.3895

'Make money, get money': how two autonomous schools have commercialised their services

Jessica Holloway ⓘ and Amanda Keddie

ABSTRACT
Using the stories of two autonomous public schools in Australia, this paper demonstrates how commercialisation can simultaneously position schools as both consumer and for-profit producer. Drawing on Foucault's articulation of discourse as that which constitutes and makes available what is possible to be said, done and imagined, the paper illustrates how the current marketised articulation of education is allowing for new possibilities of commercialisation in schools. Together these stories demonstrate that there are creative ways that these schools have embraced their autonomy, while relying on market solutions to acquire the resources they deem necessary for their students and their communities. However, it also shows how these resources and the attainment for them are inextricably constituted by the market orientation of education more broadly and how this presents potential dangers for what schools may *be* and *become* as a result.

Introduction

Over the past decade, there has been a great deal of research on the privatisation of education, focusing primarily on the ways in which market orientations of education provide pathways for external organisations to influence education systems, policies and practices (Ball, 2007, 2009; Ball & Youdell, 2009; Burch, 2006; Lubienski, 2006). Ball and Youdell (2009) argued that there are two main forms of school privatisation: endogenous – 'the privatisation *in* education', and exogenous – 'the privatisation *of* education' (p. 74). Endogenous privatisation deals with the ways in which the logics of business are taken up within education, while exogenous deals with the ways in which the private sector has found ways of marketing and selling education products. The former has been the source of extensive research, especially as it relates to contemporary education policy reforms associated with raising standards, increasing accountability, and the expansion of school 'choice' and 'autonomy' (Ball, 2009; Berliner & Glass, 2014; Ravitch, 2013). The latter, however, is still a relatively new and under-explored area of research (Lingard, Sellar, Hogan, & Thompson, 2017), despite the growing influence and presence of commercial businesses in public education (Burch, 2009; Verger, Steiner-Khamsi, & Lubienski, 2017). The purpose of this paper is to contend with these matters, specifically associated with the marketisation and commercialisation of education. While growing attention has been paid to global corporations (e.g. Pearson) and their manoeuvring to (1) participate in education policy agenda-setting and (2) deliver for-profit education services and products (e.g. Hogan, Sellar, & Lingard, 2016; Verger et al., 2017), this study looks instead at how some schools participate as both consumers and producers (and sellers) of these services. Using the stories of two autonomous public schools in Queensland, Australia, this paper demonstrates how commercialisation can simultaneously position schools as both consumer and for-profit producer.

Drawing on Foucault's (1970) articulation of discourse as that which constitutes and makes available what is possible to be said, done and imagined, the paper illustrates how the current marketised articulation of education is allowing for new possibilities of commercialisation in schools. Specifically, we argue that while schools might participate in what could be considered more 'typical' marketing strategies, such as advertising their school 'brand' using high test scores, honours programmes, and school facilities (see Lubienski, 2007 for more examples), some schools are taking these strategies and commercialising them to make a profit. We begin by mapping the conditions that have made this form of commercialisation possible; and we conclude by signalling the new possibilities that might emerge from these arrangements.

Privatisation, commercialisation and marketisation

Privatisation, commercialisation and marketisation are interrelated, but unique, concepts that are profoundly influencing education globally (Rizvi & Lingard, 2009; Verger et al., 2017). These terms are slippery and often overlapping, but documenting their nuances can help us trace how schools and schooling are being remade within new orientations of education. Lingard et al. (2017) distinguish 'privatisation' from 'commercialisation' as follows:

> Commercialisation is something that happens *in* schools, as opposed to privatisation which is something that happens *to* schools … The interesting distinction between the commercialisation of schooling and the privatisation of schooling is that private providers are working *with and within* public schools to support schooling processes, rather than taking over the delivery and running *of* schools on their own. (p. 14. Emphasis added)

These private organisations work in tandem with the state, enabling the alignment of private and public-sector agendas and values, while simultaneously positioning themselves as the necessary provider of the services required by the new policies (e.g. Pearson testing services). We see this in the way that private-sector logics and values have become commonplace in education policy reform efforts related to accountability, choice, evaluation and performance-based pay, just to name a few. These concepts have become so entrenched within our purview of understanding education so as to render them completely 'normal' and expected (i.e. endogenous privatisation). This is key to understanding the conditions that have made it possible for external agencies to infiltrate policy agendas and classrooms (e.g. exogenous privatisation). Take, for example, the emergence of technology companies in education, as they are able to appeal to the 'deeply held cultural belief in the power of technology as a key driver of progress and the need for educational systems' (Roberts-Mahoney, Means, & Garrison, 2016, p. 405). This cultural belief is met with the motivations and abilities of for-profit technology companies to carve out a prominent role within education that is both politically influential and monetarily rewarding. In this sense, commercialisation, or the selling of education products and services, is made possible and rational through the private-sector logics that are framing contemporary educational values and needs. As such, commercialisation has emerged as an integral component of twenty-first century schools, as schools grow to depend on the external services to respond to reform demands (Burch, 2009) and address the needs of their diverse students (Hogan, Enright, Stylianou, & McCuaig, 2017). At this time, however, we are just beginning to scratch the surface in terms of what we know about their presence or degree of influence in schools, as well as the ways in which educators are selecting the services/products that are most suitable for their contexts (Hogan et al., 2017; Lingard et al., 2017; Roberts-Mahoney et al., 2016).

Similarly, as education is organised by private-sector logics, and where schools are positioned within competitive orientations to one another, schools are compelled to market themselves as distinct and superior to their competitors. As the 'autonomous school' (e.g. US charters, UK academies) movement advances in various countries worldwide, marketing has become a 'normal' operation of public schools, and running a school 'like a business' has become common practice (Blackmore, 2004; Kimber & Ehrich, 2011). Research on charter schools in the USA (Lubienski & Lee, 2016; Ravitch, 2010, 2013; Renzulli & Evans, 2005), academies in the UK (Keddie, 2014; Wilkins, 2015), and independent schools in Australia (Forsey, 2009; Gobby, 2013, 2016; Gobby, Keddie, & Blackmore, 2017) have documented the many ways that 'autonomy' has re-positioned public schools as competitive organisations that need to market their 'brand' accordingly and manage themselves in entrepreneurial ways. This rendering of public schools as market entities has ushered in a suite of business-like interests, logics and private investments (Burch, 2009; Verger et al., 2017), with the economic logic being that competition will drive innovation and the delivery of best services (Lubienski, 2007).

It must also be noted that autonomy in and of itself is not necessarily bad. Indeed, it is not uncommon for education scholars and practitioners to recommend that local decisions be made by local school actors who are closest to the community, and who know the needs of the students and faculty. This was one of the key reasons for implementing the Independent Public Schools (IPS) programme in Queensland. However, we must also understand autonomy as being situated within a larger regime of accountability, where the work of principals is structured by the external demands of audit, evaluation and competition (Blackmore, 2004; Gobby et al., 2017; Kimber & Ehrich, 2011), regardless of how devolved school management has become. As school autonomy is the product of this configuration, so too must we understand how competitive conditions shape the way autonomy is both conceptualised and enacted. On the one hand, we can think of autonomy as providing schools the freedom to make decisions about what is best for their students and their communities. On the other hand, we must also consider the types of performance and practices that are valued by a marketised configuration of education. This presents a complicated tension between autonomy as being potentially good for students, schools and the public, and how autonomy gets constituted through and by the conditions of privatisation, commercialisation, and marketisation. The purpose of this paper is to contend with these tensions by providing illustrative evidence of how two autonomous schools have embodied a private-sector ethos, while using their most valuable services to distinguish themselves from their competitors (marketisation) and turn their products and services into profits (commercialisation). As we learn more about how external actors are commercialising education products and services, this paper challenges the relationship between schools and the market, while potentially blurring the lines between 'endogenous' and 'exogenous' understandings of privatisation. The stories we present below show how two schools have created new means for participating in the market.

Context and method

This paper is part of a larger study that looks at the IPS initiative in Australia. As a federally-backed initiative, IPS provides $70 million to promote school autonomy through the devolution of school authority to local school principals. While remaining publicly funded and accountable to external audits and evaluation, IPS principals are provided freedom primarily over their budgets and hiring (but not termination) practices. The various states have had their own histories with autonomous schooling, but the recent federal push has invigorated new debates about what it means for schools to be independent and to do 'autonomy' in ethical and effective ways (Gobby et al., 2017; Keddie, 2017; Keddie, Gobby, & Wilkins, 2017). Queensland, which had 250 IPS schools as of 2017, are –

> expected to look outwards, working in partnership with their community, other IPS, other state schools, state school regions and central office to create an enabling force of connected school leaders that impact positively on student outcomes. (Queensland Department of Education and Training, 2016, p. 5)

They are to innovate and experiment with new educational practices, then share their learnings across the state system.

While school autonomy is often touted as the way to build efficiency, drive innovation, and improve student outcomes (e.g. Hamilton Associates, 2015), its formation and enactment is shaped and constituted by a market discourse that also shapes the actions and decisions of the principals and faculty within the school. As such, autonomous schools operate in ways that are inextricably constituted through and by the accountability discourse that structures all education matters more broadly. Against this backdrop, we relate the stories of two autonomous schools in Queensland that have embodied a marketised ethos, making it possible for them to imagine creative ways to sell various services, symbolically and materially.

We draw on various forms of data, including (1) interviews with the lead principals, (2) publicly available statistics and reports, such as school demographics, strategic plans, and budget reports, and (3) public profiles, such as school websites and social media accounts where available (i.e. Facebook and YouTube for the second school). The interviews sought to explore the principals' thoughts about: (1) the key possibilities and challenges of school autonomy reform in general; (2) how the IPS policy supported or undermined their autonomy and freedom as leaders; (3) the location of IPS policy within increasing accountability demands; (4) the equity implications of the IPS policy at a student, school, systemic and community level; (5) the factors of school context that they viewed as supporting their productive take up of IPS; and (6) any future challenges that they projected for their school and the system within the context of school autonomy reform. Employing the discursive tools of Bacchi's (2000, 2012) 'policy-as-discourse', we illustrate how the conditions of privatisation and marketisation have created new possibilities for schools to *become* a business. We also bring into conversation the recent work on commercialisation (Hogan et al., 2017; Lingard et al., 2017) to provide unique ways that these schools are using their autonomy to commercialise their own services.

Data analysis was a reflexive and iterative process. We started by conducting a first round of initial coding (Charmaz, 2014) of the interview transcripts, reports and the content of the school websites and social media profiles. This allowed us to begin understanding the scope of the data, as well as identifying the specific data sources that would enable us to get at the general ways in which the schools were using their 'autonomy' to make decisions about their schools (e.g. budget, hiring practices, etc.). For the reports, websites and social media profiles, we worked from the assumption that 'documents [and media representations] are "social products" that must be examined critically because they reflect the interests and perspectives of their authors' (Saldaña, 2013, p. 61). We used these materials to question the types of 'values and ideologies' that were represented in the documents and profiles (Hitchcock & Hughes, 1995, p. 231). Then we focused specifically on the interview data to understand how the principals articulated their schools as autonomous operations, paying particular attention to how they embodied the 'autonomous' ethos. We used this to think about how the schools have operationalised 'autonomy' to frame the schools' values, 'problems' and 'solutions', which we ultimately saw as being shaped by a market discourse. Bringing these analyses together, we were able to map how autonomy, as constituted by and through a market discourse, has produced 'problems' defined by audit and competition, and thus requiring 'solutions' that are also market-oriented. Throughout the coding and analytical processes, we maintained individual analytic memos (Saldaña, 2013), but we met regularly to 'shop-talk' (Saldaña, 2013) the data, allowing us to think through the data together while using theory to ground our ongoing sense-making and theorising.

Below are the stories of Ann at Buford High School and Jeff at Starke State School (SSS) (pseudonyms). We conclude by bringing these stories together and situating them back into the literature, arguing that marketisation and commercialisation produce and constitute both the 'problems' and 'solutions' (Bacchi, 2000) for these schools. We also highlight the slipperiness of 'endogenous privatisation' (Ball & Youdell, 2009) *within* schools and how this sets the conditions for further 'exogenous privatisation' *of* schools.

Buford high school: 'YouTube will pay us'

Buford State School (BHS) is new to the IPS network, having received its IPS status in 2017. It serves approximately 800 students in grades 7–12, nearly half of whom speak English as a second language. According to Ann (pseudonym), the principal, the school's demographics have shifted over the years, as students of higher socioeconomic status have moved to other suburbs. As a non enrolment-managed school (i.e. there is no cap on how many out-of-precinct students BHS can enrol), and its geographic location, BHS must compete with neighbouring schools to attract students. This requires a strategic marketing plan, which has been established as one of the four Improvement Priorities for the school's 2016–2019 Strategic Plan. Marketing strategies include promoting the school's motto and increasing the school's presence on various social media platforms. Ann describes the importance of having a positive public perception:

I am in a competitive educational landscape [and I] need to have a point of difference from the schools around me, particularly because I'm not enrolment managed. And I do believe we have got a great product. My teachers do a great job.

Ann has adopted a market language ('product') to describe her school, while employing market logics to identify the problems her school faces. This is consistent with the autonomous school movement, where schools are framed as business-like entities that must promote themselves within the market (Lubienski, 2007; Lubienski & Lee, 2016). Like private businesses must do, BHS has focused on developing a positive image, using public platforms such as Facebook, YouTube, and the school's website to promote their school's brand. Their Facebook page is updated regularly with postings about upcoming events, photographs and videos of school happenings, and celebratory announcements. To make the school's website more aesthetically appealing and user-friendly, the school has decided to replace the state's endorsed website to develop its own, allowing them to include features that make enrolment queries easier for potential customers. Ann describes the decision as such:

> [I]n terms of lifting the game around … our public perception, 'that we care, that we are interested in these people', all this stuff, that's what this new website can do, that my current website doesn't do … We are going to use another piece of software … [that is] mobile-friendly; they have automation … [W]e are thinking about enrolment. We have got these booking times for enrolment. So you say [click], 'I am interested to enrol'. Automatically, a little email will pop back to the person saying, 'Thank you, we have received your email. Someone will contact you within the next day to arrange an appointment'.

This 'customer service' design helps BHS address a market problem, but it diverts resources (e.g. time, money, human capital) from educative purposes to market operations. Perhaps the most unique and time-intensive market endeavour, however, is the school's YouTube channel. The channel currently has 18 videos that have been viewed more than 10,000 times. Interestingly, the videos rarely feature students, nor do they necessarily appeal to students or their parents. Rather, the topics range from short how-to tutorials (e.g. photography, cooking) to school event videos. Not only does the school use the channel to market its brand, but now Ann is exploring options for monetising the channel, as she describes below:

> I found out if we do YouTube clips and we are successful enough, then YouTube will pay us money. It is a thing called 'monetisation'. So I am now going through the machine, going through the bureaucracy [laughs], to find the right person to talk to, about whether or not I can do monetisation.

The YouTube channel is a part of their marketing scheme, as noted in their budget and strategic plans. Again, this school has turned to market solutions to address the problems associated with the positioning of schools as market-oriented enterprises. These new orientations make possible what was once unthinkable for public schools, such as the need to explicitly budget and plan for strategic marketing. When schools are arranged in a competitive field, the need for issues like 'recruitment' emerge and become necessary elements of running a successful school. BHS has embodied this new responsibility and has developed techniques for increasing its market value. The school's YouTube channel has become a way for BHS to positively represent itself to potential customers and *funders*, such as future students, philanthropic parties, or even advertisers. All of these groups become sources of capital that help position BHS as a competitive and valuable entity in the market. Although these extra sources of revenue also help the school attain the resources they deem necessary for their students, we must question whether public schools should be in the position of marketing their services. The traditionally accepted market logic has been that competition will drive schools to improve their services (Lubienski, 2007). But in the case of BHS, it is difficult to accept their YouTube channel as something that is directly improving their educative services. Rather they must redirect resources from educative services to marketing ones. This not only changes the role of the school, but it also changes the role of school leaders, as pointed out by Ann: '[P]art of my role as a principal is to get that good message out there'.

But what choice does the school have? Between declining student numbers, and an increasingly competitive landscape, BHS is forced to differentiate itself from its neighbours. Employing a marketing scheme based on 'symbolic and emotional appeals' (Lubienski, 2007, p. 131), the school uses social media and its school website to establish its place in the local community, demonstrate its commitment to a common school mission, and attract potential funders and customers. The Facebook announcements and videos celebrate student and faculty accomplishments, while the YouTube videos invite viewers to learn both trade (e.g. cooking) and academic (e.g. mathematics) skills. Rather than relying on test scores and other annual reports and accolades to brand itself, BHS has sought a more holistic approach to its branding scheme. Not only did this move allow for BHS to distinguish itself amongst its peers, but it also positioned itself as a provider of services (beyond traditional educative ones). By appealing to a wide audience via the YouTube videos, BHS is able to commercialise its services, regardless of their viewers' interests in enrolment. If all goes as planned, the channel will eventually attract advertisers, which will translate to financial income for the school.

SSS: 'Like running a corporation'

Serving nearly 1000 students from prep to grade 6, SSS positions itself as part of a global community. The school has adopted the International Baccalaureate (IB) programme as its primary curriculum source, and its website frequently refers to its commitment to instilling students with a global perspective. As Jeff, the principal, stated: '[W]e have been able to be part of that greater network, which gets our school, again, more in the global stage'. He went on to explain that IB will 'set [students] up to be better learners for life'.

Jeff has found that the school's autonomy status has offered him opportunities to create a school that 'cater[s] for every single student who lives in [his] local area'. He describes the responsibility of public schools as needing to serve the public, which means that all students should have access to their local school, and competition should not drive schools to discriminate in terms of enrolment. He criticises the media's reporting of league tables, arguing that the top-performing schools are always 'private schools which offer scholarships, have entrance exams, who only take the top kids who should be performing anyway'. He also describes his multi-cultural and multi-ethnic school as 'harmonious', given that 'acceptance and tolerance' are two of the fundamental pillars of the IB framework.

As one of only 11 Queensland primary schools to offer the IB programme, SSS offers a unique curriculum option for students. At the same time, it creates unique challenges in terms of networking with nearby schools. While Jeff consistently praises the school's decision to implement IB, he also describes the challenges that an IB school faces in his geographic location. For one, he sees the benefits of building collaborative networks between schools, but there is only so much his teachers can learn from neighbouring schools that are non-IB. He explains how his public school has come to collaborate with both private and international schools as:

> As an autonomous school – a lot of our network is actually other IB schools ... [T]hey are all independent Catholic schools, private schools. So it is probably unheard of previously ... that State schools really had a relationship with the private sector ... [I]t is McDonalds meeting Hungry Jacks. We have been able to talk to, and we regularly network with our teachers and co-plan now with many private schools; and international schools, who come and visit. I took some staff overseas last year to visit schools in France and Switzerland, so they got an understanding of how the IB worked.

Jeff appreciates the ability to use his school's autonomy to 'choose who you want to network with', but acknowledges the steep cost associated with partnering with international IB schools. These costs, coupled with the costs of other resources deemed necessary to the school, force Jeff to encourage his deputy principals to 'feel like politicians', and to be innovative to 'think of ways to make money and get money or to do things within the box, or outside the mainstream rules, or the mainstream interpretation of those rules'. He explains how 'a big part of our admin [sic] meetings are about what we can do to generate income; how we can position our school to be a school that people want to visit and pay money [to visit]'. The school's response has been to 'open [their] school to many international visits that are now money-making.' This provides the means for SSS to 'do a lot of these extras around PD [professional development], to keep our IB licence, [and] to send staff overseas'.

Like Ann from BHS, Jeff has also assumed a market language and ethos that shapes his actions and decisions about his role and his school. While he criticises the effects of competition on public schools, the 'problems' faced by his school are nonetheless market-oriented. Making money has become a fundamental goal of the school's faculty, which, like BHS, diverts resources and energy from educative objectives to market ones. There is little, if any, evidence to suggest that Jeff and SSS have anything but the best of intentions for their students and their community. Their school reports (e.g. budget and strategic plans, curriculum and pedagogy frameworks), as well as Jeff's articulation of their school's autonomous approach to education, suggest a commitment to embracing diversity and respecting multicultural perspectives.

This commitment, however, brings challenges associated with a limited budget and geographic location. To overcome these challenges, SSS has turned to market solutions to make money from their most valuable product – their teaching practices. In this respect, autonomy provides Jeff and SSS the freedom to commercialise its services and to use the market to increase revenue for arguably decent goals (i.e. maintaining IB status). However, it is also the conditions of autonomy and the market that position the school as needing to sell their services and to spend the precious resources of time and human capital to 'think of ways to make money and get money' to remain on the 'global stage' (Jeff). This global-positioning puts SSS in competition with private schools moreso than public ones, as he explains:

We are the only State primary school in Queensland to run that framework; but because many of our students are international or come from the surrounding private schools which run with the IB program, the independent public school initiative has allowed us to change our curriculum for what we need. So we are actually taking students back from the private system into the State system, instead of previously we were losing them.

SSS's strategic positioning as globally-focused demonstrates their resonance with contemporary renderings of school success that are geared towards developing globally-competitive students. This focus is embedded within their school mission and curriculum, marketing itself as internationally relevant, but also locally aware of its community's needs. These are goals that are both enabled *by*, but also enabling *of*, business-like orientations of schools (of which 'autonomous' management is also consistent).

Concluding discussion

Our analysis illustrates the complicated nature of school autonomy, as shaped by the market rules that are setting the conditions for schools to operate. Together these stories demonstrate that there are creative ways that these schools have embraced their autonomy, while relying on market solutions to acquire the resources they deem necessary for their students and their communities. However, it also shows how these resources and the attainment for them are inextricably constituted by the market orientation of education more broadly and how this presents potential dangers for what schools may *be* and *become* as a result. As Ball (2009) has warned us, private providers and edu-businesses are well-positioned to sell 'turnaround services ... market[ing] to those schools and colleges that are "struggling" to achieve national targets and benchmarks or under-performing relative to their "competitors" or have management difficulties' (p. 85). These might be professional development packages, consultation visits, coaching services, etc. These vendors adopt the discourses of reform movements and tailor their products and services accordingly. The schools of the current study, however, disrupt this model by positioning *themselves* as the for-profit service-providers. They package and sell their own best practices, but, somewhat ironically, use the revenue to purchase other educational services and products that are deemed necessary to meet the needs of their specific students.

As mentioned earlier, it is critical that we understand how business logics create the conditions for business endeavours (Ball & Youdell, 2009). If schools are run like businesses, then it paves the way for external vendors (e.g. for-profit providers, philanthropic investors, etc.) to involve themselves in steering education matters and making a profit while doing so. As witnessed in the technology industry, eventually we reach a point where schools have to rely on the services provided by the ones setting the agenda. As the schools of this study have demonstrated, it is possible for the schools to be the ones selling the products (literally and figuratively), but when we follow this logic through, we might predict the emergence of new configurations, potentials and partnerships that value profits and competition over other educative and social purposes. In the case of Ann and BHS, their YouTube channel is poised to attract advertisers who possess their own motives and expectations for the content on the channel. It is feasible to question the influence this may eventually have on the school's YouTube image and the content it presents. As the school has already begun embodying the corporate ethos –

as demonstrated by its overall marketing scheme – its business with YouTube is but another small step in aligning itself with the image of the market and thus creating new possibilities for further privatisation and/or commercialisation. In the case of Jeff and SSS, their competitive edge is designated by their IB programme. The only way to maintain this programme, however, is to find creative ways to bring in extra income through selling teacher workshops.

Both BHS and SSS have embraced an entrepreneurial spirit that is afforded by their autonomous status. They recognise the competitive conditions within which they must operate, and they turn to market solutions to address the challenges they face. This puts the schools in precarious dilemmas, as they navigate a competitive terrain, they must spend precious resources to promote their brand or think of creative ways to 'make money' (Jeff). But then on the other hand, they have the autonomy to use their resources as they see fit, enabling them to commercialise their services. Important here is that these 'dilemmas' are a product of market understandings of 'problems' and 'solutions'. Thus, the very 'problem' that schools face regarding meeting the needs of their students is constituted through market renderings of 'success' (e.g. competitive, world-class, etc.).

These dilemmas also change the role and responsibility of the government as it relates to education. It perpetuates the idea that schools are responsible for fixing problems associated with social inequality. By shifting the responsibility of creating equitable schools from the government to the individual school, we can continue to ignore the societal factors that will continue to perpetuate social inequalities (while continuing to blame schools in the meantime). This begs the question of whether public schools should really be compelled to commodify their schooling practices in order to address the needs that are more suitable for the State to address. We should question the time commitment these endeavours cost, and how this reduces time spent on educative matters, as well as the new norms that might be set in doing so.

Hogan et al. (2017) raise an important point that not all commercialisation is necessarily bad. First, schools have purchased commercial products (e.g. textbooks) for over 100 years; and there are contemporary instances where teachers actively seek commercial products to help supplement their curriculum. We take this point that commercialisation might help support teachers in attaining the materials and resources they need to address the needs of their students. In a similar way, the schools of this study used a form of commercialisation to raise the funds necessary to support their students and their needs. Also, in the case of SSS, in particular, their IB workshops offer new choices in the market, competing with the likes of international conglomerates, like Pearson (e.g. Pearson Global Schools). One of the major issues with these global organisations is that they are often too far removed from classrooms to offer anything more valuable than 'what works' solutions (Kamens, 2013; Lewis, 2017; Lewis & Hogan, 2017). Jeff and SSS, however, have upended this model, producing on-the-ground teaching services that are developed *by* and *for* teachers, rather than international companies that can only offer de-contextualised, generic products for any school or teacher to adopt.

However, we also caution that in doing so, these schools have set up new conditions that enable new ways for public school services to be made into something that *can* and *should* be profitable. This is particularly applicable in Queensland – where BHS and SSS are located – as there is an explicit condition of their IPS status that they are to 'innovate, trial and share good practice across the state school system' (Queensland Department of Education and Training, 2016, p. 5). This makes IPS schools important places to watch for identifying new trends and arrangements – the positive and the potentially dangerous. In Jeff's words, 'a lot of the initiatives that IPS schools were allowed to undertake or entrusted with in that autonomy, have actually flowed into the non IPS schools'. Therefore, it is important that we document these conditional shifts as we continue to make ontological sense of what education *is* and what it is *becoming*. Bacchi (2000) implores us to 'recognize the non-innocence of how "problems" get framed within policy proposals, how the frames will affect what can be thought about and how this affects possibilities for action,' (p. 50). Perhaps most importantly, we should question the ways in which this form of commercialisation establishes new norms for what schools might be and be able to do. In other words, if we take an onto-epistemological perspective, we can argue that once we *know* schools as business operations, then schools will *become* business operations. Invoking Foucault's (1979) expression, these sorts of practices are 'apparently innocent, but profoundly suspicious' (p. 139, cited in Ball, 2009, p. 93) and should be documented and interrogated. In orienting 'problems' by a market discourse, and framing autonomous schools as empowered to use market 'solutions' in response, schools are fundamentally changed in terms of how they think and operate. In doing so, there is a perpetuation of endogenous and exogenous forms of privatisation that redefine the purpose and function of public schools and the individuals that inhabit them.

Disclosure statement

No potential conflict of interest was reported by the authors.

ORCID

Jessica Holloway ⓘ http://orcid.org/0000-0001-9267-3197

References

Bacchi, C. (2000). Policy as discourse: What does it mean? Where does it get us? *Discourse: Studies in the Cultural Politics of Education, 21*(1), 45–57.

Bacchi, C. (2012). Introducing the 'what is the problem represented to be?' approach. In A. Bletsas & C. Beasley (Eds.), *Engaging with Carol Bacchi* (pp. 21–24). Adelaide: The University of Adelaide.

Ball, S. J. (2007). *Education plc: Understanding private sector participation in public sector education*. New York: Routledge.

Ball, S. J. (2009). Privatising education, privatising education policy, privatising educational research: Network governance and the 'competition state'. *Journal of Education Policy, 24*(1), 83–99.

Ball, S. J., & Youdell, D. (2009). Hidden privatisation in public education. *Education Review, 21*(2), 73–83.

Berliner, D. C., & Glass, G. V. (2014). *50 myths and lies that threaten America's public schools: The real crisis in education*. New York: Teachers College Press.

Blackmore, J. (2004). Leading as emotional management work in high risk times: The counterintuitive impulses of performativity and passion. *School Leadership & Management, 24*(4), 439–459.

Burch, P. (2006). The new educational privatization: Educational contracting and high stakes accountability. *Teachers College Record, 108*(12), 2582–2610.

Burch, P. (2009). *Hidden markets: The new education privatization*. New York: Routledge.

Charmaz, K. (2014). *Constructing grounded theory*. Thousand Oaks: Sage.

Forsey, M. (2009). The problem with autonomy: An ethnographic study of neoliberalism in practice at an Australian high school. *Discourse: Studies in the Cultural Politics of Education, 30*(4), 457–469.

Foucault, M. (1970). *The order of things.* New York: Pantheon Books.

Foucault, M. (1979). *Discipline and punish.* Harmondsworth: Peregrine.

Gobby, B. (2013). Principal self-government and subjectification: The exercise of principal autonomy in the western Australian independent public schools programme. *Critical Studies in Education, 54* (3), 273–285.

Gobby, B. (2016). Putting 'the system' into a school autonomy reform: The case of the independent public schools program. *Discourse: Studies in the Cultural Politics of Education, 37*(1), 16–29.

Gobby, B., Keddie, A., & Blackmore, J. (2017). Professionalism and competing responsibilities: Moderating competitive performativity in school autonomy reform. *Journal of Educational Administration and History, 1,* 1–15.

Hamilton Associates. (2015). *School autonomy: Building the conditions for student success.* Report commissioned by the Western Australian Department of Education.

Hitchcock, G., & Hughes, D. (1995). *Research and the teacher: A qualitative introduction to school-based research.* New York: Routledge.

Hogan, A., Enright, E., Stylianou, M., & McCuaig, L. (2017). Nuancing the critique of commercialisation in schools: Recognising teacher agency. *Journal of Education Policy, 8,* 1–15. doi:10.1080/02680939. 2017.1394500

Hogan, A., Sellar, S., & Lingard, B. (2016). Commercialising comparison: Pearson puts the TLC in soft capitalism. *Journal of Education Policy, 31*(3), 243–258.

Kamens, D. H. (2013). Globalization and the emergence of an audit culture: PISA and the search for 'best practices' and magic bullets. In H.-D. Meyer & A. Benavot (Eds.), *PISA, power, and policy: The emergence of global educational governance* (pp. 117–141). Oxford: Symposium.

Keddie, A. (2014). It's like Spiderman … with great power comes great responsibility: School autonomy, school context and the audit culture. *School Leadership & Management, 34*(5), 502–517.

Keddie, A. (2017). School autonomy reform and public education in Australia: Implications for social justice. *The Australian Educational Researcher, 44*(4–5), 373–390.

Keddie, A., Gobby, B., & Wilkins, C. (2017). School autonomy reform in Queensland: Governance, freedom and the entrepreneurial leader. *School Leadership & Management, 59,* 1–17.

Kimber, M., & Ehrich, L. C. (2011). The democratic deficit and school-based management in Australia. *Journal of Educational Administration, 49*(2), 179–199.

Lewis, S. (2017). Governing schooling through 'what works': The OECD's PISA for schools. *Journal of Education Policy, 32*(3), 281–302.

Lewis, S., & Hogan, A. (2017). Reform first and ask questions later? The implications of (fast) schooling policy and 'silver bullet' solutions. *Critical Studies in Education, 44,* 1–18. doi:10.1080/17508487. 2016.1219961

Lingard, B., Sellar, S., Hogan, A., & Thompson, G. (2017). *Commercialisation in public schooling (CIPS).* Sydney: New South Wales Teachers Federation.

Lubienski, C. (2006). School choice and privatization in education: An alternative analytical framework. *Journal for Critical Education Policy Studies, 4*(1), 1–26.

Lubienski, C. (2007). Marketing schools: Consumer goods and competitive incentives for consumer information. *Education and Urban Society, 40*(1), 118–141.

Lubienski, C., & Lee, J. (2016). Competitive incentives and the education market: How charter schools define themselves in metropolitan Detroit. *Peabody Journal of Education, 91*(1), 64–80.

Queensland Department of Education and Training. (2016). *Independent public schools policy framework.* Retrieved from http://education.qld.gov.au/schools/independent-public-schools/resources/ ips-policy-framework.pdf

Ravitch, D. (2010). *The death and life of the great American school system: How testing and choice are undermining education.* New York: Basic Books.

Ravitch, D. (2013). *Reign of error: The hoax of the privatization movement and the danger to America's public schools.* New York: Vintage.

Renzulli, L. A., & Evans, L. (2005). School choice, charter schools, and white flight. *Social Problems, 52* (3), 398–418.

Rizvi, F., & Lingard, B. (2009). *Globalizing education policy*. Abingdon: Routledge.

Roberts-Mahoney, H., Means, A. J., & Garrison, M. J. (2016). Netflixing human capital development: Personalized learning technology and the corporatization of K-12 education. *Journal of Education Policy*, *31*(4), 405–420.

Saldaña, J. (2013). *The coding manual for qualitative researchers*. London: Sage.

Verger, A., Steiner-Khamsi, G., & Lubienski, C. (2017). The emerging global education industry: Analysing market-making in education through market sociology. *Globalisation, Societies and Education*, *15*(3), 325–340.

Wilkins, A. (2015). Professionalizing school governance: The disciplinary effects of school autonomy and inspection on the changing role of school governors. *Journal of Education Policy*, *30*(2), 182–200.

Care of the self, resistance and subjectivity under neoliberal governmentalities

Stephen J. Ball and Antonio Olmedo

Resistance is normally thought of as a collective exercise of public political activity. In this article, Ball and Olmedo approach the question of resistance in a different way, through Foucault's notion of 'the care of the self'. Neoliberal reforms in education are producing new kinds of teaching subjects, new forms of subjectivity. It makes sense then that subjectivity should be the terrain of struggle, the terrain of resistance. A set of e-mail exchanges with teachers, based around Ball's work on performativity, enable the authors to access the work of power relations through the uncertainties, discomforts and refusals that these teachers bring to their everyday practice. By acting 'irresponsibly', these teachers take 'responsibility' for the care of their selves and in doing so make clear that social reality is not as inevitable as it may seem. This is not strategic action in the normal political sense. Rather it is a process of struggle against mundane, quotidian neoliberalisations, that creates the possibility of thinking about education and ourselves differently.

In this article, we want to take up a 'different' approach to the issue of resistance – one which draws on the work of Michel Foucault. We can already hear the collective groans – what does Foucault, theorist of domination and nihilist, have to say about resistance and freedom? We want to suggest that he has a great deal to offer, particularly at this point in time, particularly to the teacher. We have nothing critical to say about, and nothing but admiration for, the efforts of collective resistance based on what Michael Apple (2012) calls 'decentred unities'. However, we want to address the particular plight of the teacher who stands alone in their classroom or their staff common room, and sees something 'cracked', something that to their colleagues is no more than the steady drone of the mundane and the normal, and finds it intolerable. How do they respond? To put it simply, to the extent that neoliberal governmentalities have become increasingly focused upon the production of subjectivity, it is logical that we think about subjectivity as a site of struggle and resistance.

Nowadays, the struggle against the forms of subjection – against the submission of subjectivity – is becoming more and more important, even though the struggles against forms of domination and exploitation have not disappeared. Quite the contrary. (Foucault, 1982, p. 213)

We focus here both on an analysis of the neoliberal modes and technologies of governmentality and these modes and technologies as points of agonism and struggle where different possibilities of the teaching subject can be glimpsed. This is an attempt to approach power relations differently, following the flows of power in the 'opposite direction'. What we intend to do is to sketch the basis of a 'new economy of power relations' and to do it in a different way, 'a way which is more empirical, more directly related to our present situation, and which implies more relations between theory and practice' (Foucault, 1982, p. 211). This 'different' approach takes as a starting point specific forms of resistance, that is, as Foucault suggests, we want to examine resistance to *practices*, and specifically the practices of performativity, and then use those *practices of resistance* 'as a chemical catalyst so as to bring to light power relations, locate their position, find out their point of application and the methods used' (Foucault, 1982, p. 211).

'Performance has no room for caring' (Ball, 2003, p. 224). In this article, we want to go back and revise that affirmation. More concretely, we reflect upon a set of cases that represent a particular type of struggle against/with the *practices* of performativity. 'The main objective of these struggles is to attack not so much 'such and such' an institution of power, or group, or elite, or class, but rather a technique, a form of power' (Foucault, 1982, p. 211). These cases consist of a small set of email exchanges between Stephen Ball and teachers (from primary, secondary, Further Education and Higher Education, UK and United States) which were initiated by the teachers in response to Stephen's writing on *performativity*, and seemed to speak to their present concerns.[1] Later, we will also briefly consider the significance of the form of these exchanges. Our aim is to open a space in which we might begin to understand the daily experiences and practices of freedom of individual teachers. These are 'normal' teachers, as they would categorise themselves, who may not feel 'different' but whose struggles 'make a difference' in the 'normality' of their classrooms. These are struggles that surface when the teacher begins to question the necessity of and think about the revocability of his or her own situation. That is, when the teacher begins to look for answers to questions about the *how(s) of power*[2] inside and around him or her, the *how(s)* of his or her beliefs and practices. In these moments, the power relations in which the teacher is imbricated come to the fore. It is then that he or she can begin to take an active role in their own self-definition as a 'teaching subject', to think in terms of what they do not want to be, and do not want to *become*, or, in another words, begin to *care for themselves*. Such care also rests upon and is realised through practices, practices of critique, vigilance, reflexivity, and of writing. The initial lines of Nigel's first email powerfully frame the scope and practices with which we will be dealing in this article:

> I am a small rural school head teacher. My job is being destroyed by reductive specifiers and performative maniacs. I have engaged in a fight back but that just makes it worse. To think differently – that is to engage in learning rather than pseudo-measuring – is to be subjected to a totalitarian human and public relations meltdown, subjected to a public barrage of disparagement on 'leadership' (not thinking pure thoughts) and self-evaluation (ditto). (Nigel)

We are also very aware that these are not 'their' struggles, they are also 'our' struggles. These accounts enable us to visualise the gaps between power and domination and offer opportunities to think about ourselves differently.

By focussing on particular cases of struggle we hope to address some of the questions that guided Foucault's thinking in his later work. That is, he was interested in the modes by which 'human beings are made subjects' (Foucault, 1982, p. 208). He asks: 'How are we constituted as subjects of our own knowledge? How are we constituted as subjects who exercise or submit to power relations? How are we constituted as moral subjects of our own actions?' (Foucault, 1997a, p. 318).

Teaching subjects

Let us clarify some concepts that we will be using here and, particularly, the terms *subject* and *teaching subject*. For Foucault, the word subject has two meanings, both of which suggest 'a form of power which subjugates and makes subject to'. On the one hand, subject relates to the state of subjection 'to someone else by control or dependence'; on the other hand, it refers to the self-configuration of an identity 'by a conscience or self-knowledge' (Foucault, 1982, p. 212). Furthermore, in an interview in 1984, Foucault suggested that he saw the subject not simply as a *substance*, but as a *form*. The latter rests on the idea the subject 'is not primarily or always identical to itself' (Foucault, 1997a, p. 290), and he clarifies:

> You do not have the same type of relationship to yourself when you constitute yourself as a political subject who goes to vote or speaks at a meeting and when you are seeking to fulfil your desires in a sexual relationship. Undoubtedly there are relationships and interferences between these different forms of the subject; but we are not dealing with the same type of subject. In each case, one plays, one establishes a different type of relationship to oneself. And it is precisely the historical constitution of these various forms of the subject in relation to the games of truth which interests me. (Foucault, 1997a, pp. 290–291)

The subject is the result of endless processes of construction of identities that are to a greater or lesser extent, but never completely, constrained by the contingencies of the particular historical moment in which they are inscribed. As suggested elsewhere (Ball, 2012), this perspective allows us to approach the idea of subjectivity as *processes of becoming* that focus on *what we do* rather than on *what we are,* that is to say, the work of *the care of the self*. The point here is that there is no individual, no self, that is ontologically prior to power. There is no subject that is already formed. In this sense, the self is not only a constant *beginning* but also a constant *end* (in the double sense of the word, both as consummated entity and envisioned objective), or, as McGushin puts it, it is 'the real basis of the self as both agent and object' (2011, p. 129). The subject is then governed by others and at the same time governor of him/herself. It is within this paradox that the idea of resistance becomes a central aspect in the analysis of power relations: 'In power relations there is necessarily the possibility of resistance because if there were no possibility of resistance (of violent resistance, flight, deception, strategies capable of reversing the situation), there would be no power relations at all' (Foucault, 1997a, p. 292). The power/resistance paradox is unresolvable. As Dean neatly puts it, 'our understanding of ourselves is linked to the ways in which we are governed' (2010, p. 14). The constraining historical, political and economic contextual factors are therefore central to the understanding of the limits of the horizon of possibilities and practices through which the subject actively constitutes him/herself, including the practices of resistance: 'These practices are nevertheless not something invented by the individual himself. They are models that he finds in his culture and are proposed, suggested, imposed upon him by his culture, his society, and his social group' (Foucault, 1997a, p. 291).

We are interested here in what could be termed the *teaching subject*, the teacher as a subject that has been constituted and that has constituted him/herself through certain practices of power and games of truth in a particular epistemological context. In our case, we want to disentangle in this context the mechanisms put into play by neoliberalism as a new regime of truth. Though it shares certain principles with classic liberalism, neoliberalism differs from the previous iteration replacing the logic of exchange with that of competition (Foucault, 2010a). This represents a broader epistemological shift that involves changes in the form and functions of the state, or a move from government to governance, from hierarchies to heterarchies (Jessop, 2002), and also a 'new anthropology': the *homo œconomicus*, characterised as being an 'entrepreneur of himself' (Foucault, 2010a, p. 226).

Neoliberalism is therefore both 'out there' and 'in here' (Peck & Tickell, 2002), it is realised and constituted within mundane and immediate practices of everyday life (Ong, 2007). It 'does us' – speaks and acts through our language, purposes, decisions and social relations (Ball, 2012). Altogether it sets the cultural and social limits to the possibilities of the care of the self but, at the same time, opens new spaces for struggle and resistance, as Rose (1996, p. 58) suggests: 'the reconfiguring of the subject of government confers obligations and duties at the same time as it opens new spaces of decision and action'.

Irresponsibility as resistance

In what follows we will focus on the specific practices of resistance and *self-overcoming* of a group of individual teachers who directly confront the discourse and enactment of neoliberalism and its technologies. In particular, the practices of performativity that impact upon the ways in which they are governed and are *able to be* in their classrooms and their schools. We understand the concept of government here not only in relation to 'political structures or the management of states', but more generally, in Foucault's sense, to designate 'the way in which the conduct of individuals or of groups might be directed' (Foucault, 1982, p. 221). This relates to Martin's experience. He struggles with performativity as it works to define what he does and what he does not want to become. This is a 'fundamental challenge', as he puts it:

> I find that one of the most fundamental challenges of my job is trying to avoid becoming incorporated into market modes of thinking. Of course, the more time you spend at work trying to please your superiors, the more you use the language of performativity and begin to believe in it yourself. (Martin)

Neoliberalism requires and enacts a 'new type of individual', that is a 'new type of teacher and head teacher' formed within the logic of competition. The apparatuses of neoliberalism are seductive, enthralling and overbearingly necessary. It is a 'new' moral system that subverts and re-orients us to its truths and ends. It makes us responsible for our performance and for the performance of others. We are burdened with the responsibility to perform, and if we do not we are in danger of being seen as irresponsible. 'There are two technologies at play here turning us into governable subjects – a technology of *agency* and a technology of *performance*' (Davies & Petersen, 2005, p. 93). We are produced rather than oppressed, animated rather than constrained! This is Martin's experience:

> My participants[3] see no problem in their focus on impression management. They proudly see themselves as promoting their institutions – and one could hardly blame them as they must compete for funding, for student enrolment, for allocation of resources within their districts, etc. The neoliberal or marketized environment has certainly created a new sort of principal. And one of the most interesting points is that many of them claim to reject the system of rankings/comparisons that has become the dominant mode of governance. Frequently, the school principals' own language says the opposite. (Martin)

These techniques of regulation and self-regulation are creating a new episteme of public service through a 'reshaping of "deep" social relations' (Leys, 2001, p. 2) which involve the subordination of moral and intellectual obligations to economic ones (Walzer, 1984) so that 'everything is simply a sum of value realised or hoped for' (Slater & Tonkiss, 2001, p. 162). Martin continues:

> Since practitioners (like me!) have become normalized into the discourse of 'constant improvement' and instrumentality/usefulness, it is difficult to see outside of this paradigm . . . . Every principal I interviewed was interested in constant or continuous improvement – and I'd be hard-pressed to find someone who didn't think this was a reasonable goal of the educational institution.

The rationality of performativity is presented as the new common sense, as something logical and desirable. Indeed, performativity works best when we come to want for ourselves what is wanted from us, when our moral sense of our desires and ourselves are aligned with its pleasures. Resisting performativity at a discursive level implies problematising the essence and 'raw material' of our own practices. It requires the deconstruction and recreation of the self and a certain capacity to examine ourselves critically. This is exactly what these teachers are doing throughout their correspondence:

> For example, when each of my participants says that his/her goal is to make sure that each student is college/career ready, it seems like a perfectly rational thing to say. Of course we want that for our students! But, would you say that this is something that should give me pause? Is this yet another example of performance accountability at work? Have the principals simply been normalized (as Foucault might put it) into using the discourse of the discipline? 'College/Career readiness' is, after all, the language of government documents, politicians, and state curriculum standards. I guess my issue is that it's difficult to get people to see that making such statements is problematic – that it leaves something out of schooling. (Martin)

Martin unsettles the mundane and rational truths of neoliberal education and questions the *obviousness* of things. Such questions fuel processes of introspection and allow the teachers to expose the power relations in which they are immersed. Walter is also troubling the inner logic of performativity. In a letter attached to his school's annual staff questionnaire, Walter confronts his school's new policy on internal evaluation. The new regulation consists of the introduction of termly lesson observations using the Ofsted [Office for Standards in Education] grade system.[4] While not rejecting the need for the evaluation of teachers' work he distinguishes between constructive and collegiate forms of feedback and those that he understands as 'beguiling but harmful' practices:

> Feedback must be a dialogue . . . . From a top-down perspective the requirement of termly judgements and re-judgements makes sense and is helpful as it produces reassuring spread sheets of data and hard evidence of 'Teacher X' moving from a 4 to a 3, a 1 to a 2 and so on. From the ground up however it looks and feels quite different. It is, for a number of teachers, demoralising, depressing, frustrating and very stressful. The judgement is made and without any dialogue there is no way to state your case; to draw attention to the shortcomings of the observations themselves, that is to shine a light on the limited perspective of the observer. (Walter)

These teachers are uncovering the often misleading and controversial line that separates practices of power from those of domination. Walter might be using different words but he is contextualising what Foucault says when he explained that 'power relations are not something that is a bad thing in itself' (Foucault, 1997a, p. 298). Power becomes a problem when 'an individual or social group succeeds in blocking a field of power relations, immobilizing them and preventing any reversibility of movement by economic, political, or military means' (1997a, p. 283). These situations are what could be termed *states of domination*, and they imply the almost total impossibility of developing practices of freedom. Foucault illustrates this idea more graphically as follows:

> I see nothing wrong in the practice of a person who, knowing more than others in a specific game of truth, tells those others what to do, teaches them, and transmits knowledge and techniques to them. The problem in such practices where power – which is not in itself a bad thing – must inevitably come into play is knowing how to avoid the kind of domination effects where a kid is subjected to the arbitrary and unnecessary authority of a teacher, or a student put under the thumb of a professor who abuses his authority. (1997a, pp. 298–299)

The effects of such impositions are experienced at symbolic and physical levels by many teachers. 'Demoralisation, depression, frustration, and stress' are tropes of experience that recur in the email correspondence quoted here. These are also signs of what Foucault (1982) understands as 'processes of confrontation', often not fully recognised by the actors but already on-going. This is resistance *to practices*. In these examples, neoliberalism is experienced and perceived in the classroom and in the soul, which confers a sense of 'immediacy', both in temporal and spatial terms. It is precisely at this level where 'people criticize instances of power which are the closest to them, those which exercise their action on individuals. They do not look for the "chief enemy," but for the immediate enemy' (Foucault, 1982, p. 211). Here, critique of externally imposed regimes of truth, represented in this case in the Ofsted inspection, is put to use not so much as a political tool in the usual sense but as a means of self-formation. This makes it more difficult to act and think 'as usual' and makes it possible to rethink our relationship to ourselves and to others, and our possibilities of existence, differently from what is expected.

The critiques of these teachers represent an attitude of 'hyper and pessimistic activism' as Foucault (1997a, p. 256) called it. They are uncovering in their everyday practices what Lazzarato (2009, p. 111) identified as the core strategies of the 'neoliberal transformation of the social', 'individualization, insecuritization and depolitization' (p. 109), all embodied in the enterprising subject. But, as Walter suggests, there is more to it than that. It is more than *simply* understanding the teaching subject as the 'entrepreneur of him/herself'. Performativity implies also accepting that 'these are things that we do to ourselves and to others' (Ball, 2003, p. 224).

> The 'Ofsted-style' grading is divisive and unhelpful. It's wrong for Ofsted to do it every few years and it's even more wrong for staff within a school to do it to each other every term . . . . The observer should not be jury and judge. It might make good TV like The Apprentice but it's no way to build morale and build a team. (Walter)

At the same time as it isolates the subject through processes of individualisation, performativity introduces a routine of constant reporting and recording of our practice. It installs a set of informational structures and performance indicators that become the principle of intelligibility of social relations. The latter become increasingly 'ephemeral, disposable, serial, fleeting' (Ball, 2004, p. 21), and are 'replaced by judgemental relations wherein persons [here we would include teachers and also students] are valued for their productivity alone. Their value as a person is eradicated' (Ball, 2003, p. 224). Another teacher explained it this way:

NEOLIBERALISM AND EDUCATION 137

> The whole thing is so weird. I obviously haven't found a resolution or I wouldn't be harping on about it. Just before Ofsted, County [the local education authority] wrote about seeing me as an 'outstanding teacher with my training and workshops I do in schools etc – they were full of praise and my head was full of nothing but praise – and I was really enjoying my work. Then in one fell swoop, Ofsted said that I had come into the school with 'my ideas' and was limiting progress in all pupils and gave me a 'satisfactory'. Then nobody believed anything I said about music and the rest is history. (Sarah)

In the realms of performativity, as Peters puts it, 'value displaces values' (2001, p. 17). Results are prioritised over processes, numbers over experiences, procedures over ideas, productivity over creativity. Furthermore, the technologies put in place here are a manifestation of 'dividing practices' that work to identify, valorise and reward successful and productive subjects (Miller & Rose, 2008, p. 98), and target for exile or for reform, the 'irresponsible', those who fail to re-make themselves in 'the image of the market' (Gillies, 2011, p. 215).

> I am currently working in a failing college context – where values/ethos are highly disregarded because they are 'soft' concepts and not quickly translated into measurable impact, and where instead, monitoring at every level is preferred (internal and external) amid a deep seated lack of trust (from a leadership perspective). (Alice)

Resisting what works!

This group of teachers is struggling to produce identity and meaning within the structural and discursive limitations of their everyday practice. For instance, as one of the head teachers acknowledges, one of the mechanisms by which these limitations are enacted in classrooms is what he identified as 'the audit-managerial monolith' and which he portrays as functioning as follows:

> The effects are dire – harming the real job to an extreme degree, and undermining confidence in the service so that parents are at our throats. They are confused by a mismatch of rhetoric, reality and expectation and here it is descending into a mire of confusion and despondency. The work overload of drowning in specificatory garbage to irrelevant notions, which ever-change and for which you are damned for the impossibility of keeping up, dealing with damage and somehow trying to find the space for real work which 'they' are not in the slightest bit interested in, is exhausting. How to break out? (Nigel)

In the midst of these cold, machinic, calculative techniques, 'we become ontologically insecure' and 'uncertain about the reasons for actions' (Ball, 2003 p. 220). Teachers are no longer encouraged to have a rationale for practice, account of themselves in terms of a relationship to the meaningfulness of *what they do*, but are required to produce measurable and 'improving' outputs and performances, what is important is *what works*. We are in danger of becoming transparent but empty, unrecognisable to ourselves – 'I am other to myself precisely at the place where I expect to be myself' (Butler, 2004, p. 15).

What is being called into question here is what Foucault calls the '*régime du savoir*', that is 'the way in which knowledge circulates and functions, its relations to power' (Foucault, 1982, p. 212). Below Paul highlights the need to question the truths of education and those of the teaching profession and to rearticulate the teacher as a pedagogical subject whose responsibility, as Foucault suggested, is 'to keep watch over the excessive powers of political rationality' (1982, p. 210).

> Perhaps the years of SATs and National Strategies [literacy and numeracy], the colonisation of state schooling by neoliberal definitions and values which have ousted those of public service (as Stephen Ball has made clear) and the huge increase in central government reach and diktat have re-shaped what education-in-schools means fundamentally, so that certain (oppositional/submerged) discourses have become unintelligible. (Paul)

This re-imagining of power involves bringing the teacher back into the sphere of the *political*, as an actor who takes up a position in relation to new discourses and truths and who looks critically at the meaning and enactment of policy. It implies an analysis of the structural conditions of the educational system alongside a critical scrutiny of our own practices and beliefs:

> The data-drivers, or the engine of hyper-accountability now, is mainly to do with tracking each student's progress through the levels, and expecting everyone to make 3 levels' progress across secondary school. There are ways this can be presented as positive, though I'd maintain it directs teachers to teach-the-test and is reductive of both students and a notion of education. (Paul)

Two regimes of truth are in opposition here, two systems of value and values. One produces measureable teaching subjects, whose qualities are represented in categories of judgement. The other is vested in a pedagogy of context and experience, intelligible within a set of collegial relations:

> I have known staff to engage with the most challenging and disaffected children, and gain their interest, respect and productive engagement (some of the time). Walk into the room and nothing leaps out as 'excellent'. But get to know those pupils, and those staff, and you will find they have genuinely excelled themselves in what they have achieved, over time. (Nigel)

Nigel here refuses the credibility of external metrics and judgements that tell the teacher what he or she is, including both internal procedures in the form of observation protocols developed within the schools, among colleagues, and external inspections and evaluations. Neither relate to what Nigel understands as the central and defining aspects of the work of the teacher. More fundamentally, these struggles have to do with the right to define ourselves according to our own judgements, or, in other words, to develop a particular *technology of the self* according to our own principles, an aesthetics of the self (Foucault, 1992, 2010b), which are focused on the question of *who we are* and *who we might become*, that is on *askesis* and 'the labour of becoming' (Venn & Terranova, 2009, p. 3). As Foucault points out, they 'revolve around the question: Who are we? They are a refusal of these abstractions, of economic and ideological state violence which ignore who we are individually, and also a refusal of a scientific or administrative inquisition which determines who one is' (Foucault, 1982, p. 212).

> But what about those teachers judged 'good' or 'outstanding'? Firstly I'm not convinced that the best teachers ever think of themselves as 'outstanding'. You are a teacher, always learning. More importantly where does a teacher go who is labelled 'outstanding'? This label may well be applied within the first year or two of a teacher's career! Can you be 'outstanding' after 2 or 3 years teaching? I think you can but only if 'outstanding' is defined as the possession of a limited set of skills combined with the ability to comply with your individual school's lesson protocol. The minority of inadequate teachers can be dealt with, and the few outstanding teachers, and it is a few if this term is going to have any real meaning, can be led towards Advanced Skills Teacher (AST) status or similar. This leaves the vast majority of teachers on a level playing field – your goods and adequates – working on their skills/knowledge/expertise in a mutually supportive environment. (Walter)

Walter is undertaking a 're-problematisation' of the present that 'dismantles the coordinates of his or her starting point and indicates the possibility of a different experience' (Burchell, 1996, p. 31).

All of this relates back to and rests on Foucault's efforts at making the subject historically mutable and thus the possibility of 'making ourselves open to transformation' (Taylor, 2011, p. 112). As he said in an interview: 'My role – and that is too emphatic a word – is to show people that they are freer than they think' (Martin, 1988, pp. 10–11). These words seem directed to Walter:

> A new curriculum direction sprang to the fore here – the ill named Curriculum for Excellence, and our control system set about subverting it, not from the outside by opposing it, but by undermining it conceptually, procedurally and linguistically, from the inside . . . . Somehow I can 'see' this. But not hard when you live it, since they swamp you with performative goo. If you resist they add thickening agent,[5] . . . And all I wanted was to do my job! (Walter)

Walter's apparent pessimism could be seen from another perspective as a calculative process of decision-making. It represents a strategic recess, a pause for assessment – he is aware that the risks of 'truth-telling' (Tamboukou, 2012) stand over and against the costs of silence (see below). This exercise sets the basis for ethical responses which are founded on the existence of practices of freedom: 'Freedom is the ontological condition of ethics. But ethics is the considered form that freedom takes when it is informed by reflection' (Foucault, 1997a, p. 284). The practices of resistance apparent here are about deciphering, understanding, unravelling and retranslating.

> We as a University have a great reputation of drawing in students who are often the first in family to go to Uni, who live in the local area, who have families, jobs etc and who come to us because they know we have a great reputation for student support, valuing diversity focus . . . . However our Uni's aim is to be in the 1st quartile of the league tables and I am not sure the two things can actually co-exist. I want to work in an organisation known for the difference it makes to the local community as much as the international community, increasing entry tariffs has already seen a shift in the backgrounds of the students that come to us. (Natalie)

A conclusion in becoming

Resisting the flows of neoliberalism is different from past struggles. For now it also encompasses resisting our own practices, it is about confronting oneself at the centre of our discomforts. If one follows the logic of critique we end up finding out that we are precisely the ones to be blamed. Resistance to dominant discourse(s) and the technologies in which they are shaped, implies that we must change our understanding of what being a teacher is all about. All of this involves constant and organised work on the self, that is, the 'establishment of a certain objectivity, the development of a politics and a government of the self, and an elaboration of an ethics and practice in regard to oneself' (Foucault, 1997a, p. 117).

We said at the beginning that we would say something about the form of these cases. They are all drawn from email exchanges initiated by the teachers. The emails, we would suggest, are part of the process of struggle against, of critique, of making things intolerable, of 'unsettling' and the struggle to be different. 'One's idea of what one is struggling against has a direct impact on what one becomes as one struggles' (Blacker, 1998, p. 357). The emails provide a way for these teachers to articulate themselves and their practice differently by opening up spaces of doubt. Foucault saw writing as a key technique of the 'arts of the self', and a means for exploring the 'aesthetics of existence' and for inquiring into the government of self and others (Foucault, 1997b). He presented self-writing as a deliberate, self-conscious attempt to explain and express oneself to an audience within which one exists and from whom one seeks confirmation (see Peters, 2000). The email may be understood as both part of an attempt to 'mark out an ethical space' (Burchell, 1996, p. 34) within which the teacher might teach differently and ways of exploring the possibilities and impossibilities of transgression.

However, there are *costs* to be considered here, the costs of constant vigilance, the costs of a commitment to a kind of 'permanent agonism' (Burchell, 1996, p. 34), the possibilities of ridicule and precarity – what Lazzarato calls the 'micro-politics of little fears' (2009, p. 120). Over and against these there are the costs of silence, and who bears them – in what is nonetheless an increasingly one-sided 'parrhesiastic game' (Foucault, 2001, p. 13). If we take Foucault seriously we must confront the problem of standing outside our own history, outside of ourselves, and do ethical work on ourselves.

We are not suggesting that the analysis we have laid out above is clear-cut, or indeed that the tensions between domination and freedom in Foucault's later work were ever fully resolved; their development was ended by his death and taken up by others. But Foucault's work provides a way of thinking about resistance and freedom which focuses on subjectivity, transgression and possibility that does not rely on the mobilisation of grand narratives, or simple normativities, but rather recognises the courage displayed in refusing the mundane, in turning away from excellence, in unsettling truths – or the 'activity of self-overcoming [that] is constituted through transgressing social practices' (Owen, 1994, p. 205). It is an invitation to the practice of 'concrete liberty', which is localised and flexible, a liberty which is created in and through acts of resistance and processes of self-definition. We write here in part as audience, but also as fellow strugglers, to validate these attempts at self-overcoming, as we at the same time attempt our own. These attempts may also have more general significance in helping to distinguish 'between those elements of present social reality which remain necessary and unchangeable from those which are open to change' (Patton, 1995, p. 357). All of this involves recognition of the possibilities of power, the fragility of freedom and the limits of contingency and domination, while seeking a space within them. The focus of our analysis and discussion has been on individuals and their struggles to recognise different possibilities of power. One such possibility is clearly offered in relations with others who share the same discomforts. These others might not be available in the staffroom but they may be within everyday social relations, union meetings or on social media sites. That is to say: 'It is not that a politics informed by aesthetics would necessarily eschew or discourage social consensus and solidarity' (Pigantelli, 1993, p. 426). There are already examples described by the teachers in the email exchanges of campaigns, discussions and meetings in which singular struggles are shared and common experiences recognised. The point is that these commonalities are not established from a priori political positions but through work on and over and against practices and on what it means to be a teacher, what it means to be educated, and what is means to be revocable.

Notes

1. The teachers quoted in the text initially contacted Stephen to indicate ways in which his writing on performativity 'spoke' to their experience and aligned with their sense of fear and anger. It was later that the ensuing exchanges were recognised as offering a way of understanding situated struggles over subjectivity. The interlocutors were asked whether their emails could be used and quoted in a paper and all were willing and interested. Pseudonyms have been used. There is no 'method' involved here apart from a careful reading and re-reading of the email texts.

2. Foucault explains his particular use of the article *how*: "*"How," not in the sense of "How does it manifest itself?" but "By what means is it exercised?" and "What happens when individuals exert (as they say) power over others?"*' (Foucault, 1982, p. 217; emphasis in the original).
3. Michael is a primary school head teacher doing a PhD. He is in the process of analysing his interviews with a group of fellow head teachers.
4. The Ofsted evaluation system is compounded of four grades, defined as: 1: Outstanding; 2: Good; 3: Satisfactory; 4: Inadequate (for more information about Ofsted evaluation scheme see: http://www.ofsted.gov.uk/schools).
5. From this Autumn, Ofsted inspections in England will be carried out without the need to give notice to schools prior to the visit of the inspectors. According to Sir Michael Wilshaw, HM Chief inspector, this measure will allow inspector to see the classroom 'as they really are' (Wilshaw on The Guardian, 01/10/2012). Alongside, the House of Commons Education Committee released on May 1st, its Ninth Report of Session 2010–2012 entitled: 'Great teachers: attracting, training and retaining the best'. The title itself summarises many of the aspects and relates to the technologies referred to in our correspondence with the teachers. The Committee openly suggests that: 'No longer should the weakest teachers be able to hide behind a rigid and unfair pay structure. We believe that performance management systems should support and reward the strongest teachers, as well as make no excuses (or, worse, incentives to remain) for the weaker' and a bit further summarises, 'We further recommend that the Department develop proposals (based on consultation and a close study of systems abroad) for a pay system which rewards those teachers who add the greatest value to pupil performance' (House of Commons Education Committee, 2012, p. 47).

References

Apple, M.W. (2012). *Can education change society?* New York, NY: Routledge.
Ball, S.J. (2003). The teacher's soul and the terrors of performativity. *Journal of Education Policy*, *18*, 215–228.
Ball, S.J. (2004). *Education for sale! The commodification of everything? The annual education lecture 2004*. London: King's College London.
Ball, S.J. (2012). *Foucault, power and education*. New York, NY: Routledge.
Blacker, D. (1998). Intellectuals at work and in power: Toward a Foucauldian research ethic. In T.S. Popkewitz & M. Brennan (Eds.), *Foucault's challenge: Discourse, knowledge and power in education* (pp. 348–368). New York, NY: Teachers College Press.
Burchell, G. (1996). Liberal government and the techniques of the self. In A. Barry, T. Osborne, & N.S. Rose (Eds.), *Foucault and political reason* (pp. 19–36). London: UCL Press.
Butler, J. (2004). *Undoing gender*. New York, NY and London: Routledge.
Davies, B., & Petersen, E.B. (2005). Neo-Liberal discourse and the academy: The forestalling of (collective) resistance. *Learning and Teaching in the Social Sciences, 2*, 77–79.
Dean, M. (2010). *Governmentality: Power and rule in modern society* (2nd ed.). London: Sage Publications.
Foucault, M. (1982). The subject and power. In H. Dreyfus & P. Rabinow (Eds.), *Michel Foucault: Beyond structuralism and hermeneutics* (pp. 208–226). Chicago, IL: University of Chicago Press.
Foucault, M. (1992). *The history of sexuality, vol. 2: The use of pleasure*. Harmondsworth: Penguin.

Foucault, M. (1997a). *Ethics: Subjectivity and truth. The essential works of Michel Foucault, 1954–1984* (Vol. 1). New York, NY: The New Press.

Foucault, M. (1997b). Writing the self. In A. Davidson (Ed.), *Foucault and his interlocutors* (pp. 234–247). Chicago, IL: University of Chicago Press.

Foucault, M. (2001). *Fearless speech*. Los Angeles, CA: Semiotext(e).

Foucault, M. (2009). *Security, territory, population: Lectures at the College de France 1977–78*. New York, NY: Palgrave Macmillan.

Foucault, M. (2010a). *The birth of biopolitics. Lectures at the Collège de France 1978–1979*. Basingstoke: Palgrave Macmillan.

Foucault, M. (2010b). *The government of the self and others: Lectures at the College de France 1982–1983*. Basingstoke: Palgrave Macmillan.

Gillies, D. (2011). Agile bodies: A new imperative in neoliberal governance. *Journal of Education Policy, 26*, 207–223.

House of Commons Education Committee. (2012). *Ninth report. Great teachers: Attracting, training and retaining the best* (Vol. 1). London: The Stationery Office Limited.

Jessop, B. (2002). *The future of the capitalist state*. Cambridge: Polity Press.

Lazzarato, M. (2009). Neoliberalism in action. Inequality, insecurity and the reconstitution of the social. *Theory, Culture & Society, 26*, 109–133.

Leys, M. (2001). *Market-driven politics*. London: Verso.

Martin, R. (1988). Truth, power, self: An interview with Michel Foucault. In L.H. Martin, H. Gutman, & P.H. Hutton (Eds.), *Technologies of the self. A seminar with Michel Foucault* (pp. 9–15). Amherst, MA: University of Massachusetts Press.

McGushin, E. (2011). Foucault's theory and practice of subjectivity. In D. Taylor (Ed.), *Michel Foucault: Key concepts*. Durham: Acumen.

Miller, P., & Rose, N.S. (2008). *Governing the present*. Cambridge: Polity Press.

Ong, A. (2007). Neoliberalism as a mobile technology. *Transactions of the Institute of British Geographers, 32*, 3–8.

Owen, D. (1994). *Maturity and modernity: Nietzsche, Weber, Foucault and the ambivalence of reason*. London: Routledge.

Patton, P. (1995). Taylor and Foucault on power and freedom. In B. Smart (Ed.), *Michel Foucault: Critical assessments* (Vol. 5, pp. 352–370). London: Routledge.

Peck, J., & Tickell, A. (2002). Neoliberalizing space. *Antipode, 34*, 380–404.

Peters, M. (2000). Writing the self: Wittgenstein, confession and pedagogy. *Journal of Philosophy of Education, 34*, 353–368.

Peters, M. (2001). Education, enterprise culture and the entrepreneurial self: A Foucualdian perspective. *Journal of Educational Enquiry, 2*, 58–71.

Pignatelli, F. (1993). What can I do? Foucault on freedom and the question of teacher agency. *Educational Theory, 43*, 411–432.

Rose, N.S. (1996). Governing 'advanced' liberal democracies. In A. Barry, T. Osborne, & N.S. Rose (Eds.), *Foucault and political reason: Liberalism, neo-liberalism and rationalities of government* (pp. 37–62). Chicago, IL: University of Chicago Press.

Slater, D., & Tonkiss, F. (2001). *Market society*. Cambridge: Polity Press.

Tamboukou, M. (2012). Truth telling in Foucault and Arendt: Parrhesia, the pariah and academics in dark times. *Journal of Education Policy*. doi/abs/10.1080/02680939.2012.694482

Taylor, D. (2011). Practices of the self. In D. Taylor (Ed.), *Michel Foucault: Key concepts*. Durham: Acumen.

Venn, C., & Terranova, T. (2009). Introduction. Thinking after Michel Foucault. *Theory, Culture & Society, 26*(6), 1–11.

Walzer, M. (1984). *Spheres of justice: A defence of pluralism and equality*. Oxford: Martin Robertson.

Nuancing the critique of commercialisation in schools: recognising teacher agency

Anna Hogan ⓘ, Eimear Enright ⓘ, Michalis Stylianou ⓘ and Louise McCuaig

ABSTRACT
This paper investigates the commercialisation of Social and Emotional Learning (SEL) in Australian schools. Specifically, it focuses on understanding why teachers value commercial resources, and how they enact these in their classrooms. Theorising around teacher agency suggests teachers are now choosing to use a range of commercial resources and view these as important additions to their pedagogical toolbox. Teachers want high quality resources, and they prefer resources that are easy to import, scaffold and modify according to their specific needs. Teachers did not readily see the benefit of a prescriptive SEL program. Instead, they wanted multiple resources that they could pick and choose the best bits from. Our data suggests that teachers are not being seduced by commercialisation and the 'easy fix' it promises, but are in fact presenting as agentic professionals who care deeply about students' social and emotional wellbeing and are working to tailor bespoke learning experiences to meet the needs of their students within their specific school contexts. We argue that it is worth nuancing the critique about commercialisation offered in the literature to date, and suggest that commercialisation is not inherently bad, rather it is the 'intensity' of commercialisation that needs to be regulated and further investigated.

Introduction

This paper reports on teacher and school leader perceptions of commercialised Social and Emotional Learning (SEL) resources in Australian schools using data generated through a series of focus group interviews. As private providers are now major suppliers of education products and services to schools, there is urgent need for research that investigates the affordances and dangers of commercialisation. A common critique in recent scholarship is that commercialisation undermines the role of schools as equitable and just learning centres, positioning them instead as centres of capital investment for private interests (Kenway, Bigum, and Fitzclarence 2006). Moreover, there is a general consensus that schools and teachers accept these services uncritically as they have been primed to view commercialisation as pragmatic (in terms of time and investment) and educationally valuable (Powell 2015). Indeed, commercial providers have been labelled as offering ready-made 'solutions' to various education 'problems' across large scales (Ball 2012) and as such, are now firmly entrenched in schools as a seemingly necessary way to deliver education in the twenty-first century (Burch 2009).

While there has been much debate about the appropriateness of commercialisation, this has largely focused on questions of morality, equity and social justice. Research has critiqued private providers from large, multinational firms to much smaller local providers, and argued that despite their scale, these corporations tend to be driven by generating profits through the sale of their goods and services (Au and Ferrare 2015; Verger, Lubienski, and Steiner-Khamis 2016). We agree that this characterisation might be true in many cases, but we also argue that to date, very little research has considered commercialisation from the perspective of teachers and school leaders. In fact, we argue there is room to explore a more nuanced argument, and investigate whether commercial resources have the potential to support teachers in delivering learning experiences for students, just as the traditional commercialised textbook has done for over a century (Callaghan 1964).

This paper proceeds by, first, defining commercialisation and contextualising the use of commercial SEL resources in Australian schools. Drawing from Priestley, Biesta, and Robinson's (2015) work, we highlight that teacher agency is an important consideration in understanding the use and influence of commercial resources in schools and classrooms. Second, the paper presents data from teachers and school leaders expressing their perceptions about the affordances of commercial SEL resources and how these allow them enhanced opportunities to create meaningful learning experiences for their students. In presenting these data, we also highlight the hidden dangers of commercialisation, including the fact that private providers have considerable influence over what SEL competencies are taught and valued in schools, that the SEL marketplace is fragmented and overcrowded, and that there is a considerable flow of public education money to the private sector. Notwithstanding these issues, this paper argues that teachers are becoming discerning actors within the commercialised schooling marketplace and are enacting their agency to control the extent to which their classrooms become commercialised.

Defining commercialisation

We define commercialisation, for the purposes of this paper, as the creation, marketing and sale of education goods and services to schools by private providers (Hogan and Thompson 2017). By private providers we mean both for-profit and not-for-profit organisations, as distinct from government agencies. The sale of education goods to schools has had a long and relatively uncontroversial history. If we consider the private provision of textbooks, computers, transport services and food supplies, commercialisation is a practice that has always existed to some extent in state schooling systems (Molnar 2007). However, recent work has suggested that corporations are now investing in education in unprecedented (and divisive) ways. Over the past few decades there has been a dramatic proliferation of the commercialised products and services on offer to schools. The reasons for this increase have been shaped by shifting logics in the governance of public institutions and subsequently, their economisation through market forces (Verger, Lubienski, and Steiner-Khamis 2016).

In schooling this tends to play out through decentralisation discourses and the global adoption of education policies such as standardised testing, accountability infrastructures and performance management techniques (see Verger, Lubienski, and Steiner-Khamis 2016,

6–11). These policy logics create quasi-markets in which commercial providers can prosper (Hogan and Thompson 2017). For instance, Burch (2009) argues that policies that focus on 'education reform' through testing and accountability have worked to create the need for commercial products and services targeted at improved student outcomes. As Molnar (2007, 622) observes, the intense external pressure schools now face to raise student performance 'makes commercialized offers of assistance, if not very attractive, at least politically convenient'. These services often include the provision of curriculum content, assessment services, data infrastructures, digital learning, remedial instruction, professional development for staff and administrative support. The important distinction between commercialisation and privatisation is that commercialisation involves providers working with and within public schools to support educational processes, rather than taking over the establishment and management of schools (e.g. privatised school models such as low-fee for-profit schools, U.S. Charter Schools, U.K. Academies and Swedish Free Schools) (Ronnberg 2016). Thus, in commercialised school systems public monies fund commercial businesses. In fact, the multiple profit opportunities that now exist in schooling and education more broadly has led to the emergence of a 'global education industry' already worth $4.3 trillion annually (Robertson and Komljenovic 2016).

The extent of the commercialisation of teaching and learning processes is often hidden because there is little empirical research on commercialisation in schools. One line of inquiry has been focused on large multinational corporations like Pearson, where it has been critiqued for creating a global monopoly in the education marketplace and selling products at scale with very little variation for national contexts (Riep 2017). Another example has been the burgeoning literature associated with the investigation of the 'outsourcing' phenomenon in schools where private providers are hired to deliver subjects like Health and Physical Education, displacing the pedagogical expertise of teachers and value of the curriculum (Williams, Hay, and Macdonald 2011; Penney, Petrie, and Fellows 2015; Powell 2015; Sperka and Enright 2017). This paper focuses on the case of SEL in Australia as an increasingly common manifestation of commercialisation in schools.

Contextualising SEL commercialisation in Australia

Commercialised SEL is an increasingly popular phenomenon in Australia. Similar to the way it is conceived in the UK and USA, there is a prevailing logic that SEL can be implemented in schools as an easy 'fix' to a diverse range of issues that young people face today. Research argues that effective SEL programs can work to reduce problem behaviours, decrease emotional distress, improve social and emotional skills and even increase standardised test scores for students (see Durlak et al.'s (2011) meta analysis of SEL programs in the USA). The weight of evidence suggests that SEL is a worthwhile addition to any school context (Elias 2006; Banerjee, Weare, and Farr 2014; Durlak et al. 2015). Interestingly, SEL in Australia is not conceived as a formal learning area, however, it is described as a general capability of the Australian curriculum, meaning that all teachers, across all learning areas, from Foundation to Year 10, have the responsibility to develop students' personal, social and emotional capabilities. Thus, the problem that most Australian schools and teachers encounter when adopting SEL is deciding where, and how, it fits within the formal school curriculum and who has the responsibility for teaching it (Humphrey 2013).

One solution to this complexity has been provided by private sector organisations. In Australia, for example, the government endorsed and funded initiative, KidsMatter, is a website that provides comprehensive information about SEL for Australian primary schools. Included within this is the 'Programs Guide' to assist 'schools in making informed decisions about appropriate and effective SEL programs'. KidsMatter identifies over 100 commercially available SEL programs and provides information on each of these to 'help schools make an informed choice when selecting a program to address the particular needs of their students'.[1] KidsMatter even provides a range of free survey tools for schools to ascertain what these needs might be. The interesting point here is that a government-endorsed organisation highlights commercial programs as the most effective way for schools to enact SEL.

Research to date has predominately focused on how likely these SEL programs are to improve student outcomes (see Durlak et al. 2011, 2015). While this is important research, particularly considering the significant investment some schools are making in purchasing commercial SEL programs, our argument is that there are potentially broader issues at play that are also worth considering. For example, no research has yet considered the rationale underpinning why schools and teachers are so readily purchasing commercial SEL programs. Some scholars have expressed unease about this phenomenon in terms of schools uncritically adopting SEL programs (Humphrey 2013), particularly programs that are underpinned by pedagogies of 'direct instruction' and are supported by basic resources that constrain how young people understand and engage with social and emotional issues (Ashdown and Bernard 2012). Gard and Pluim (2014, 202) have further cautioned that SEL might be used as 'rhetorical camouflage for commercial activity' where private providers are capitalising on a concern for student health and wellbeing as a way to establish a presence within schools. The idea that private providers are selling SEL programs to schools on a for-profit basis is a complex phenomenon that requires in-depth investigation. We argue that an important step towards addressing this issue is to first comprehend the rationale for SEL commercialisation from the perspective of school leaders and teachers. The aim of this paper is to do this within the Australian context, and draw some inferences about teacher agency and thus, the skills and capabilities that teachers might need to employ when working within the commercialised school landscape.

Teacher agency and the appeal of commercialisation

To better understand the rationale for using commercial SEL programs we draw from Priestley, Biesta and Robinson's work on teacher agency. While various definitions of teacher agency abound, it is important to highlight that in this paper, following Priestley et al. (2012, 211), we have taken the view that 'teacher agency is largely about repertoires for manoeuvre, or the possibilities for different forms of action available to teachers at particular points in time'. While individual agency has been extensively theorised to understand the different factors that affect social action, teacher agency, that is, 'agency that is theorised specifically in respect of the activities of teachers in schools', has been subject to little explicit research or theory development (Biesta, Priestley, and Robinson 2015, 624). As Biesta, Priestley and Robinson argue, this is a significant issue because of the acknowledged importance of how teacher agency constructs the day-to-day reality of educational practice in schools and classrooms.

Teachers use their agency to adopt, adapt or oppose education policy directives (Lasky 2005). However, teacher agency is not only constructed by an individual teacher's identity – that is their past experiences, current setting and envisaged future possibilities, but also the structural and cultural features of the school in which they work (Biesta, Priestley, and Robinson 2015). This means a teacher's agency shapes and is shaped by the demands, opportunities and constraints of their work, including workplace conditions, professional relationships, school leadership and structural organisation (Buchanan 2015). This ecological view of agency shifts the emphasis from what teachers have (skills, knowledge and capacity), to what they can do and achieve by means of the environment in which they act (MacLean 2016).

For Biesta, Priestley, and Robinson (2015), this suggests that teacher agency is an emergent phenomenon of an 'actor-situation transaction'. Framing agency in this way means understanding the dialectic between how teachers are interpreting and responding to the demands of practice (Edwards 2015). For example, in the context of SEL in Australia, teachers may interpret the general capability of SEL as important to enact in their classrooms, but may either face opportunities or constraints for enactment given the broader culture of their school. Biesta (2010) argues that in matters of curriculum reform, school leadership should ensure teachers have access to resources that support their capacity to plan for change, as well as structures to ensure they have sufficient time to actually enact the change. Thus, in this example, we can see teacher agency is an interplay of individual motivation, resources and time.

Of course, agentic factors always interact in unique ways and contemporary policy actually works to influence this relationship. Often policy is construed to either give enhanced opportunities for teachers to exert judgement and control over their work (e.g. greater teacher autonomy), or reduced opportunities to critically engage with decisions around their work through moves to deprofessionalise teachers via highly prescriptive curricular, enhanced accountability infrastructures and performance management systems (Biesta 2010). These structures can obviously shape agency, and how teachers understand and define their role and their successes. As Buchanan (2015) notes, teachers often talk about standardised testing in contradictory ways, where they dislike the testing climate in their schools, but also feel professionally validated when their students are successful on those measures of assessment. Thus, teachers are generally motivated to find time and resources to help prepare students for high stakes standardised assessments, and returning to Burch's (2009) argument, it is in this environment that private providers have prospered.

Beyond assessment, education products and services are now marketed at schools and teachers across a plethora of learning areas, and it appears these commercial services are in high demand (Lingard et al. 2017). Teachers cite an overcrowded curriculum, time constraints, lack of content expertise and the usefulness of commercial resources in developing innovative learning experiences as key reasons to access commercial services (Williams, Hay, and Macdonald 2011; Lingard et al. 2017). In fact, teacher belief is highlighted by Biesta, Priestley, and Robinson (2015) as an important component of agency that, coupled with teacher capacities and school structures, can make certain things seem impossible for teachers to enact. Thus, using the theory of teacher agency, we seek to identify both the challenges and affordances to teachers' perceived capacity to teach SEL, and the relationship between teacher agency and the commercialisation of teaching and learning resources.

The case of SEL commercialisation in Australia

In this paper we report on data gathered from 5 focus group interviews with 35 participants from Queensland and South Australia (see Table 1). The participants included currently practicing teachers, school leaders, school counsellors and chaplains whose voices were seen as necessary to provide contextualised insight into the commercialisation of SEL delivery in Australian school settings. Informed consent documentation was collected at the beginning of each focus group with each session taking between 90 and 120 min.

The focus groups involved a semi-structured interview process that was guided by an interview protocol comprising a series of open-ended questions. The questions focused on participants' understandings of SEL and the current practices of SEL in schools, including the barriers and enablers that support the teaching of SEL. Focus groups were conducted by one to three researchers, with all conversations recorded on a digital voice recorder. Following the interviews, all recorded information was transcribed in full. Data from the focus groups were analysed using a qualitative deductive approach based on a pre-determined coding scheme aligned with a series of interrelated questions (Elo and Kyngäs 2008). In this paper we present data through these interrelated questions that ultimately explicate the underpinning rationale for the use of commercial SEL programs in Australian schools.

As a brief overview, we found teachers' perspectives about what constitutes SEL, why it is important to teach SEL in schools, and the challenges teachers face in delivering relevant SEL content to students largely aligned with findings from previous research (Durlak et al. 2015; Humphrey 2013). For example, participants referenced that SEL competencies, including 'sympathy', 'empathy', 'resilience', 'stamina', 'grit', 'acceptance', 'the ability to read body language', 'how to recognise and deal with emotion', and the capacity to 'form and develop productive relationships' are not only necessary for a happy, productive life, but are also essential for enhancing a student's ability to learn and succeed academically. Moreover, there was a general narrative amongst participants that teaching these competencies to students was part of the broader shift of teachers having to compensate for parental deficits and engage in 'pseudo parenting':

> I would say when I first started teaching... that they were the skills that parents really took responsibility for, and just the way society's changed, that for some reason the pendulum for who needs to have responsibility for teaching those skills is more weighted on schools now. (Teacher, SA 2)

Despite this largely shared understanding, teachers also agreed that implementing a meaningful SEL program in their classrooms was not a straightforward matter. Challenges cited by teachers included finding time in an already overcrowded Australian curriculum as well as their perceived lack of confidence and competence to teach SEL to their students. This was evident for example, when a teacher shared her thought process during a SEL discussion at her school:

> Then I started thinking, I wonder if I'd be able to teach that part? Would I feel comfortable enough, not having had that background training in it? I think it's important to make sure people have the skills to teach it effectively. (Teacher, QLD 2)

Another teacher suggested that sometimes it is easier to say nothing than say the wrong thing, and that despite having good and honest intentions, without the knowledge to have the 'right' conversations, situations could be made worse and harm done to students. She summarises, 'I think we just sort of go, "maybe someone else can do that for us" ...' (Teacher,

SA 1). These expressed feelings are not uncommon and research has highlighted that class-room teachers need not only knowledge of their students, but expertise in the delivery of social and emotional competencies to respond to students' needs and create learning experiences that allow students to better develop these skills (St Leger 2006). Perhaps unsur-prisingly then, participants unanimously argued that for them to effectively implement SEL in their classrooms they required high-quality commercial resources. It is this finding that we want to focus on in order to better understand the affordances (and potential hidden dangers) of commercialised products in the day-to-day practices of teaching and learning.

Perceived affordances (and hidden dangers)

Teachers perceived commercial SEL resources as serving multiple functions, including the highlighting of relevant SEL content that can be taught to students, provision of ideas for innovative student learning experiences and articulation of relevant links between SEL con-tent and the Australian curriculum. As one school leader commented, commercial resources provide an important starting point for her teachers to implement an SEL program (Deputy Principal, QLD 2) and similarly, a teacher argued some of her 'best ideas' and 'strategies' have come from these (Teacher, SA 3). Others made a more pragmatic point that they felt 'time poor' in their classrooms and commercial programs allowed them to 'tick off' aspects of the curriculum without them 'having to go searching for the links themselves' (Focus Group, QLD 1). As Burch (2009) argues, teachers have welcomed commercial products into their classrooms not only for content-specific instructional material, but also for technical assistance in how they might improve their teaching practice. She does observe, however, that this acceptance has resulted in private sector organisations having considerable influ-ence over what is taught and valued in schools.

Our data reveals that SEL providers are assuming responsibility for the design and imple-mentation of SEL in Australian schools, and often market their products as a 'solution' to a particular 'problem' students might be facing. Indeed, participants, and particularly school leaders, referenced they selected commercial SEL programs dependent on the needs of their school community: 'Okay, we've got a whole lot of Grade 6 [11–12 years old] boys that are disengaged. What can we do? Then we match a program to what's suitable, what funding we've got, what time we've got.' (School Principal, QLD 2). From one perspective, this selection process represents efforts by school personnel to leverage market resources in order to meet specific student needs. However, from a more precautious perspective, when a school purchases SEL products they are essentially hiring a private provider to act as a critical extension of educationally sound practice – to set preferences for what educational outcomes matter and to design interventions based on these outcomes.

The effects of this, as warned by Bulkley and Burch (2011), is that the SEL marketplace has become fragmented, with more providers selling more and different kinds of prod-ucts and services. Scholars have argued that some private providers, such as Pearson, have been able to offer schools a 'one stop shop' to school improvement, offering a full gamut of services from curriculum and learning materials to assessment needs, data infrastruc-tures and teacher professional development (Ball 2012). Yet, it is clear from participants' perspectives that no one SEL provider (yet) offers holistic SEL development to Australian schools. This means that teachers were constantly evaluating the programs they had access to, and numerous teachers noted that fidelity to any one resource was not productive. As one teacher explained:

> I guess as teachers we don't want to be the school that takes a program off the shelf, and says, here, [solve] that. We've not done that for anything really ... we really want to look at what is the research that this is based on as well, in terms of 'Is this something that might fill our needs, or help in some way to fill our needs?' (Teacher, QLD 2)

Similarly, another teacher discussed: 'We're not just sticking to one program, and this is what we're doing for the next 20 years ... we're constantly looking for up-to-date things' (Teacher, SA 1). Another argued, 'we take the best bits of lots of stuff' as 'there is never going to be a program that covers everything ... so certainly more than one is good' (Teacher, SA 2). As a teacher (QLD 1) summarised:

> Once you have all the information, you make the decision about what you can and can't do. It needs to suit the kids on the day. Sometimes you might think, 'you know what, doing this is going to work better today'. So, we're going to do that.

Thus, from the perspective of teachers, it is obvious they draw on these commercial resources to enact agency. As Priestley, Biesta, and Robinson (2015, 3) reminds us, these resources allow teachers to exercise agency in translating and adapting curricular to fit the cultural, social and material structure of their individual school and their particular student needs. Indeed, these data suggest that schools and teachers were not reliant on any one commercial program but were using a range of resources to fit their own unique situation. Again, this underscores the notion that agency is not something teachers possess, but is something teachers do in critically shaping their responses to problematic situations, which in this case, is using commercial resources to fill a gap in teacher knowledge.

Yet, to play devil's advocate, we would also argue that because of the fragmented nature of SEL resources that tend to focus only on one key problem/solution, rather than the holistic development of SEL curriculum and teacher pedagogy, schools and teachers are often investing in more and different resources to attempt to fill the void. The following extract from a school counsellor gives an indication of the proliferation of commercial SEL resources and models in schools, and the multiple influences on how SEL is delivered in his school:

> Program Achieve was the main program happening, but teachers were doing varying things ... Kimochis is used in junior primary a little bit now ... We've also done training in Play Is The Way, but ... the [outside] games don't happen a great deal ... Circle Solutions is something that most of our staff have done training in recently and that's happening to varying degrees. So some people are doing SEL where it's scheduled in once a week now, but not everybody as yet. Other programs that we use are Seasons for Growth, that's a small group program, Literature for Life is – I do that with Year 6/7s and that's a challenge/change/grief/loss program ... Connected and Respected is another program from the States that I use in classes as well. (School Counsellor, SA 1)

In researching the costs of each of these programs, it is clear that this school had a significant SEL resource outlay. For example, 'Program Achieve' is $695 for a primary set of resources with additional resources and workshops available; a class set of 'Kimochi' puppets costs $145 and 'Play Is The Way' another $363; Circle Solutions involves teacher professional development at a cost of approximately $750 per teacher; 'Seasons for Growth' is $15 per student; 'Literature for Life' $70 per grade; and 'Connected and Respected' costs $40 per book. The cost of these services deserves particular scrutiny considering these private providers are capturing public education revenue for selling these products to schools. It also appears that schools pay for these services in the absence of evidence for student outcomes or a coherent strategy for longevity in the school. As the excerpt above highlights, SEL is often engaged with in ad hoc ways within schools. Additionally, the following dialogue between teachers from SA 1 further reflects not only the multiple SEL programs that exist in schools, but also the fast pace of change within the SEL space in schools:

Teacher 1: Seasons for Growth is a program that's been done just with specific students that have been pulled out to do that. And What's the Buzz? is done now consistently throughout the primary, but we've also done small targeted groups in years.

Teacher 2: And we've had staff development and training on wellbeing… Positive psychology and mindfulness and [they] kind of inform my teaching.

Teacher 1: We had the local psychologist come in, and she created her own program that we ran within the school, which I think was great. Because she sees a lot of these people, and she's aware of the needs within the community, so she created this wonderful program that we can teach to our kids, which is really beneficial.

Teacher 3: With Shine, which is a sexual health and relationships program, that gets put into Health and PE at the corresponding year levels. Because it's pretty much a prescribed unit, but you can adapt it. And that's got a lot to do with, more so relationships and communication than anything else, really. Yeah so that's one that goes into a subject.

Teacher 1: I think also, like we have 20 minute care groups in the morning, which is quite a significant amount of time. So when we did Pathways to Resilience last year that was done during care group time. And I know mindfulness was promoted quite a bit.

These excerpts highlight the complex environment of SEL in schools and the multitude of commercial programs and providers that schools and teachers now have access to in supporting their delivery of SEL. What is clear from these data is that commercial resources and programs are at the heart of SEL practices in schools and are seen as necessary in how teachers exercise agency to teach SEL. Indeed, each participant's articulation of their perception on teaching SEL was always informed by their individual confidence and competence, the resources available to them and the structural conditions of their school in terms of accommodating SEL obligations/responsibilities/requirements into an already crowded curriculum. Yet, there was also evidence of hidden dangers in the data. Clearly, the SEL market in Australia is fragmented with many schools purchasing multiple programs in an attempt to deliver a holistic SEL curriculum. In terms of market-based theory, schools should be holding SEL providers to account through their program choices (and continuation of using the same programs over time), however there are such significant fluctuations within schools in a single year around SEL resources that it is nigh impossible to get a sense of what resources are working and why. As one teacher summarised, 'We need a program, we get a program, but if you don't keep talking about it, if you don't keep it central, if you don't keep committing to it, it just sort of fades away' (Teacher, QLD 2). This raises an interesting tension between teachers' perceived need for commercial SEL resources, and how they actually utilise these in their individual school contexts.

Achieving and articulating teacher agency in a commercialised learning area

SEL in Australian schools is, and exists within, a complex space. Clearly, our participants revealed a shared perception that to implement SEL effectively, teachers need high-quality, curricular-relevant SEL resources that will assist them to design and deliver engaging learning experiences for their students. On this point, our data strongly suggests that teachers do not see commercial SEL providers or resources as threats to their professionalism or agency, rather they see these resources as having the potential to enhance their ability to implement high-quality learning experiences with their students. As one school principal argued, the programs his school implemented might be multifarious, but they fit within the school's strategic plan:

> So, we're at a conference, or we're reading something from here, or we're in Melbourne, or we're involved with something. We say, 'this is outstanding', because we have that umbrella view of what our school, all the pieces of our body of our school. So, if we think – if there's a little thing there that is a, righto that's something we really have been talking about but I haven't got to, we will bring it back and then go through that process. (Principal, QLD 2)

Thus, while school personnel value and have high aspirations for SEL and its delivery, they recognise that they do not necessarily have the capacities (time, skills and knowledge) to deliver effective SEL independently. Given the proliferation of commercial SEL resources, some teachers thought it would be ridiculous to even try to do so.

Commercialised SEL resources, then, are viewed as important additions to teachers' pedagogical toolbox or repertoire, additions that open up new pedagogical pathways of possibility and opportunities for teachers to devise creative responses to curriculum and policy imperatives that might match their schools' needs. Teachers want high quality SEL resources, and they prefer resources that are digital, malleable, have articulations with various curricular areas and are easy to export, import, scaffold and modify according to their specific needs. As one teacher expressed, he needed to change prescriptive commercial SEL programs to allow him to feel 'more comfortable, making it more real to me ... otherwise it would just be instant failure. I would probably give up half way through the lesson' (Teacher, SA 1). Similarly, teachers did not readily see the benefit of a highly structured, yearlong, prescriptive program. Instead, they wanted a resource that they could pick and choose the 'best bits' from, according to their local needs and the programs available to them. Thus, we would argue that teachers are not looking for commercialised quick fixes and they are certainly not looking to abdicate responsibility for the teaching of SEL. This speaks back to the general concern in literature that private providers are displacing the educative value of curriculum through the sale of simple, highly prescriptive programs that are marketed as being able to 'solve' the 'problems' students might have. Instead, what emerged very clearly from the perspectives of our participants was the image of a creative, agentic professional who cares deeply about students' social and emotional wellbeing and is working to tailor bespoke learning experiences to meet the needs of their students and to enrich (or challenge) official discourses in their schools.

From this perspective, we argue that although environmental affordances (conditions of possibility and constraint) vary from context to context, teachers and school leaders are clearly enacting 'ecological agency' (Priestley et al. 2012) in the commercial SEL school landscape. They are mobilising SEL in line with their beliefs, values and priorities and those of their schools. Even though the types of agentic activities they engage with are often constrained, teachers appear to be engaging productively with the constraints or tensions that influence their constructions of, and the decisions they make about, SEL. Of course, teacher agency is always circumscribed to some extent by, for example, the context in which s/he teaches, the various intellectual and pedagogical resources s/he has the capacity to recruit, confidence, prior experience and aspirations. A variety of ecological factors will always influence the possibility and practicality of achieving particular ends, including time constraints and standardised assessment pressures. However, how teachers spoke about their engagement with the prescribed curriculum, various commercial SEL resources and the decisions they made regarding their enactment of an SEL curriculum, revealed the clear role their reflexivity played in their agentic orientations towards the SEL possibilities they pursued. Whether driven by 'the head or the heart', by cost-benefit analyses, evidence-based innovation or intuition, teachers' translations and enactment of SEL curricula were always imbued with their broader educational philosophies, and framed by the complex and contingent, concrete realities of their schooling context.

Conclusion

There are caveats and obvious challenges associated with schools' and teachers' adoption of various commercial SEL resources. From our perspective these caveats and challenges are not, however, all located where others have previously encouraged critique. Research to date has critiqued the private sector organisations offering these services. They have characterised these organisations as being motivated by profit agendas, aggressively marketing their products and pushing these into schools with little connection to curriculum or concern for student outcomes. This characterisation is true in many cases, but by focusing on the 'commercial = bad' trope, we are diverting attention away from some key questions that we feel are under-researched and under-theorised. Specifically, why do schools and teachers value these commercial resources, how are these resources taken up by teachers to assist them in their core business of teaching and learning, and why a market has emerged at this time for commercial providers to prosper in?

Our data speaks to some of these issues, and clearly suggests that teachers view commercialised resources as necessary in successful delivery of an SEL program. In many of the discussions about commercialisation in/of schooling to date, we have not sufficiently recognised teachers as 'courageous counterpoints' (Ball 2016). Our data suggests that teachers are not being seduced by commercialisation, but are often discerning actors in the schooling marketplace. They are not employing a single commercialised resource as an easy fix, one size fits all approach, nor are they seeking a standardised SEL program. They are enacting moral agency (Campbell 2012) and governing their professional practice according to deeply held values and beliefs about teaching and learning. Thus, if we were to 'draw a line in the sand', we would argue that commercialised products and services are not necessarily problematic if the teachers and schools that choose to use them are aware of the significance of their choices and how those choices influence their educative responsibilities. In this regard, a parallel can be drawn between these commercialised programs and the commercialised textbook that has been a prominent feature of schooling since the early twentieth century (Callaghan 1964).

If, however, commercialisation becomes about the product or service itself and teachers' articulated beliefs and convictions do not manifest in practice, then this is a significant concern. To explicate, imagine a school purchases a commercial SEL program and then stops worrying about developing and evaluating students' social and emotional competencies because the program does this for them. In this case, the classroom has become commercialised and the teacher de-professionalised as the focus is on the product itself, and not on the potential of the product to help teachers. We argue that investigating the 'intensity' of commercialisation in schools is an important research agenda moving forward to better characterise the impact of commercial resources on teaching and learning practices.

In light of our findings, we wish to advocate for a more nuanced critique of commercialisation in schools than has been offered in the literature to date. The teachers in this study suggest commercial resources are a necessary component of schooling in the twenty-first century, as one could argue they have been throughout history. However, as these commercial resources become increasingly common in classrooms, and even promoted by education authorities as a useful means to address curriculum intentions (as per the government-endorsed KidsMatter website in Australia), it seems necessary for these education authorities to work proactively with the private sector to better regulate these resources. For example, authorities could ensure resources align with both curricular frameworks and pedagogical intentions. Similarly, they could offer support and guidance to the teaching profession by ensuring suitable policy shapes and regulates the use of commercial products in schools. Responding to these implications must sit within a policy context of ongoing debate concerning the appropriate intensity of commercialisation in schools, the regulatory environment that surrounds the development and sale of commercial products, the potential equity issues that surround the ability of all schools and teachers to access these services, and the enhancement rather than diminishment of teachers' agential capacities, particularly through ongoing professional development and critical understanding and engagement about commercialisation. Policies emerging from these debates may further protect schools, teachers and students from being enmeshed in a web of commercial activities, which at times, involve ethically questionable practices undertaken by global corporate entities at a considerable remove from local classrooms (Hogan, Sellar, and Lingard 2016; Reckhow 2013; Verger, Lubienski, and Steiner-Khamis 2016).

All of these issues are not insignificant and warrant increased scrutiny in future research. Regardless, we are undoubtedly witnessing a radical shift in the scope and scale of commercial resources now available to schools, and while these resources vary significantly in their quality and educative value, it is probable that schools and teachers will continue to seek, access, and enact these resources. As a consequence, private actors and organisations will become more closely entwined with the daily operations of schooling, and the 'repertoires of manoeuvre' (Priestley et al. 2012, 211) available to teachers and school leaders to interpret and translate commercial resources will become even more important.

Note

1. It is worth noting that KidsMatter includes this disclosure statement on its website: 'From time to time, programs offer discounts or special arrangements to KidsMatter schools/ services. KidsMatter does not endorse these programs and does not prioritise one program over another. KidsMatter encourages schools and services to use the Program Guides to explore the available programs and determine the best choice to meet their needs' (https:// www.kidsmatter.edu.au/primary/resources-for-schools/other-resources/programs-guide).

Acknowledgements

The authors would like to acknowledge the support of Lions Quest Australia who funded the project.

Disclosure statement

No potential conflict of interest was reported by the authors.

ORCID

Anna Hogan ⓘ http://orcid.org/0000-0003-0213-7097
Eimear Enright ⓘ http://orcid.org/0000-0001-7206-4781
Michalis Stylianou ⓘ http://orcid.org/0000-0002-5905-8229

References

Ashdown, D., and M. Bernard. 2012. "Can Explicit Instruction in Social and Emotional Learning Skills Benefit the Social-emotional Development, Well-being, and Academic Achievement of Young Children?" *Early Childhood Education Journal* 39 (6): 397–405.

Au, W., and J. Ferrare. 2015. *Mapping Corporate Education Reform: Power and Policy Networks in the Neoliberal State*. New York: Routledge.

Ball, S. J. 2012. *Global Education Inc. New Policy Networks and the Neo-liberal Social Imaginary*. Oxon: Routledge.

Ball, S. J. 2016. "Neoliberal Education? Confronting the Slouching Beast." *Policy Futures in Education* 14 (8): 1046–1059.

Banerjee, R., K. Weare, and W. Farr. 2014. "Working with 'Social and Emotional Aspects of Learning' (SEAL): Associations with School Ethos, Pupil Social Experiences, Attendance, and Attainment." *British Educational Research Journal* 40 (4): 718–742.

Biesta, G. J. J. 2010. *Good Education in an Age of Measurement: Ethics, Politics, Democracy*. Boulder: Paradigm.

Biesta, G., M. Priestley, and S. Robinson. 2015. "The Role of Beliefs in Teacher Agency." *Teachers and Teaching* 21 (6): 624–640.

Buchanan, R. 2015. "Teacher Identity and Agency in an Era of Accountability." *Teachers and Teaching* 21 (6): 700–719.

Bulkley, K., and P. Burch. 2011. "The Changing Nature of Private Engagement in Public Education: For-Profit and Nonprofit Organizations and Educational Reform." *Peabody Journal of Education* 86 (3): 236–251.

Burch, P. 2009. *Hidden Markets: The New Education Privatization.* Hoboken: Routledge.

Callaghan, R. E. 1964. *Education and the Cult of Efficiency.* Chicago, IL: University of Chicago Press.

Campbell, E. 2012. "Teacher Agency in Curriculum Contexts." *Curriculum Inquiry* 42 (2): 183–190.

Durlak, J., C. Domitrovich, R. Weissberg, and T. Gullota. 2015. *Handbook of Social and Emotional Learning: Research and Practice.* New York: The Guilford Press.

Durlak, J., R. Weissberg, A. Dymnicki, R. Taylor, and K. Schellinger. 2011. "The Impact of Enhancing Students' Social and Emotional Learning: A Meta-analysis of School-Based Universal Interventions." *Child Development* 82 (1): 405–432.

Edwards, A. 2015. "Recognising and Realising Teachers' Professional Agency." *Teachers and Teaching* 21 (6): 779–784.

Elias, M. 2006. "The Connection between Academic and Socio-emotional Learning." In *The Educator's Guide to Emotional Intelligence and Academic Achievement: Social-emotional Learning in the Classroom*, edited by M. Elias and H. Arnold, 4–14. Thousand Oaks, CA: Corwin Press.

Elo, S., and H. Kyngäs. 2008. "The Qualitative Content Analysis Process." *Journal of Advanced Nursing* 62 (1): 107–115.

Gard, M., and C. Pluim. 2014. *Schools and Public Health: Past, Present, Future.* Lanham: Lexington Books.

Hogan, A., and G. Thompson. 2017. "Commercialization in Education." In *Oxford Research Encyclopedia of Education*, edited by G. Noblit. New York: Oxford University Press.

Hogan, A., S. Sellar, and B. Lingard. 2016. "Commercialising comparison: Pearson puts the TLC in soft capitalism." *Journal of Education Policy* 31 (3): 243–258.

Humphrey, N. 2013. *Social and Emotional Learning: A Critical Appraisal.* London: Sage Publications.

Kenway, J., C. Bigum, and L. Fitzclarence. 2006. "Marketing Education in the Postmodern Age." *Journal of Education Policy* 8 (2): 105–122.

Lasky, S. 2005. "A Sociocultural Approach to Understanding Teacher Identity, Agency and Professional Vulnerability in a Context of Secondary School Reform." *Teaching and Teacher Education* 21: 899–916.

Lingard, B., S. Sellar, A. Hogan, and G. Thompson. 2017. *Commercialisation in Public Schooling.* Sydney: News South Wales Teachers Federation.

MacLean, J. 2016. "Teachers as Agents of Change in Curricular Reform: The Position of Dance Revisited." *Sport, Education and Society.* Advance online publication. doi: 10.1080/13573322.2016.1249464.

Molnar, A. 2007. "The Commercial Transformation of Public Schools." *Journal of Education Policy* 21 (5): 621–640.

Penney, D., K. Petrie, and S. Fellows. 2015. "HPE in Aotearoa New Zealand: The Reconfiguration of Policy and Pedagogic Relations and Privatisation of Curriculum and Pedagogy." *Sport, Education and Society* 20 (1): 42–56.

Powell, D. 2015. "Assembling the Privatisation of Physical Education and the 'inexpert' Teacher." *Sport, Education and Society* 20 (1): 73–88.

Priestley, M., G. Biesta, and S. Robinson. 2015. *Teacher Agency: An Ecological Approach.* London: Bloomsbury Publishing Plc.

Priestley, M., R. Edwards, A. Priestley, and K. Miller. 2012. "Teacher Agency in Curriculum Making: Agents of Change and Spaces for Manoeuvre." *Curriculum Inquiry* 42 (2): 191–214.

Reckhow, S. 2013. *Follow the Money: How Foundation Dollars Change Public School Politics.* New York: Oxford University Press.

Riep, C. 2017. "Fixing Contradictions of Education Commercialisation: Pearson Plc and the Construction of its Efficacy Brand." *Critical Studies in Education.* Advance online publication. doi: 10.1080/17508487.2017.1281828.

Robertson, S., and J. Komljenovic. 2016. "Unbundling the University and Making Higher Education Markets." In *World Yearbook of Education 2016: The Global Education Industry*, edited by A. Verger, C. Lubienski, and G. Steiner-Khamis, 211–227. London: Routledge.

Ronnberg, L. 2016. "From National Policy-making to Global Edu-business: Swedish Edu-preneurs on the Move." *Journal of Education Policy* 32 (2): 234–249.

Sperka, L., and E. Enright. 2017. "The Outsourcing of Health and Physical Education: A Scoping Review." *European Physical Education Review*. Advance online publication. doi: 1356336X17699430.

St Leger, L. 2006. *Health Promotion and Health Education in Schools – Trends, Effectiveness and Possibilities. Research Report 06/02*. Melbourne: Royal Automobile Club of Victoria RACV.

Verger, A., C. Lubienski, and G. Steiner-Khamis. 2016. *World Yearbook of Education 2016: The Global Education Industry*. London: Routledge.

Williams, B., P. Hay, and D. Macdonald. 2011. "The Outsourcing of Health, Sport & PE Work: A State of Play." *Physical Education & Sport Pedagogy* 16 (4): 399–415.

Students as consumers? A counter perspective from student assessment as a disciplinary technology

Rille Raaper

ABSTRACT

The notion of students as consumers who exercise educational decisions based on economic self-interest leads to interesting questions about their perceptions of current higher education assessment practices. Guided by a Foucauldian theorisation and the findings from focus groups carried out with students from two European universities, one from the UK and another from Estonia, the article argues that globally dominant consumerist policy discourses have altered but not removed the student experience of constraint in assessment. I argue that students' response to disciplinary power in assessment has become highly strategic and differs depending on the institutional assessment systems: students from Estonia recognise the powerful position of academics as assessors and find ways to create a good social impression of themselves; their counterparts from the UK, however, demonstrate a tactical approach to their learning and study processes.

Introduction: a neoliberal positioning of students as consumers

Higher education institutions today exist in a context where market-driven demands and accountability measures are fundamental organising principles of university work (Jankowski and Provezis 2014), promoting competition within and between them. Universities, like other public sector organisations are pressured to become entrepreneurial to ensure their competitiveness in national and global higher education markets (Allen 2011). Foucault (2004) would term this shift towards economic discourses of competition as neoliberalism. Within a neoliberal environment, students are increasingly addressed – both in policy and scholarly discourses – as consumers who practise economic decisions and choose their universities based on league tables that measure teaching and research quality (Pritchard 2005). In the UK setting, for example, the universities are required to comply with consumer law that formalises student-university relations in terms of information provision, terms and conditions, and complaints handling (CMA 2015). Furthermore, the recent Higher Education and Research Act 2017 in the UK promotes consumer relations between universities and students. In particular, the Act introduces a new quality assurance exercise branded as the Teaching Excellence Framework (TEF) which aims to measure teaching quality across universities and to potentially link tuition fee increase with the outcomes of the exercise (Morris 2017). The TEF development has been surrounded by the rhetoric of 'placing students at the centre of higher education' where student is seen as a consumer who engages in a rational financial transaction to develop one's employability (Gourlay and Stevenson 2017, 391). This re-conceptualisation of consumer relations in higher education reflects an assumption that if students act as consumers, they will pressure universities to develop high quality courses and academic practices (Naidoo and Williams 2015).

The phrase 'the student experience' has become particularly dominant in higher education policies over the last decade, and has 'acquired the aura of a sacred utterance' (Sabri 2011, 657). The National Student Survey (NSS) in the UK, for example, evaluates the experiences of final-year undergraduate students and makes the results publicly available ostensibly to inform the choices of future applicants (Naidoo and Williams 2015). No equivalent exists in Estonia, but most universities pay increasing attention to promoting and evaluating student satisfaction at institutional levels, with the aim of promoting competitiveness to recruit more home and international students. The *Internationalisation Strategy 2008–2015* in the Estonian University of this study illustrates the impact neoliberal discourses of competition have on wider institutional policy:

> Adding an international dimension to the curricula and offering the opportunity to study in English undoubtedly increases the attractiveness of the university among local student candidates. These students will be better prepared for a successful career in an integrated European labour market.

Universities, however, not only provide (educational) experience to students or train future workers, but as part of their relationship they shape students' subjectivities: '[their] identities, values, and sense of what it means to become citizens of the world' (Giroux 2009, 460). Student as subject from a Foucauldian perspective is in a constant process of being produced (Butler 1997). There are no 'universal necessities in human nature', only various technologies through which the individual is created or creates him/herself (Besley and Peters 2007, 6). The process of becoming a subject – subjectification – is therefore a never-ending process through which subject positions are created, negotiated, accepted and transformed (Lehn-Christiansen 2011). Subjectification of students happens through everyday discursive practices in which discourse is a space of positions and functioning for the subjects (Foucault 1972). In this article, discourse is understood as a social practice through which not only meanings but particular student subjectivities are constructed (Fairclough 1992; Graham 2011). It encompasses policy and scholarly discourses that enforce particular subject positions as well as student discourses (created through focus groups in this study) that allow certain subjectivities to be constructed and negotiated. Hay and Kapitzke (2009, 155), for example, argue that neoliberal higher education policy discourses promote 'entrepreneurial citizens' for the competitive global economy. By addressing students as consumers, students are expected to act as 'private investors' who seek a financial return in the form of enhanced employability skills (Naidoo and Williams 2015, 213). This repositioning of students is unsurprising as in the current economic context, university degrees move from being desirable to being a necessity in many fields (Svensson and Wood 2007).

This study does not propose that students necessarily act as consumers but it recognises that the consumerist positioning has been increasingly enforced on students by various policy frameworks, making it an influential discourse worldwide. There is some evidence to suggest that students from the UK in particular have been influenced by a consumerist mind-set. For example, a recent large scale survey led by the Universities UK (2017) suggests that 50% of student participants identified themselves as consumers of higher education. However, the findings also indicated that this consumer relationship in higher education is unique, including trust and collaboration (Universities UK 2017). In critiquing the neoliberal positioning of students as consumers, this article questions the ways in which student subjectivity emerges in assessment situations, a context traditionally characterised by academic domination. The article draws on a small scale exploratory research project involving focus groups with 15 students from two universities: a well-established Russell Group[1] university in the UK and a relatively new university in Estonia. These universities were selected based on their different historical and political backgrounds and diverse assessment systems. Guided by a Foucauldian theorisation of the subject, this study engages with the following research questions: (a) To what extent does a consumerist positioning of students emerge in assessment situations? (b) How do students experience and negotiate power dynamics within different assessment regimes?

Disciplinary power in student assessment

Assessment in its traditional form can be understood as 'a normalising gaze, a surveillance that makes it possible to qualify, to classify and to punish' (Foucault 1975, 184). It enhances students' visibility, helping to differentiate and judge them. From this perspective, academics as assessors are institutional agents with authority to make judgements about learners (Leach, Neutze, and Zepke 2000), and their role is to guard the norms. Disciplinary power is organised around norms (Foucault 1973) which define what 'normal' behaviour is and what one must do. Authority is rooted in the logic of the liberal university that legitimises academic freedom and academics' ownership over their practices (Mampaey and Huisman 2015), particularly judgment in assessment contexts.

Neoliberal policy developments attempt to challenge disciplinary power which exists between teacher and student, and reforms are often justified in terms of professionalisation of assessment (Murphy 2006). For example, the European Association for Quality Assurance (ENQA) emphasises that students should be assessed by published and consistent criteria, regulations and procedures (ENQA 2009). It is therefore unsurprising that this 'professionalisation' priority in assessment has resulted in increased use of criteria and anonymised marking in higher education. Bloxham, Boyd, and Orr (2011) argue that it is criterion rather than norm referencing that is now prevalent, and Yorke (2008) explains that anonymised marking is increasingly applied to reduce bias in respect of gender, ethnicity and other demographic characteristics. These reforms can be understood as part of wider attempts to reorganise academic work and create so-called 'managed academics' who rely on standards and performance targets (Fanghanel 2012, 15), and whose assessment practices are constrained by institutional regulations rather than underpinned by pedagogical principles (Raaper 2016, 2017a).

Policy developments on academic practices, however, do not necessarily alter power relations in the classroom (Gipps 1999; Reynolds and Trehan 2000). Both students and staff bring their previously-learned notions of behaviour and power dynamics into assessment situations (Tan 2004). Furthermore, Taras (2008, 83) shows that the power of academics in assessment is crucial as 'the role of the tutor as final arbiter of assessment is often unchallenged'. Power in assessment not only operates in sovereign forms between assessor and assessed, but exists in less visible forms where assessment practices set expectations for student behaviour in universities and beyond. Becker, Geer, and Hughes (1968) conceive grades as personal and institutional currency: a measure of worth to oneself and others. Assessment, then, has a function of 'gate-keeping in terms of enabling or restricting entry into a professional career' (Harman and McDowell 2011, 50), judging whether students are even considered, let alone suitable for a job or a credential (Leach, Neutze, and Zepke 2000). As assessment affects individuals' potential opportunities, careers and feelings of worth, it is unsurprising that students experience it as constraining (Reynolds and Trehan 2000). While recognising disciplinary power in assessment, this research project aimed to explore the impact consumerism has on traditional power relations associated with assessment. It questions whether the freedom that supposedly makes students act as 'potential wealth creator(s)' as Bansel (2015, 8) explained it, also includes opportunities to practise freedom (Foucault 1984, 282) in such disciplinary situations as assessment. This is particularly the case in neoliberal universities, as according to Foucault (2004), the idea of freedom and self-interest are key conditions for the formation of a neoliberal subjectivity of 'homo economicus': the student as a consumer in this article.

Research setting and methodology

This study included two European universities with different historical, political and social backgrounds: a Russell Group university from the UK and a relatively new university from Estonia.

UK University

The UK University is a medieval university that belongs to the prestigious Russell Group universities. The UK University, like most other British higher education institutions, has been affected by increasing bureaucratisation, both in terms of regulating academic practices and managing academics (Barnett 2011). In the UK University, the number of assessment regulations has increased over the past years, resulting in 113 pages of text. The university has an assessment policy and regulations, as well as three guidance and strategic documents accompanying the regulations. All these documents need to be read together to gain a complete understanding of the regulatory context, causing confusion and stress amongst the academics (see Raaper 2017a). As regards practice, the UK University applies anonymised marking based on a 22 point marking scale which encourages detailed differentiation of student performances. Assessment is often carried out by diverse markers, including casual academic staff who may be employed to teach a number of lectures and seminars on particular courses and/or to carry out some assessments (Evans 2011).

Estonian University

Located in North East Europe, the Estonian University was founded in the 2000s as a result of uniting several higher education institutions in the local area. As a newer university from a post-soviet country,[2] neoliberalisation is a more recent process. Until the regaining of independence from the Soviet Union in 1991, the higher education sector in Estonia was under direct government control (Unt and Lindemann 2013). Saar and Mõttus (2013, 9) describe the sector as currently undergoing major modernisation, including significant reforms for integrating universities 'into European models and practices of education and research'. These reforms in Estonia, however, conflict with a traditional understanding of academic authority (Tomusk 1996). In terms of assessment regulations, for example, it still has a single document, regulating learning, teaching and assessment processes in the university. The section on assessment is 2.5 pages long. The policy is descriptive, highlighting the assessment timeline and the process for appeals. The document also confirms the academics' ownership over their practices, non-anonymised assessment process and the use of marking scale A to F or pass/fail categories.

Method and participants

Three focus groups were carried out as part of this study: one in the UK and two in Estonia during the academic year 2014/15. The focus group in the UK university included three undergraduate (UG) and two postgraduate (PG) students, and the two focus groups in the Estonian University included six students (4 UG and 2 PG) and four students (2 UG and 2 PG) respectively. Due to standard ethical practice in the UK University, I was not allowed to use mailing lists for participant recruitment. Alternative methods (e.g. emailing student representatives and student clubs, advertising through posters and programme leaders), however, resulted in only five participants over five months research period. Unlike some other disciplinary areas (e.g. Psychology), this research did not offer any incentives to participants and this might have caused students' low participation. In order to accommodate all volunteers in both institutions, the composition of focus groups required flexibility in terms of size and programme levels. Each focus group lasted about 1.5 h and was moderated by the researcher.

Participants were from a wide range of disciplinary areas; however, only one student volunteered from the disciplinary area of the Arts and Humanities. Most participants were female: the UK study included one and the Estonian focus group two male students. While the sample size does not permit any generalisation about disciplinary and/or study level differences, when such differences emerge, the findings will emphasise the students' background. The main focus of this exploratory study was on the two institutional settings. Future research with a more targeted focus on students' background would be essential to understand disciplinary and/or study level differences.

Focus group questions were informed by a Foucauldian (1982) perspective on student subjectivity that is discursively constructed. The questions addressed the following thematic areas:

- students' higher education choices;
- understandings of the assessment purposes;

- experiences of assessment practices;
- opportunities to negotiate assessment practices.

The key analytic focus in this study is on discourse which from a Foucauldian perspective can be understood as a postmodern concern with how language produces particular subjects (Graham 2011). Discourse is therefore a term that not only applies to policy that produces particular understandings of students as consumers (as argued earlier in this article) but to student interviews which also have an effect on students' understanding of themselves within the dominant policy structures. The study borrowed practical tools from Fairclough's (1992) three-dimensional model of discourse analysis. As I have argued elsewhere (see Raaper 2017b), I find Fairclough's approach to discourse complementing Foucault's work. Fairclough (1992) explains discourse as a form of social practice, which constitutes social entities, relations and subjects. Fairclough's critical discourse analysis is therefore a dialectical method, making it possible to explore the relations between discourse and social practices and subjects (Fairclough 2001).

Each interview transcript was approached as discursive artefact and analysed in a spreadsheet format as a text, a discursive practice and a social practice (Fairclough 1992, 2001). Firstly, the textual analysis focused on examining textual structure in terms of vocabulary, metaphors and grammar used by student participants. Secondly, the interpretative analysis of discursive practice focused on the ways in which the text relates to other discourses/texts (e.g. dominant policies), and how different influences might be incorporated into the specific discourse (Fairclough 2003). Finally, the analysis of discourse as a social practice questioned how the students' accounts (discourses in this study) operate in the world (Fairclough 2001). My particular interest here was targeted towards power relations relating to the discourses and how student subjectivities emerge in assessment situations.

These three stages of analysis overlapped in practice, and were used to deconstruct the student discourses and to trace the ways in which students position themselves in higher education and assessment situations. By breaking down the student discourses into different Faircloughian stages, the analysis provided a more nuanced way to explore the Foucauldian concept of subjectification and the practices of power as they are experienced in neoliberal assessment contexts. For example, the linguistic aspects related to vocabulary reflected the students' economic understanding of higher education and assessment processes, indicating some neoliberal influence on their subjectivity. In other words, linguistic focus became a resource for the author when tracing the Foucauldian processes. The findings presented in this article are therefore structured based on a Foucauldian perspective to the subject, starting with a macro context of social structures and shifting towards the micro experiences of how power gets negotiated at the individual level (Foucault 1982). The study was approved by the College of Social Sciences Research Ethics Committee, and data was de-identified by using pseudonyms.

Status, employability and students' higher education choices

Clear from participants' description of their universities was an early insight into economic discourses of higher education: UK participants from both UG and PG backgrounds described their university as '*top 50 in the world*' (Callum), '*prestigious*' (Chloe, Tracy), and '*elite*' (Tracy). These discursive accounts provide hints about the importance of league tables to student educational decisions (Naidoo and Williams 2015; Pritchard 2005). In contrast, no such reference to status appeared in Estonian students' focus groups; rather, they used words such as '*innovative*' (Merle, Karoliine) and '*creative*' (Greta, Karoliine). As Estonian universities are not represented in the top quartile of the world league tables, university rankings may not affect students to the same extent. Lacking a long or elite history, the university can pride itself on a marketing strategy that privileges its sense of identity as a 'contemporary and dynamic university that has a reputation of being the most student-friendly university in Estonia'. While the participants' descriptions of their universities differ, both groups have still adopted the dominant marketing language characteristic of particular institutions: discourses that these universities use to compete at various national and global higher education markets (Allen 2011).

The ways in which students from the two universities spoke about their subject-related choices indicated even stronger similarities. For example, Callum reflected on his experience of changing his major based on employment prospects: '*not lots of people get jobs in Politics degrees, so I decided for Geography*'. Similarly, Tracy explained that her first degree in Sociology – '*a Mickey Mouse degree*' – as she now calls it, did not help her with finding a relevant job. She assigns monetary value to her education:

> … when I went to university the first time, if you had a degree, you were guaranteed a job, you were guaranteed to start with 15 grand or above a year. It's absolute rubbish, I couldn't get a job in my field at all, you know, I ended up working in a supermarket and then trying to find out what I was going to do next … (Tracy)

Estonian students were less specific in their examples but still problematised aspects of employability as the main value of higher education. Kerli emphasised that university education should develop '*logical thinking*' rather than '*pointless factual knowledge*', demonstrating a utilitarian approach to learning. In support, Markus argued that good grades do not provide advantage in the labour market:

> Well, at today's labour market, if there's two people running for the same position, one has work experience, and the other one has a 'cum laude', then the one with the experience gets it. Yes, no one will care why you got that B or … (Markus)

These views suggest that, despite historic and structural differences between the universities and study levels, students evaluate educational choices based on work-related prospects, reflecting a globally dominant situation where they are increasingly reluctant to choose programmes from which jobs are difficult to obtain (Peters and Olssen 2005). While disciplinary differences did not emerge from the analysis, I am aware that students from the Arts and Humanities could differ in their educational decisions. The only participant from the Humanities background was a language student and her perspective to employability aligned with the mainstream view in this study: '*my field is languages, and it's connected to work practice*' (Kristiina).

I recognise that a desire for employability cannot be equalled with consumerism in higher education. The focus on employment prospects might have characterised students prior to major neoliberal reforms. Svensson and Wood (2007), however, argue that students' understanding of higher education as a preparation for work is increasingly enforced by contemporary service-based economies where job prospects are highly dependent on degrees. As highlighted earlier, students are often positioned as consumers – 'rational utility maximisers' (Olssen 2009, 445) – who need to make careful educational decisions while considering individual benefits associated with particular degree programmes (Hay and Kapitzke 2009). Like consumers buying a product, students are expected to enact their economic self-interest when evaluating universities and degree programmes. They are in a process of developing their competitiveness and therefore are expected to prioritise employment prospects when exercising choice (Canaan and Shumar 2008; Naidoo and Williams 2015). This Faircloughian (2003) interdiscursivity with economic discourses of higher education becomes further evident from the participants' perspectives to assessment purposes as will be discussed next.

Students' economic understanding of assessment purposes

Similar economic discourses characterised the participants' understanding of assessment which was explained as evaluating and comparing individual success. The PG students from the Estonian University explained assessment in relation to allocating bursaries and selecting students for qualifications:

> … purely financial reasons, giving the grants and bursaries – who gets the funding, who doesn't, who graduates with a distinction, who doesn't – they need to be filtered. (Annika)

> I find it's creating comparison within university, between universities, within Estonia and abroad etc., so that ultimately we'd be able to, based on a standard, a yardstick, to analyse you and me. (Greta)

> Not everybody can be allowed to graduate … (Liisa)

The discourses indicate the students' sense of assessment as a process enabling visibility of individual performance (Foucault 1975; Harman and McDowell 2011; Manuel and Llamas 2006). While the reasoning amongst the UG students in both universities was more limited, it still reflected a concern with selection aspects of assessment: *'otherwise it's just passing the subject for nothing more than your presence'* (Markus), and *'just testing, just to check how smart you are'* (Sophie). Selection processes through assessment might therefore contribute to students' overall experience of developing oneself as an economically minded competitive subject who sees good grades as necessary for promoting one's work prospects (Leach, Neutze, and Zepke 2000). For example, Tracy and Callum from the UK University highlight how assessment has played a crucial role in shaping their educational choices:

> … I was actually majoring in Law, and I swapped for majoring in Sociology […] because it was after I had essays, I decided that assessment in Sociology is better for me … (Tracy)

> Politics always tends to have an essay equivalent to 30% of the mark, 10% goes to tutorial participation, and then the reminder goes to your overall exam, whereas Geography was so different, you know, it would be split down to very small fractions […] say, well, if I do good at this, this and this, and not so well in this, I could still come for a good grade. So that's what I liked about Geography, and that's why I went on. (Callum)

Elements of economic mind-set surface in two very different higher education environments, and provide an example of subjects who are fundamentally influenced by the social context they are part of, shaped by the 'walls of society' as portrayed by Butler (1997, 74). It appears that neoliberal higher education discourses provide 'a space of functioning' (Foucault 1972) for students and shape the ways in which they not only reason about the value of education but assessment. The students interviewed explained assessment as being necessary for comparing students and making individual achievement – or lack of it – visible. It is therefore unsurprising that some students (e.g. Tracy and Callum in this study) have become pragmatic about their educational decisions based on how certain assessment methods can benefit or disadvantage their performance in higher education.

Students' experiences of disciplinary power in assessment practice contexts

While the analysis did not reveal strong alignment with consumerist policy discourses where students would describe themselves as passive purchasers of education or so called private investors (Naidoo and Williams 2015), there were signs of economic mind-set in terms of employability. The participants explained their relationship with higher education as what Gourlay and Stevenson (2017, 391) would describe as a matter for 'private gain in terms of employability'.

Despite the similarities in students' accounts of higher education, their experiences of being assessed differed greatly in the two universities. Students from the UK emphasised constraining experiences of limited assessment methods due to restrictive regulations: what Murphy (2006) calls the professionalisation of assessment practices characteristic of neoliberal universities. This manifests as a sense of being continuously assessed: *'we are pushed to essays'* (Chloe), *'the essays we have done are based on the standard kind of marking grid'* (Tracy) and *'it's all multiple choice'* (Rachel), reflecting some disciplinary differences between the Social and Medical Sciences. Similarly, they highlighted academics' strictness with certain standards. Callum, for instance, argues that *'with Geography they are kind of like, they are really harsh I must admit'*, and Sophie explains how academics in her courses are being strict with word limits which appear as if *'set in stone'*. The findings suggest that students sense the restrictive assessment policy context characteristic of neoliberal universities (Fanghanel 2012): they are normalised and surveilled (Foucault 1975) via particular assessment methods and standards. Unlike academics, however, who critique the regulations (Laughlin and Broadbent 1994; Raaper 2016), UG students have at most limited abilities to compare contexts, standards and regulations. They just perceive it as part of 'normal' assessment practices.

In contrast, assessment in the Estonian University is mostly practised by individual academics and not conducted anonymously, reflecting traditional trust in academic work (Mampaey and Huisman 2015). These structural differences along with student experiences of various assessment methods contribute to students' perception of assessors and themselves. Markus, for example, argues that *'there's no specific framework based on what students are assessed'* and that assessment is *'very relative'* in terms of individual academics and their preferences. Some students see academics adopting their own assessment policies:

> Some academics, at least in Natural Sciences, set the best paper as the maximum or 100% and then deduct from that. (Kerli)

... if, say, the academic feels, when we sit an assessment and many fail, and if the academic feels that they did not explain well enough what they expected of the student, they'll give them another chance ... (Marili)

The students in the Estonian University position academics as being powerful in terms of controlling assessment processes, and this relationship raises questions about academic bias (Bradley 1993). Phrases such as *'Yes, there's subjectivity in assessment'* (Karl), *'Clearly most academics don't manage to avoid marking by the face'*[3] (Kerli), and *'Sure, there are academics – like we heard – who don't mark very well'* (Marili) were common among both study levels. Assessment in the Estonian University compared to its UK counterpart, is under-regulated and does not rely on anonymity: academics know the authors of the assessed works. Kerli even argues that academics develop their opinions during their various encounters with students:

... if you're thought of well, if you're above the average and have been noticed through the years, your grades are better, and if you have been slacking and haven't done well enough, then also later you get assessed worse in relatively subjective situations. (Kerli)

This experience of assessment being relational, and depending on dynamics between the individual assessor and assessed was absent from the UK students' discourses. Rather, assessment power relations for these students exist in various 'networks of social' (Foucault 1983, 372). For example, the participants explained how assessment is increasingly divided between marking teams of varying academic status such as academics, tutors and graduate teaching assistants who may all have had an input to teaching. The NSS, every year, highlights the importance of assessment and feedback and universities manage this by co-opting a range of sometimes marginal staff in pursuit of improving timely feedback practices. Tracy, for example, is concerned by the ways marking teams operate in large programmes:

And obviously they are all marking with the same criteria but then specialism kind of intervenes as well. For example, people who are marked by language tutors tended to get marked down for grammar and things like that and structure, emm whereas I think people who are marked by maybe Maths specialists or other things, are maybe more kind of focused on the content. (Tracy)

Tracy's example above reflects her experience of assessors who act as part of marking teams and who – despite the standards – can still differ in their practices. Furthermore, Chloe explains how marking teams mediate their biases by becoming protective against student queries:

... obviously teachers as well might want to ... keep things like ... they don't want to say anything wrong about other, like a colleague [...] as a student you get the feeling like that it's you against them in a way, you are not going to win because they are going to be altogether. (Chloe)

Despite the UK students' understanding of assessment as a highly standardised process, relying on a limited number of methods, they still see disciplinary power underpinning the process. However, this power is mediated within marking teams, as assessment in the UK is no longer the domain of a single academic (Leach, Neutze, and Zepke 2000) but belongs to the complex field of regulations and marking teams that students have little access to. Chloe's quote demonstrates the ways students might want to appeal when they notice inconsistency of standards across the team but feel unable to act against academic collegiality. While the Estonian students emphasised academic bias in assessment, they also explained it in terms of traditional authority in which academics not only assess student performance but their overall behaviour and being in the university (a student's *'face'*). Assessment as a normalising technology and a domain of the teacher (Foucault 1975) might not only motivate students to perform in particular ways but also to display certain character traits. Also, their sense of wanting to appeal against academic judgements was less evident. It might be because the students from the Estonian university are used to academic authority in assessment and difference in practise: there is no 'professionalised' framework (Murphy 2006) to be constrained by or to act against.

Negotiation of disciplinary power in assessment practice contexts

Further differences emerge when tracing the ways in which the participants respond to assessment power dynamics in the two universities. In line with their constraining experiences of assessment regulations and marking teams, students from the UK University express negative emotions such as *'panic'* (Chloe, Callum), *'fear'* (Chloe), *'freak-out'* (Sophie), *'stress'* (Rachel) and *'nightmare'* (Callum). These emotions provide an impression of students as fearful and needing to perform in a 'right' way: power from a Foucauldian perspective is always productive (Foucault 1983), making people act and respond in particular ways. The examples below illustrate how the students became strategic in learning and assessment processes:

> I have now learned to think that for every hundred words in an essay if I'm not quoting somebody or mentioned somebody, I've got something wrong here. (Callum)

> I was reading my friend's essay, she was in Archaeology, she was talking about buildings, she had put her opinion in it, she had so many 'I-s', and I was like what is this … it's not correct. (Rachel)

A neoliberalised UK assessment system that has shifted power from academic judgment to regulations might make students both highly cautious but also strategic in their study processes, especially in terms of referencing, note taking, and expressing one's opinion. As soon as their understanding of the 'right' way of doing things is threatened by ambiguous instructions, confidence may be undermined leading to a feeling of vulnerability in assessment, hence the negative emotions associated with assessment. Students want to perform well, but standardised assessment practices and protective marking teams constrain their opportunities to affect assessment processes. Unlike the traditional understanding of assessment as the domain of a single assessor (Leach, Neutze, and Zepke 2000), the UK students need to cope with a diffused assessment context where regulations, individual characteristics of assessors and collegiality make power relations difficult to comprehend. Diffuse power, however, is essential to neoliberal institutions, helping to enforce responsibility and self-government (Foucault 2004) and resulting in strategically minded subjects as evident from the quotes above.

Unlike their counterparts in the UK, the UG and PG students from Estonia did not perceive themselves as utterly constrained by assessment or assessors; rather, they described themselves as being aware of and proactive in manoeuvring within existing power relations. Their key strategy relies on creating a good impression of themselves that would affect academics' assessment decisions. They want to become 'the good student' (Grant 1997, 106). For example, Markus argues that *only after the first assignment you'll know what kind of academic you're dealing with, how you should do your work for them*', and Liisa emphasises that '*as I've been studying here for five years, I know practically all academics pretty well, and they know what to expect of whom*'. This idea of '*knowing*' academics and doing '*work for them*' increases over the study years and helps students to shape their behaviour in order to enhance their chances for success. This also reflects how the Estonian students are having their behaviour shaped by the system in which assessment is highly controlled by academics without any form of student anonymity. However, this clear disciplinary power between assessor and assessed does not necessarily make students passive subjects as literature has suggested (Tan 2004; Taras 2008): they are able to reverse the power and make it work for their own advantage. Students could be seen practising their entrepreneurial mind-set within the university setting (Hay and Kapitzke 2009).

Findings from both universities demonstrate a Foucauldian notion of power that is never owned by a single person but rather exists in various networks and can be exercised only so far as the subjects are free to choose actions within a field of possibilities (Dean 2013; Foucault 1982). Adopting a strategic approach or creating a good impression of oneself seem to be possibilities that students choose to negotiate subjectivities in assessment situations. Their response to disciplinary power is therefore contextual, depending on assessment systems and opportunities available to them.

Concluding thoughts

When probing beyond simplistic measures like the NSS assessment and feedback scores characteristic of the UK higher education sector, it becomes evident that the changing discourse around the nature of higher education impacts student behaviours. From this study, it is clear that there is evidence of neoliberal influences on student understanding of higher education and assessment processes. The students from both universities exercise educational choices in the higher education market as Pritchard (2005) described, and they are interested in university education for promoting their competitiveness in the labour market (Canaan and Shumar 2008; Naidoo and Williams 2015). Furthermore, the students ascribed economic value to assessment as an institutional technology of selection and reward: a way to promote one's competitiveness. While these findings do not suggest that students are necessarily consumers as portrayed in dominant policy discourses, they indicate some neoliberal influence on students' understanding of themselves and their place in university. The functionality of education in terms of needing to secure employment has become prevalent in neoliberal societies (Naidoo and Williams 2015; Peters and Olssen 2005). However, the study also exposed that this economic mind-set was less evident in the practice context of assessment, in the relationship between assessor(s) and assessed where either codified regulation (UK) or potential for academic bias (Estonia) exist. It is clear that students in assessment situations cannot and do not position themselves as 'homo economicus' in a Foucauldian sense, acting as 'a free and autonomous 'atom' of self-interest' (Hamann 2009, 37). They are shaped by disciplinary power: whether the traditional domination of a single assessor or more diffuse power contexts in the UK.

Interestingly, however, students interviewed are not passive subjects within this power imbalance, but find ways to negotiate assessment dynamics. In the Estonian University, where the assessment system is still based on liberal ideas of academic authority and freedom, students identify assessors' power and their opportunities for manoeuvre: they make use of the ways assessment – so called *'face-based assessment'* (Kerli) – acts on them. In more regulated setting like the UK, the disciplinary technology has become more diffuse and students struggle to identify the cause of the pressure they feel: they speak about standards and academic protectiveness. Their response to these constraints results in their becoming strategic learners. However, the tactical ways in which students understand and respond to these power relations might reflect the wider impacts of neo-liberalism and increasingly promoted consumerist attitudes which expect individuals to maximise their potential for success. It should be a concern to all in higher education to recognise this changing relationship between student subjectivities, their understandings of education and behaviour.

Notes

1. The Russell Group includes 24 UK universities 'which are committed to maintaining the very best research, an outstanding teaching and learning experience and unrivalled links with business and the public sector' (Russell Group 2015).
2. The Republic of Estonia gained independence from Soviet Union in 1991 and joined the European Union in 2004. The population of Estonia is approximately 1.3 million people.
3. The word 'face' is often used in Estonian language to refer to subjective judgment (e.g. favouring someone based on their visible characteristics).

Acknowledgments

I wish to thank Dr Jan Smith for her time and generous feedback on this paper. I am also highly grateful to Dr Fiona Patrick for her support during my research project.

Disclosure statement

No potential conflict of interest was reported by the author.

Funding

This work was supported by the ESRC [grant number ES/J5000136/1 +3 Doctoral Award] and the University of Glasgow, College of Social Sciences scholarship.

References

Allen, A. 2011. "The Idea of a World University: Can Foucauldian Research Offer a Vision of Educational Futures?" *Pedagogy, Culture & Society* 19 (3): 367–383. doi:10.1080/14681366.2011.607840.
Bansel, P. 2015. "The Subject of Policy." *Critical Studies in Education* 56 (1): 5–20. doi:10.1080/17508487.2015.971839.
Barnett, R. 2011. *Being a University*. Oxon: Routledge.
Becker, H. S., B. Geer, and E. Hughes. 1968. *Making the Grade. The Academic Side of College Life*. New York: John Wiley and Sons.

Besley, T., and M. A. Peters. 2007. *Subjectivity and Truth. Foucault, Education and the Culture of Self.* New York: Peter Lang Publishing.

Bloxham, S., P. Boyd, and S. Orr. 2011. "Mark My Words: The Role of Assessment Criteria in UK Higher Education Grading Practices." *Studies in Higher Education* 36 (6): 655–670. doi:10.1080/03075071003777716.

Bradley, C. 1993. "Sex Bias in Student Assessment Overlooked?" *Assessment and Evaluation in Higher Education* 18 (1): 3–8. doi:10.1080/0260293930180101.

Butler, J. 1997. *The Psychic Life of Power: Theories in Subjection.* Stanford: Stanford University Press.

Canaan, J. E., and W. Shumar. 2008. "Higher Education in the Era of Globalization and Neoliberalism." In *Structure and Agency in the Neoliberal University*, edited by J. E. Canaan, and W. Shumar, 1–30. New York: Routledge.

Competition and Markets Authority. 2015. "Higher Education Providers: Consumer Law. 60-Second Summary." Accessed February 9, 2018. https://www.gov.uk/government/uploads/system/uploads/attachment_data/file/411392/HE_providers_60ss.pdf.

Dean, M. 2013. *The Signature of Power. Sovereignty, Governmentality and Biopolitics.* London: Sage Publications.

ENQA. 2009. "Standards and Guidelines for Quality Assurance in the European Higher Education Area." Accessed March 20, 2016. http://www.enqa.eu/wp-content/uploads/2013/06/ESG_3edition-2.pdf.

Evans, A. M. 2011. "Governing Student Assessment: Administrative Rules, Silenced Academics and Performing Students." *Assessment and Evaluation in Higher Education* 36 (2): 213–223. doi:10.1080/02602930903277727.

Fairclough, N. 1992. *Discourse and Social Change.* Cambridge: Polity Press.

Fairclough, N. 2001. *Language and Power.* 2nd ed. Essex: Pearson Education Limited.

Fairclough, N. 2003. *Analysing Discourse. Textual Analysis for Social Research.* London: Routledge.

Fanghanel, J. 2012. *Being an Academic.* London: Routledge.

Foucault, M. 1972. "History, Discourse and Discontinuity." *Salmagundi* 2: 225–248.

Foucault, M. 1973. "Truth and Juridical Forms." In *Power. Essential Works of Foucault 1954–1984*, edited by J. D. Faubion, 1–89. London: Penguin Group.

Foucault, M. 1975. *Discipline and Punish. The Birth of the Prison.* London: Penguin Group.

Foucault, M. 1982. "The Subject and Power." In *Power. Essential Works of Foucault 1954–1984*, edited by J. D. Faubion, 326–348. London: Penguin Group.

Foucault, M. 1983. "The Risks of Security." In *Power. Essential Works of Foucault 1954–1984*, edited by J. D. Faubion, 365–381. London: Penguin Group.

Foucault, M. 1984. "The Ethics of the Concern of the Self as a Practice of Freedom." In *Ethics. Essential Works of Foucault 1954–1984*, edited by P. Rabinow, 281–301. London: Penguin Group.

Foucault, M. 2004. *The Birth of Biopolitics: Lectures at the College de France, 1978–1979.* New York: Picador USA.

Gipps, C. 1999. "Socio-Cultural Aspects of Assessment." *Review of Research in Education* 24: 355–392.

Giroux, H. A. 2009. "Beyond the Corporate Takeover of Higher Education: Rethinking Educational Theory, Pedagogy, and Policy." In *Re-Reading Education Policy. A Handbook Studying the Policy Agenda of the 21st Century*, edited by M. Simons, M. Olssen, and M. A. Peters, 458–477. Rotterdam: Sense Publishers.

Gourlay, L., and J. Stevenson. 2017. "Teaching Excellence in Higher Education: Critical Perspectives." *Teaching in Higher Education* 22 (4): 391–395. doi:10.1080/13562517.2017.1304632.

Graham, L. J. 2011. "The Product of Text and 'Other' Statements: Discourse Analysis and the Critical Use of Foucault." *Educational Philosophy and Theory* 43 (6): 663–674. doi:10.1111/j.1469-5812.2010.00698.x.

Grant, B. 1997. "Disciplining Students: The Construction of Student Subjectivities." *British Journal of Sociology of Education* 18 (1): 101–114. doi:10.1111/j.1469-5812.2010.00698.x.

Hamann, T. H. 2009. "Neoliberalism, Governmentality, and Ethics." *Foucault Studies* 6: 37–59.

Harman, K., and L. McDowell. 2011. "Assessment Talk in Design: The Multiple Purposes of Assessment in HE." *Teaching in Higher Education* 16 (1): 41–52. doi:10.1080/13562517.2010. 507309.

Hay, S., and C. Kapitzke. 2009. "'Smart State' for a Knowledge Economy: Reconstituting Creativity Through Student Subjectivity." *British Journal of Sociology of Education* 30 (2): 151–164. doi:10. 1080/01425690802700206.

Jankowski, N., and S. Provezis. 2014. "Neoliberal Ideologies, Governmentality and the Academy: An Examination of Accountability Through Assessment and Transparency." *Educational Philosophy and Theory* 46 (5): 475–487. doi:10.1080/00131857.2012.721736.

Laughlin, R., and J. Broadbent. 1994. "The Managerial Reform of Health and Education in the UK: Value for Money or a Devaluing Process." *The Political Quarterly* 65 (2): 152–167. doi:10.1111/j. 1467-923X.1994.tb00442.x.

Leach, L., G. Neutze, and N. Zepke. 2000. "Learners' Perceptions of Assessment: Tensions Between Philosophy and Practice." *Studies in the Education of Adults* 32 (1): 107–119. doi:10.1080/ 02660830.2000.11661424.

Lehn-Christiansen, S. 2011. "Health Promotion Viewed as Processes of Subjectification in the Education of Danish Social and Healthcare Workers." *Journal of Social Work Practice: Psychotherapeutic Approaches in Health, Welfare and the Community* 25 (3): 311–322. doi:10. 1080/02650533.2011.597178.

Mampaey, J., and J. Huisman. 2015. "Defensive Stakeholder Management in European Universities: An Institutional Logics Perspective." *Studies in Higher Education*. Advance online publication. doi:10.1080/03075079.2015.1029904.

Manuel, J., and C. Llamas. 2006. "Technologies of Disciplinary Power in Action: The Norm of the 'Good Student'." *Higher Education* 52 (4): 665–686. doi:10.1007/s10734-004-1449-1.

Morris, D. 2017. "Be It Enacted: The Higher Education and Research Act (2017)." *Wonkhe*. Accessed Ferbuary 9, 2018. http://wonkhe.com/blogs/be-it-enacted-the-higher-education-and-research-act-2017/.

Murphy, R. 2006. "Evaluating New Priorities for Assessment in Higher Education." In *Innovative Assessment in Higher Education*, edited by C. Bryan, and K. Clegg, 37–47. Oxon: Routledge.

Naidoo, R., and J. Williams. 2015. "The Neoliberal Regime in English Higher Education: Charters, Consumers and the Erosion of the Public Good." *Critical Studies in Education* 56 (2): 208–223. doi:10.1080/17508487.2014.939098.

Olssen, M. 2009. "Neoliberalism, Education, and the Rise of a Global Common Good." In *Re-Reading Education Policy. A Handbook Studying the Policy Agenda of the 21st Century*, edited by M. Simons, M. Olssen, and M. A. Peters, 433–457. Rotterdam: Sense Publishers.

Peters, M. A., and M. Olssen. 2005. "'Useful Knowledge': Redefining Research and Teaching in the Learning Economy." In *Reshaping the University. New Relationships Between Research, Scholarship and Teaching*, edited by R. Barnett, 37–48. Maidenhead: Open University Press.

Pritchard, R. 2005. "Education Staff and Students Under Neoliberal Pressure: A British-German Comparison." *Beiträge zur Hochschulforschung* 4 (27): 6–29.

Raaper, R. 2016. "Academic Perceptions of Higher Education Assessment Processes in Neoliberal Academia." *Critical Studies in Education* 57 (2): 175–190. doi:10.1080/17508487.2015.1019901.

Raaper, R. 2017a. "Tracing Assessment Policy Discourses in Neoliberalised Higher Education Settings." *Journal of Education Policy* 32 (3): 322–339. doi:10.1080/02680939.2016.1257160.

Raaper, R. 2017b. "Discourse Analysis of Assessment Policies in Higher Education: A Foucauldian Approach." *SAGE Research Methods Cases*. doi:10.4135/9781473975019.

Reynolds, M., and K. Trehan. 2000. "Assessment: A Critical Perspective." *Studies in Higher Education* 25 (3): 267–278. doi:10.1080/03075070050193406.

Russell Group. 2015. *About Us*. Accessed February 9, 2018. http://www.russellgroup.ac.uk/about-russell-group.

Saar, E., and R. Mõttus. 2013. "Foreword." In *Higher Education at a Crossroad: The Case of Estonia*, edited by E. Saar, and R. Mõttus, 9–10. Frankfurt: Peter Lang.

Sabri, D. 2011. "What's Wrong with 'the Student Experience'?" *Discourse: Studies in the Cultural Politics of Education* 32 (5): 657–667. doi:10.1080/01596306.2011.620750.

Svensson, G., and G. Wood. 2007. "Are University Students Really Customers? When Illusion May Lead to Delusion for All!." *International Journal of Educational Management* 21 (1): 17–28. doi:10.1108/09513540710716795.

Tan, K. 2004. "Does Student Self-Assessment Empower or Discipline Students?" *Assessment and Evaluation in Higher Education* 29 (6): 651–662. doi:10.1080/0260293042000227209.

Taras, M. 2008. "Issues of Power and Equity in Two Models of Self-Assessment." *Teaching in Higher Education* 13 (1): 81–92. doi:10.1080/13562510701794076.

Tomusk, V. 1996. "Recent Trend in Estonian Higher Education: Emergence of the Binary Division from the Point of View of Staff Development." *Minerva* 34: 279–289.

Universities UK. 2017. "Education, Consumer Rights and Maintaining Trust: What Students Want From Their University." Accessed February 9, 2018. http://www.universitiesuk.ac.uk/policy-and analysis/reports/Documents/2017/education-consumer-rights-maintaining-trust-web.pdf.

Unt, M., and K. Lindemann. 2013. "From Bust to Boom and Back Again: Social Positions of Graduates During the Last Decade in Estonia." In *Higher Education at a Crossroad: The Case of Estonia*, edited by E. Saar, and R. Mõttus, 307–338. Frankfurt: Peter Lang.

Yorke, M. 2008. *Grading Student Achievement in Higher Education. Signals and Shortcomings.* Oxon: Routledge.

Preoccupied with the self: towards self-responsible, enterprising, flexible and self-centered subjectivity in education

Kristiina Brunila and Päivi Siivonen

In the neoliberal order, the ideal self is self-responsible, enterprising, flexible and self-centred. Regarding this ideal we argue that the rise of therapisation in society, and in education, particularly, links both the therapeutic and enterprising discourses. The article examines how these discourses jointly produce and legitimate the ideal, and thus, the preoccupied subjectivity of the neoliberal order. As a discursive form of power therapisation is observed here to work by directing students to focus on their inner selves – including their problems, vulnerabilities, dependencies as well as reactions to life events – in a therapeutic mode. And it does not stop there. Therapeutic discourses offer a seemingly empowering and flexible subjectivity, which is central in enterprising discourses. At the same time, however, selfhood tends to diminish to the extent that we argue for a need to understand more about the subjectivities that emerge from the alliance between therapeutic and enterprising discourses.

Introduction

At first glance, the self-centredness of therapisation as a discursive form of power may seem far removed from the enterprising discourses involving competitiveness, performance, efficiency and the compulsion to succeed in order to cope with the uncertainty and unpredictability of contemporary life and the market economy. However, despite the differences between the therapeutic and enterprising discourses, both have emerged in tandem with the neoliberal spirit driving the restructuring of education (see Brunila, 2012a; Ecclestone & Hayes, 2008; Komulainen, Korhonen, & Räty, 2009; Siivonen & Brunila, 2014). And, thereafter, they have also worked together towards shaping an autonomous, self-responsible, enterprising, flexible and self-centred ideal self of the neoliberal order (see, for example, Brunila, 2012b; Kelly, 2006; Komulainen et al., 2009; Rose, 1998).

In this article, we focus on therapisation and therapeutic discourses and how they offer to free each of us from our psychic and emotional chains so that we can become enterprising and take control of ourselves and our lives (Brunila, 2012a; Rose, 1998). Only in this way are we able to become lifelong learners who actively contribute to the flourishing market economy. As a lifelong learner, an adult becomes an entrepreneur who chooses education based on his/her individual needs and on where s/he wishes to eventually arrive in life (Fejes & Dahlstedt, 2013). Moreover, these discourses are strengthened by experts who claim that the self can achieve a better and happier life through the application of scientific knowledge and professional skill (Rose, 1998). Guidance given by experts has, at any age, become central in the process of getting to know oneself and deciding what one wants to become – a logic based on humanistic psychology which entails that the entire person is affected through learning and education (Fejes & Dahlstedt, 2013). Thereafter, in order to legitimate herself or himself, the neoliberal subject becomes both vulnerable (therapeutic) and necessarily competitive (enterprising) – a consequence of the rise of therapisation in Western societies (see, also, Furedi, 2004).

Here we examine education as involving both the therapeutic and enterprising discourses. By analysing these discourses together and as interlinked, we wish to highlight that what is shaping education today is not just competitiveness and efficiency, but even more implicit changes in the ways we perceive ourselves and others (see, also, Furedi, 2004; Kelly, 2006; Rose, 1998). The literature regarding therapisation in education, generally, is already quite vast; however, in adult education it is still lacking in maturity (see, however, Brunila, 2012a; Ecclestone, Hayes, & Furedi, 2005; Fejes & Dahlstedt, 2013). Our joint contribution, therefore, emanates from the rise of therapisation involving both the therapeutic and enterprising discourses in adult education, and how these discourses jointly participate in producing and shaping preoccupied subjectivity (see, for example, Brunila, 2012a, 2012b; Ecclestone & Brunila, in press a; Siivonen, 2010, 2013). Moreover, we will focus on some of the consequences of therapisation for adults themselves that emerged in our joint interview data. We argue that therapeutic and enterprising modes of personal understanding tend to categorise adults without problematising the categorisations in any way. These categorisations have consequences that have not yet been carefully considered.

In what follows, we will first discuss the rise of therapisation and how this intertwines with the therapeutic and enterprising discourses. After presenting our data and method of analysis, we will first discuss the role of diagnosis as a powerful tool for creating preoccupied, that is, therapeutic, as well as enterprising subjectivity. Second, we will discuss the process of self-making and self-realisation in our joint data and, finally, survivalist discourses as consequences of therapisation.

The rise of the therapeutic turn in education and the making of a preoccupied subjectivity

By 'therapeutic turn' we refer to a multifaceted spectrum of discourses and social practices that discursively and institutionally pervade social and cultural life including education. These discourses enhance the language of disorder, addiction, vulnerability and dysfunction, together with associated practices from different branches of therapy as well as psychological ideas and diagnoses (see, for example, Ecclestone & Hayes, 2008; Furedi, 2004; Wright, 2011). This concerns not only infants and children, but also adults (Burman, 2008; Ecclestone, 2013; Ecclestone et al., 2005; Furedi, 2004; Harwood, 2006). For example, in schools, universities as well as in youth work and youth educational programmes, diverse individual and group methods range from circle time, emotional education, psychodrama workshops, anger management and direct behavioural training to peer mentoring and life-coaching (Brunila, 2011, 2012b; Ecclestone & Hayes, 2008; Fejes & Dahlstedt, 2013; Wright, 2011).

The past 15 years or so have seen a therapeutic turn in the social policy systems of an increasing number of countries, including Finland, Sweden, Britain, the USA and Australia (Brunila, 2012a, 2012b; Dahlstedt, Fejes, & Schönning, 2011; Ecclestone et al., 2005; Wright, 2008, 2011). However, this therapeutic turn had been the focus of much research long before that. Philip Rieff's influential analysis *The Triumph of the Therapeutic* (1987/1966), James Nolan's (1998) *The Therapeutic State*, Michel Foucault's writings on madness and psychology (1961/2009), Nikolas Rose's (1999) discussions concerning governmentality and technologies of the self and Frank Furedi's (2004) more recent *Therapy Culture* have all provided significant understanding of the therapeutic turn.

It was, however, *The Dangerous Rise of Therapeutic Education* (2008) by Kathryn Ecclestone and Dennis Hayes that aroused a critical discussion of therapeutic interventions in educational politics and practices. The book offers examples from the British educational system of how therapeutic education is turning children, young people and adults into anxious, preoccupied individuals rather than defining them capable and potential (see, also, Ecclestone, 2013). The focus of Foucault's, Rose's and Ecclestone and Hayes' writings on the role of psychological and therapeutic discourses in the constitution of the modern self and in the operation of modern systems of power has particularly influenced our reading of the therapeutic turn.

In their previous study focusing especially on the therapeutic turn in education, Kathryn Ecclestone and Kristiina Brunila have summarised it as the influence of two inextricably linked cultural characteristics that now permeate social policy, public discourses and private life. The first combines the very large growth of targeted or specialist interventions within social policy settings in numerous countries, alongside the rise of universal approaches derived from these. Their psychological roots are diverse, *ad hoc* and eclectic: programmes might be adapted from cognitive behavioural therapy and positive psychology, while others draw on different strands of counselling, self-help, psychotherapy and psychology, sometimes embellished with neuroscience (Ecclestone & Brunila, in press b).

Therapisation as a discursive form of power

Therapisation and, as we argue here, combining both the therapeutic and enterprising discourses, work towards individualising education, and this in turn requires the right kind of subjectivity as a target in order to legitimate itself. The therapeutic discourses of the self represent the regulation of personal existence. These discourses encourage distancing the self from others, causing the self to turn inwards (see, also, Furedi, 2004). Moreover, the enterprising discourses work in the same way producing a subjectivity that is enterprising and makes an enterprise of one's life, seeking to maximise one's own human capital and to shape oneself in order to become what one wishes to be (Rose, 1999). Consequently, the aim of both the therapeutic and enterprising discourses is to produce a coherent and self-reliant subjectivity of the humanistic ideal.

In our analysis we aim to challenge this humanistic ideal which locates existence within the individual. We wish to make visible that choice stems not so much from the individual, but from the condition of possibility – the discourses which prescribe not only what is desirable but also what is recognisable as an acceptable form of subjectivity (Davies et al., 2001; Laws & Davies, 2000). We are well aware that it would be far too simplified and narrow to claim that the therapeutic and enterprising discourses work in a way that makes people emotionally and psychologically well, thereby becoming productive and thus, responsible and independent in meeting the demands of the market. As our research suggests, the consequences can actually be quite the opposite.

We share the emphasis on language referring to a domain of struggles: conflicts over what is or is not true and who has the power to pronounce what the truth is. As Nikolas Rose (1999, p. 14) writes:

> it is not, therefore, a matter of meaning but of truth, of the relations of power and truth, and the conditions under which truth in discourse comes to be established and defended, or alternatively attacked and undermined.

Our focus here is on the effects, what language does, and what it enables people to imagine and do to themselves and others. We understand the therapeutic and enterprising discourses in terms of discursive power, and acknowledge the relation between knowledge, discourse and power as productive and regulative with material effects (Davies, 2005; Foucault, 1977, 1980). Likewise, we acknowledge that power inherent in the therapisation of adult education is complex and multifaceted.

In this article, we relate therapisation to a more effective classifying and governing, resulting in an excessive concern with the self enhanced by therapeutic culture and the neoliberal order that emphasises individualisation and economic interests. Therapisation is both compelling and rewarding because it defines a cultural script for appropriate feelings and responses to events, and a set of associated practices through which people make sense of themselves and others. In this way, therapisation works as a religion-like subjectification 'that binds us to others at the very moment we affirm our identity' (Rose, 1999, p. 244; see, also, Furedi, 2004). Furthermore, therapisation entails an alliance between, on the one hand, professionals claiming to provide an objective, rational answer to the question of how one should conduct one's life to ensure normality, and success, and on the other, individuals seeking to shape a 'life-style', not in order to conform to social conventions but in the hope of personal happiness and an 'improved quality of life'. The mechanism of this alliance is the market, the 'free' exchange of those with a service to sell and those who have been prompted to buy (Rose, 1998).

To see how the forms of power work and their effects on the forming of subjectivities in adult education, we have integrated the idea of subjectification (Davies, 1993, 2005) with therapisation. This has helped us to analyse how certain discursive constructions are appropriated while others are discarded as irrelevant or even threatening. In our analysis, therapisation as a form of subjectification describes the ongoing process whereby one is placed and takes place in the therapeutic and enterprising discourses. Through these discourses, people become speaking subjects while being subjected to the constitutive force of the discourses. In addition, we consider that therapisation as a form of discursive power is always being constructed and is never fixed. In education a range of competing discourses exists, at any particular time, of which some are given more space than others. Power is thus exercised in and through these discourses.

Furthermore, it is the paradoxical simultaneity of submission and mastery, and the related ambivalence, that we explore here. As Bronwyn Davies et al. (2001) have argued, the dual nature of subjection is easily misunderstood in the binary structure of Western language as necessarily either submission or mastery, but not both. We argue that they cannot be separated because the condition of possibility for the subject requires both. Therapisation, therefore, represents a strand of regulative and productive power that intertwines with adult education, encompassing subjects that can be known and spoken about and gaining its legitimacy from the popularisation of therapeutic explanations. Crucially, it also elicits the self as a subject to be known and talked about, both by oneself and others such as educational professionals and youth workers.

Due to the nature of this approach, it is possible to see subjects as not fixed but rather continuously engaged in a process, being constituted and reconstituted through the discourses they have access to in education. The tensions and instabilities in subjectivity become visible through an examination of the discourses through which our subjectivities are constituted. Further, the discourses through which subjects are constituted are also often in a state of mutual tension, providing the subjects with multiple layers of contradictory meanings inscribed in their bodies (Davies, 1993).

Data and analysis

We draw on data from two separate studies and focus our attention on the ways in which therapeutic discourses imply and elicit a social subject that is simultaneously vulnerable and enterprising. The first, conducted by the first author of this article, Brunila, concerned short-term educational programmes targeting young adults transitioning from school, and particularly also those not engaged in education or work. The second, conducted by Siivonen, the second author, was a narrative life history study conducted with 20 young adults in Finland who had recently completed upper secondary school and were in the process of continuing their education or applying to do so. In each of these studies we found that the therapeutic and enterprising discourses in adult education were implicated in the subjectification of the young adults we interviewed.

First, we draw on Brunila's analysis based on a four-year post-doctoral research project (2010–2013), in which short-term educational programmes targeting young adults transitioning from school, and also in particular those outside educational or working life, were studied. The analysis began in 2010 with an examination of documents from 60 publicly funded programmes from the 1990s and 2000s. The documents included programme reports, web pages, marketing material, articles and newsletters. We have chosen not to mention the names of the programmes. Instead of focusing on individual projects, we wanted to highlight the importance of what has been said. This is a central point in the analysis of discursive power.

The 60 above-mentioned programmes in the field of adult education in Finland, train, guide and rehabilitate unemployed young adults. In practice, the programmes are usually short-term projects funded by the European Union (EU), government, ministries, municipalities and associations. The programmes were visited, at which time in-depth interviews were conducted with 15 youth workers and 30 young adults between the ages of 19 and 29 years. In these programmes the enterprising discourses were easily traced. In some of the projects an enterprising orientation was more implicitly included in the aims and activities that emphasised, for example, self-responsibility, flexibility and active learning. Moreover, many of these projects consistently and explicitly highlighted not just an enterprising but also a therapeutic orientation in their aims and activities, as in the following project report extracts:

> Being enterprising can be so fulfilling. You are able to decide about your own aims, who you want to be and what you want to become. (A youth-related project's report, 2009)
> Emotions were reflected in a nice and secure environment accompanied and guided by project workers. (Youth project report, 2004)

From this article's point of view it was interesting to discover both enterprising and therapeutic discourses already intertwined in the project reports. To become whole, to become what you want to be and to become yourself is also a part of the therapeutic discourses that have shaped working life and discourses on jobs, careers and unemployment (Rose, 1998). We can become self-disciplined and enterprising by taking control of ourselves and our emotions, by becoming more self-centred, as well as by working on and transforming ourselves in accordance with what is expected of us.

Second, we utilise the narrative life history data generated by Siivonen, as we noticed that in addition to the enterprising discourses in the interviews with general upper secondary school adult graduates the therapeutic discourses were also easily traced. All in all, 20 adult students were interviewed in 2004–2005, of which 10 were re-interviewed in 2012. At the time of the first interviews the participants had just graduated from general upper secondary school for adults (GUSSA), which provides publicly funded formal general education for adults of all ages. The students had earned a general upper secondary school certificate and/or had passed the school leaving matriculation examination for Finnish upper secondary school. By the time of the second interviews in 2012, all except one of the interviewed GUSSA students had applied for further education, and eight had gone on to study in vocational education, at polytechnic, or university. The data extracts of the GUSSA students will be referred to as GUSSA 1/2 (interview 1/interview 2). Pseudonyms are used to refer to all interviewees.

We have chosen to read all of our multiple interview data together in order to understand how the therapeutic and enterprising discourses in adult education are intertwined. We examine how the adult students we interviewed have engaged in the discourses, taking them as part of their subjectivities in the ambivalent process of simultaneous submission and mastery of these discourses. The analysis permits an examination of the multi-layered politics and practices regarding the therapeutic and enterprising discourses in adult education, as well as some of the consequences of the discourses for adults participating in adult education in diverse educational settings. In our analysis we will first explore how the therapeutic discourses work together with the enterprising discourses, and second, what kinds of consequences this has for the adults we interviewed. In addition, we jointly asked how the students engaged in the ambivalent process of therapeutic subjectification and what effects this had on the construction of their subjectivities. Therapisation is related to discursive regularities, and we also explore the possibility of speaking and acting otherwise.

Demand for a diagnosis

A vast array of literature has noted the rise of diagnostic practices in society (see, for example, Conrad, 1992; Furedi, 2004; Harwood, 2006; Teittinen, 2011). Accordingly, in an age of disorders and diagnoses, the therapeutic ethos is pushing education to interpret problems through the prism of illness. Based on our data and analysis, it seems that adult education, too, is claiming legitimacy by engineering human existence through making therapeutic interventions such as diagnoses:

> Kirsti, adult educationalist: We are of course not licensed to make official diagnoses. But when a customer has done this test [the project developed its own test that measures concentration skills and learning difficulties], we write a statement that shows the test results and further recommendations.
> Pia, adult educationalist: Making diagnoses for our customers helps and eases our work.
> Kaija, adult educationalist: Our customers usually think that they do not want to study anything; they feel that they are not capable of studying. Of course this is anchored in previous experiences of failures [in school] and their very low self-esteem. But then when we have done tests [diagnosing learning difficulties] and investigations, then – wonder of wonders – believing in themselves begins to occur.

In a therapeutic culture, recognition requires an accepted diagnosis and label. In our data, therapeutic diagnostic practices that resulted in diagnoses such as Attention Deficit Hyperactivity Disorder (ADHD) were described by the youth workers as being soothing and relieving for those diagnosed, and were subjected to little critical attention (cf. Davies, 2005; Harwood, 2006; Teittinen, 2011). This shows how receiving a diagnosis itself has the capacity to relieve anxiety. In addition, therapisation is raising a call for a therapeutic authority that actively shapes and transforms subjectivities and exercises power through a variety of innovations and mechanisms (see, also, Rose, 1999).

Brunila's data showed cases of 10 specialists working with young adult students to help them develop abilities and skills considered important. However, the call for a therapeutic authority reaches even further. The interviewed project workers were not licensed to make official diagnoses, but instead utilised tests that gave indications of learning difficulties and ADHD. The extracts above describe how the therapeutic discourses foster a climate in which people seek to be recognised according to the language of therapeutics. According to Furedi (2004), such a language becomes easily confused with a diagnosis, so that the demand for a diagnosis has become a key motif in contemporary societies. Further, Valerie Harwood (2006) has acknowledged a shift in education which she calls psychopathological. According to her, diagnostic practices in particular are increasingly emphasised (see, also, Conrad, 2006). Although Harwood's work pertains to the education of children and not adults, her argument is also relevant in the context of adult education, as our analysis shows.

While full subject status requires being constrained by the rules and structures of the social world, and at the same time acting as if one were an autonomous agent, the subject status of those adults who are marked by diagnoses is never fully guaranteed. In the interviews we were able to trace how the therapeutic and enterprising discourses work in the making of imperfection, vulnerability and failure in the adult students' sense of self. A striking feature of the interviews was the adults' worry about their ability and competence to study and learn (see, for example, Siivonen, 2010, 2013). Before becoming recognised as legitimate lifelong learners and enterprising subjects, they had to prove their ability and competence as students and learners. This could be achieved through a diagnosis of dyslexia, as shown in the following interview with Riitta. Having been labelled as a 'poor' student in primary and secondary school, the therapeutic and enterprising discourses worked in constructing vulnerability and an incapability to learn as well as a keen desire to be categorised as a 'normal' student and learner:

> It was like a hell of a relief 'cause you've always like thought of yourself as a bit dumb or not really dumb but that you understand things but a bit slowly
> But it's like kind of much better to be like … to be diagnosed different than to be just otherwise different if you understand what I mean …
> (GUSSA 1/Riitta)

In the interview extract with Riitta, and also in the following with Mervi, a diagnosis of dyslexia and ADHD brings a great relief as it provides a legitimate explanation: not being unintelligent but just learning more slowly than others. Riitta's interpretations of herself as a person who can make choices and act upon the world are based to a large extent on both therapeutic and enterprising discourses. The diagnosis releases her inner potential and enables a management of the self as a way of reaching one's goals in life:

> Mervi, adult educationalist: Our customers become so relieved and happy when they get these statements saying that they have learning difficulties or ADHD.

In the above extracts, and especially Riitta's case, the validation of a particular claim of suffering is important, and requires an accepted diagnosis and label that permits normalcy and the potential to act. Consequently again, the diagnosis itself begins to relieve anxiety and uncertainty on the personal level (Furedi, 2004). It can even become a resource in education for both students and teachers. This also raises the question of whether the pressure on health professionals to recognise a variety of new diseases is also shared among adult educationalists.

The advantage of a medical explanation of a learning difficulty or a behavioural problem is that it removes the stigma attached to poor academic performance. Logically, an individual cannot be held responsible for something s/he has no control of (Erchak & Rosenfeld, 1989). Similarly, Walkerdine, Lucey, and Melody (2001, p. 130) argue that of the two competing narratives low ability versus dyslexia, the latter is more positive as it allows 'to maintain some sense of self-respect'. In the same vein, the diagnosis rescues young adults like Riitta from being victims of low expectations and failure. The diagnosis verbalised by a teacher – no testing is needed – provides legitimate enough proof that she is able to learn, even though more slowly than what is considered the healthy person's norm. In such ways teachers nurture and direct these individual strivings, 'the pedagogies of self-fulfilment' (Rose, 1998, p. 17). In the end, in a culture that values inner entrepreneurship and lifelong learning, it is more acceptable for an individual to be a different kind of learner than not to be able to learn at all.

A diagnosis marks individual subjectivity with such qualities as self-control, autonomy, self-directedness, as well as being an active student and learner who takes responsibility for her/his own actions. These are all qualities of an enterprising subjectivity. The diagnosis offers more flexibility in the sense that it is possible to actively control one's learning when the 'problem' is known and 'talked about'. Medicalisation may, then, act as a salvation for individuals who would otherwise be permanently excluded from the learning society ideal.

Therapisation works not only to render its targets as subjects of power but also to construct them as agentic. During her interview, Mervi described how her students were aware that it is their learning difficulties or ADHD that define them, and that they also learn to utilise their diagnoses in public as a statement of who they are, for example when applying to a school or taking a driver's test. However, a more critical approach was also brought up by another adult educationalist who had trained young adults in several educational programmes:

> Saija, adult educationalist/project worker: These young people who come to these projects, they show me a long list of diagnoses they have been given from other educational organisations. It's a mess. Many of them are medicated, especially because of ADHD. And the funny thing is I just can't see anything wrong with them.

These discussions with educationalists and also with the adult students revealed critical perspectives, reminding us that therapisation 'does us' by speaking and acting through language and social relations whilst also allowing us to think about how we are 'reformed' by therapisation, how we continuously learn to act in these power relations, and how to utilise them (cf. Brunila, 2009). It is also worth remembering that individuals do not simply internalise ideas regarding therapisation; they are also exposed to many other kinds of discourses in the process of making sense of themselves according to their various experiences.

However, therapisation in education has not come without consequences. Students have learned to demand therapeutic interventions such as diagnoses in order to feel that they have received enough attention from society (see, also, Furedi, 2004). A diagnosis provides a 'medical excuse' for learning more slowly than what is expected. It gives comfort, and no further treatment is needed. The diagnosis suffices to exercise self-control, which results in better learning outcomes. However, it is important to note that the problem is placed squarely within the individual, and therefore needs to be dealt with and solved by the individual alone.

Self-making and self-realisation

The so-called 'new adulthood' (Koski & Moore, 2001) does not mean being 'ready'; rather, it is characterised by incompleteness, imperfection and uncertainty. Learning and education has become an important, or even the only, way to full adulthood, consisting of demands for personal growth and development, self-knowledge and self-mastery as well as fulfilling one's potential. The focus of adult education has been switched to working upon oneself and displaying individual distinctiveness. This focus privileges the insights gained through self-reflection. This is also the case with Riitta, who after the relieving diagnosis of dyslexia finds her inner potential for self-development:

> R: At least I'm getting closer to myself more quickly … [laughter]. It's difficult to say who I am but at least at a good speed I'm finding out what I'll start doing and what I want out of this life … and try to find myself … I know that you are never ready and it gives you a positive direction.
> A2: Yes, it's perhaps important to be on the road to something.
> R: Yes, that's right, otherwise it would be boring, if you reach your goal you have nothing to aim at anymore. If you are ready, perfect … there's no fun anymore, just the opposite, it's so much fun to be on the road and to stray from a straight path. (GUSSA 1/Riitta)

Riitta's extract also shows that discourses are never fixed because they shift in meaning according to the context and the positioning of the subjects within them (Davies, 1993). 'Getting closer to myself', 'realising my inner potential' and 'trying to find myself' demonstrate a humanist understanding of a stable and coherent identity enhanced and strengthened by therapisation (see, Brunila, 2014). However, expressions such as 'it's difficult to say who I am' or 'to be on the road' demonstrate subjectivity that is more fluent and in a constant process of becoming. Nevertheless, the 'journey to oneself', even a difficult one, is an endless opportunity for learning and self-improvement, a strenuous route to one's own goals in life. The case is rather similar with other adult students, such as Joonas who described during his interview how he began to believe in himself because of the programme. When asked what has been most rewarding for him in the project, Joonas replied:

> I guess I didn't believe in myself earlier that much, I had all kinds of (emotional) problems, but luckily this project helped. Now I know it's all up to me, I can manage if I really want to. I know of course, that I have to work hard.

As Rose (1998, p. 157) writes:

> [c]ontemporary individuals are incited to live as if making a *project* of themselves: they are to *work* on their emotional world, ... their relations with employment ... to develop a 'style' of living that will maximize the worth of their existence to themselves.

In a similar way, Lisa expresses the idea that every work task is an opportunity for learning and self-development:

> I notice it here, too, as I'm working on terribly many projects at the same time. And perhaps my work is like that, too, so that I have taken up many things, as I'm really eager to learn and do things. And then I still have this terrible fear that I should know how to do a million things and be better than everyone else. So that I should learn everything really quickly, as I have this one year's chance to learn a thousand things. (GUSSA 2, Lisa)

However, continuous self-making and striving towards self-realisation, self-esteem and self-fulfilment are not without consequences: fear of not learning and developing fast enough is constantly present. The following excerpt from Lisa's interview shows how the enterprising discourses can bring about therapeutic interpretations of one's subjectivity:

> A2: Where do you think this lack of concentration comes from?
> Lisa: It started when I went to upper secondary school for adults. And then because of those kids, I then had a total burnout and ... I'm like really hyperactive all the time. (GUSSA 2, Lisa)

Trying so hard for so long may result in concentration problems and a diagnosis of burnout. The whole person is at stake; such personal qualities as being a nice person, taking responsibility, being active, having initiative and being ready to learn as well as doing new things have become at least as important as actually doing the job. When nothing is enough the important question becomes: How can I find new ways to develop myself? According to Rose (1998):

> the prevailing image of the worker is of an individual in search of meaning and fulfilment, and work itself is interpreted as a site within which individuals represent, construct, and confirm their identity, an intrinsic part of a style of life. (p. 160)

He continues that:

> work has become an essential element in the path to self-realization, and the strivings of the autonomous self have become essential allies in the path to economic success. (Rose, 1998, p. 161)

As a consequence, the neoliberal subject becomes both vulnerable and necessarily competitive. Therefore, it is not surprising that educational activities related to adults are more and more informed by the view that the particular problem at hand is some type of psychological deficiency (see, also, Brunila, 2011, 2012a, 2012b; Ecclestone et al., 2005; Ecclestone & Brunila, in press b; Furedi, 2009).

Adult education as a survival game?

> I have had emotional problems and all kinds of problems, but this project has taught me how to survive. (Pasi)
> Some time ago I did not know if I would survive but I have learned to get rid of old survival models and to use new ones, better ones. (Teppo)

During their interviews, Pasi and Teppo positioned themselves as students who had become in touch with their real selves, free from previous emotional and psychological chains by becoming survivors. Davies (2005) has argued that the neoliberal discourse has shifted in a significant way towards survival being seen as an individual responsibility. This is a crucial element of the neoliberal order – the removal of dependence on the social combined with the dream of wealth and possessions for each individual who gets it 'right'. According to Davies, vulnerability is closely tied to individual responsibility. Workers are disposable and there is no obligation on the part of the 'social fabric' to take care of the disposed. As well as success, the individual remains responsible for any failure and its negative effects.

Kenneth McLaughlin (2011) has written how political claims today are being increasingly made on the basis of experienced trauma and inherent vulnerability while the previous political demand for recognition has resulted in therapeutic solutions. In his view, the survival discourse is a consequence of the therapeutic ethos (McLaughlin, 2011). Moreover, in several educational programmes the discourse of survival is already central (Brunila, 2014) in the way that the therapeutic discourse of vulnerabilities and emotional problems is able to find a powerful expression in the position of the victim, and the solution is to become a survivor.

In the therapeutic and enterprising discourses above, students such as Pasi and Teppo comply with such demands in order to be recognised as 'properly' flexible, active, self-disciplined and responsible. The ideal subjectivity is built on ideas of what is desirable, what is possible, and how to be heard. These extracts describe how young adults' existence is shaped, and how as a consequence they begin to position themselves as survivors (see, also, Brunila, 2014; McLaughlin, 2011). The position of a survivor appears to be seductive. The survivor concept allows for a flattering representation of the emotional self, for it suggests that despite intense pain and suffering, these individuals have survived. This makes survivor status all the more authoritative and remarkable, as Furedi (2004) has written. The problem here is that in order to be heard, the young person must play the role of a victim. The position from which people are heard is established through recognising their vulnerabilities, injuries and emotional problems including low self-esteem, anxiety and stress. The assumed identity is one of victimhood or traumatisation; it is the therapeutic identity required for recognition (see, also, McLaughlin, 2011). This risks depoliticising the problems people face in society such as unemployment, lack of education and poverty.

Conclusion

We have argued that therapisation including both the therapeutic and enterprising discourses is effective in linking political rhetoric and regulatory programmes to the 'self-steering' capacities of the subjects themselves (cf. Rose, 1998). The removal of dependence on the social is combined with the dream of empowerment, wealth and possessions for anyone who gets it 'right'. However, instead of autonomous and rational individuals, what therapisation actually produces is vulnerable and fragile as well as imperfect and incapable subjectivities. When vulnerability is tied to individual responsibility, there is no obligation on the part of the 'social fabric' to take care of the disposed. Failure as well as success is up to each individual to bear.

In an era of individualisation and the decline of wider collective identities (Furedi, 2004), people are forced to rely on their own resources. Understanding one's self becomes crucial. The vocabulary of both enterprising and therapeutic discourses offers a means to self-discovery. The ideal therapeutic discourses offer to free each of us from our psychic and emotional chains so that we can become enterprising and take control of ourselves and our lives. In practice, the result seems to be a 'vicious circle' where the individual is constantly obliged to improve his/her ever fragile and vulnerable self in perpetual competition with others. The risk of not achieving what is expected is therefore ever present. This shows how choice stems from the condition of possibility.

In previous work (Brunila, 2012b; Siivonen, 2010, 2013; Siivonen & Brunila, 2014) we have argued that vulnerability is a key element of the enterprising discourses and the rise of what we have identified not just as enterprising but also the 'therapeutic' discourses along with the broader effects of 'therapisation', in compulsory and post-compulsory education. In this article, we aimed to continue analysing therapisation, because this vulnerability is the main feature of the new worldview and moral order: the removal of dependence on the social and the emphasis on individual responsibility central to neoliberal subjectivity. It may be difficult to accept how subtle and pervasive these discourses of therapisation are, discourses through which students tend to learn to know their places and remain within them. However, within the framework of this kind of understanding it makes it easier to introduce students, educationalists and other specialists to therapisation, which may enable them to see how the discourses of preoccupied subjectivities are constructed and how more and more people are caught up in them.

In therapeutic culture, we are all expected to shape ourselves by continuously updating our knowledge and skills to the needs of the market economy, and to do so willingly and in an upbeat state of mind. The ideal individuals for such a task are those who are healthy, adaptable, autonomous, self-responsible, enterprising, flexible and self-centred. In education, this reinterprets problems previously defined as social through a psychological prism, as personal problems or as the wrong kinds of attitudes, emotions or mindsets. This, in turn, undermines the idea of people acting as socially responsible students and citizens.

References

Brunila, K. (2009). *PARASTA ENNEN. Tasa-arvotyön projektitapaistuminen* [Best before. The projectisation of gender equality]. Helsingin yliopisto kasvatustieteen laitoksen julkaisuja 222. Väitöskirja. Helsinki: Yliopistopaino.

Brunila, K. (2011). The projectisation, marketisation and therapisation of education. *European Educational Research Journal. Special Issue: Philosophy of Education and the Transformation of Educational Systems, 10*, 425–437.

Brunila, K. (2012a). A diminished self: Entrepreneurial and therapeutic ethos operating with a common aim. *European Educational Research Journal*, *11*, 477–486. doi:10.2304/eerj.2012.11. 4.477

Brunila, K. (2012b). From risk to resilience—The therapeutic ethos in youth education. *Education Inquiry*, *3*, 451–464. doi:10.3402/edui.v3i3.22046

Brunila, K. (2014). The rise of survival discourse in the era of therapisation and marketisation of education. *Education Inquiry*, *5*(1), 7–23.

Burman, E. (2008). *Deconstructing development psychology* (2nd ed.). London and New York: Routledge.

Conrad, P. (1992). Medicalization and social control. *Annual Review of Sociology*, *18*, 209–232. doi:10.1146/annurev.so.18.080192.001233

Conrad, P. (2006). *Identifying hyperactive children. The medicalization of deviant behaviour* (Expanded ed.). Hunt and Burlington: Ashgate.

Dahlstedt, M., Fejes, A., & Schönning, E. (2011). The will to (de)liberate: Shaping governable citizens through cognitive behavioural programmes in school. *Journal of Education Policy*, *26*, 399–414. doi:10.1080/02680939.2010.516841

Davies, B. (1993). *Shards of glass. Children reading and writing beyond gendered identity*. Sydney: Allen & Unwin.

Davies, B. (2005). The (im)possibility of intellectual work in neoliberal regimes. *Discourse: Studies in the Cultural Politics of Education*, *26*(1), 1–14. doi:10.1080/01596300500039310

Davies, B., Dormer, S., Gannon, S., Laws, C., Rocco, S., Taguchi, H. L., & Mccann, H. (2001). Becoming schoolgirls: The ambivalent project of subjectification. *Gender and Education*, *13*, 167–182. doi:10.1080/09540250124848

Ecclestone, K. (Ed.). (2013). *Emotional well-being in policy and practice: Interdisciplinary perspectives*. London: Routledge.

Ecclestone, K., & Brunila, K. (in press a). Governing emotionally-vulnerable subjects: Mechanisms and consequences in the 'therapisation' of social justice. *Pedagogy, Culture and Society.*

Ecclestone, K., & Brunila, K. (in press b). The goal of emotional well-being in British and Finnish adult education: The implications of 'therapeutic' approaches to social justice for subjectivity and images of the 'self'. *Pedagogy, Culture and Society.*

Ecclestone, K., & Hayes, D. (2008). *The dangerous rise of therapeutic education*. London: Routledge.

Ecclestone, K., Hayes, D., & Furedi, F. (2005). Knowing me, knowing you: The rise of therapeutic professionalism in the education of adults. *Studies in the Education of Adults*, *37*, 182–200.

Erchak, G. M., & Rosenfeld, R. (1989). Learning disabilities, dyslexia, and the medicalization of the classroom. In J. Best (Ed.), *Images of issues: Typifying contemporary social problems* (pp. 79–97). New York, NY: Aldine de Gruyter.

Fejes, A., & Dahlstedt, M. (2013). *The confessing society: Foucault, confession and practices of lifelong learning*. New York, NY: Routledge.

Foucault, M. (1977). *Discipline and punish: The birth of the prison*. London: Penguin Books.

Foucault, M. (1980). Power/knowledge: Selected interviews and other writings, 1972–1977. London: Harvester.

Foucault, M. (1961/2009). *History of madness*. New York, NY: Routledge. (Preface to the 1961 edition.)

Furedi, F. (2004). *Therapy culture: Cultivating vulnerability in an uncertain age*. London: Routledge.

Furedi, F. (2009). *Wasted. Why education isn't educating*. London and New York: Continuum International.

Harwood, V. (2006). *Diagnosing 'disorderly' children. A critique of behaviour disorder discourses*. London: Routledge.

Kelly, P. (2006). The entrepreneurial self and 'youth at-risk': Exploring the horizons of identity in the twenty-first century. *Journal of Youth Studies*, *9*(1), 17–32. doi:10.1080/13676260500523606

Komulainen, K., Korhonen, M., & Räty, H. (2009). Risk-taking abilities for everyone? Finnish entrepreneurship education and the enterprising selves imagined by pupils. *Gender and Education*, *21*, 631–649. doi:10.1080/09540250802680032

Koski, L., & Moore, E. (2001). Näkökulmia aikuisuuteen ja aikuiskasvatukseen [Perspectives on adulthood and adult education]. *Aikuiskasvatus*, *21*(1), 4–13.

Laws, C., & Davies, B. (2000). Poststructuralist theory in practice: Working with "behaviourally disturbed" children. *International Journal of Qualitative Studies in Education, 13*, 205–221. doi:10.1080/09518390050019631

McLaughlin, K. (2011). *Surviving identity: Vulnerability and the psychology of recognition.* London: Routledge.

Nolan, J. (1998). *The therapeutic state: Justifying government at century's end.* New York: New York University Press.

Rieff, P. (1987). *The triumph of the therapeutic: Uses of faith after Freud.* Chicago: University of Chicago Press. (First published 1966.)

Rose, N. (1998). *Inventing our selves. Psychology, power and personhood.* Cambridge: Cambridge University Press.

Rose, N. (1999). *Governing the soul. The shaping of the private self.* London: Free Association Books.

Siivonen, P. (2010). *From a 'student' to a lifelong 'consumer' of education? Constructions of educability in adult students' narrative life histories.* Finnish Educational Research Association. Research in Educational Sciences, *47.* Jyväskylä: Jyväskylä University Press.

Siivonen, P. (2013). 'A bad head for maths?' Constructions of educability and mathematics in adult students' narrative life histories. *Scandinavian Journal of Educational Research, 57*, 507–525. doi:10.1080/00313831.2012.696208

Siivonen, P., & Brunila, K. (2014). The making of entrepreneurial subjectivity in adult education. *Studies in Continuing Education, 36*(2), 160–172.

Teittinen, A. (2011). Onko diagnoosi tarpeellinen? Pohdintoja lääketieteellisten diagnoosien yhteiskunnallisista merkityksistä. Teoksessa Suvi Vaarla (toim.): *Alkoholin vaurioittamat. FASD-lasten ja -nuorten mahdollisuudet hyvään elämään* [Damaged by alcohol. FASD children's and young people's chances for good life]. Helsinki: Kehitysvammaliitto.

Walkerdine, V., Lucey, H., & Melody, J. (2001). *Growing up girl: Psychosocial explorations of gender and class.* Houndsmills: Palgrave.

Wright, K. (2008). Theorizing therapeutic culture: Past influences, future directions. *Journal of Sociology, 44*, 321–336. doi:10.1177/1440783308097124

Wright, K. (2011). *The rise of therapeutic society.* New York, NY: Academia.

Index

Note: Page numbers followed by "n" denote endnotes.

academics 4, 6, 111, 160–162, 166–169
accountability 5, 6, 8, 9, 85–87, 90, 91, 109, 110, 113, 119, 120
accreditation 11, 78, 88, 90
actually existing neoliberalism 11, 26, 64, 65, 74
adult education 13, 175, 177–180, 182, 184
adult educationalist 180, 181
adult students 179, 180, 182, 183
Andhra Pradesh 11, 62–66, 72
Andrzejewski, J. 92
Apple, M. W. 91, 93, 131
assessment 13, 107, 109, 147, 149, 160–162, 165–169; processes 162, 163, 167–169; situations 160, 161, 163, 169
assessors 160, 161, 166–170
Attention Deficit Hyperactivity Disorder (ADHD) 180–182
austerity 10, 18, 22, 46, 52, 58, 99
Australia 12, 113, 119–121, 145–148, 151, 154
Australian schools 13, 143, 144, 148, 149, 152
autonomous schools 118–121, 125, 128
autonomy 12, 72, 118, 120–122, 125–128, 181

Bacchi, C. 121, 128
Ball, S. J. 6, 118, 126
Baltodano, M. 92
Bansel, P. 84, 161
Becker, H. S. 161
Biesta, G. 144, 147, 150
Bloxham, S. 160
Blyth, M. 22
Boyd, P. 160
Brenner, N. 65
Brexit 10, 43, 44, 51–58
British state 50, 53, 58
Brown, W. 84
Buchanan, R. 147
Buford State School (BHS) 122–127
Bulkley, K. 149
Burawoy, M. 39

Burch, P. 145, 147, 149
Butler, J. 166

capital relation 47, 48, 104, 114
caste politics 68, 73
Centeno, M. A. 18
charter schools 79, 85, 86, 91, 120, 145
Chicago Public Schools 87
Codd, J. 80
Cohen, J. N. 18
coherence 3, 7–10, 14, 31
Collier, S.J. 31, 33, 34
commercialisation 5, 6, 11–13, 119–122, 127, 143–145, 153, 154
commercialised learning area 152–153
commercialised social and emotional learning (SEL) 143, 145; resources 144, 150–153
commercial resources 13, 144, 147, 149–151, 153, 154
commodification 8, 9, 11, 29, 72, 73, 88, 100
commodities 47, 86, 99, 101–104
conjunctural shifts 51–52
contemporary capitalism 103
contradictions 30, 35, 36, 38, 39, 47, 48, 65, 100–105, 112
corporatization 73, 78
critical policy analysis 79, 80
Crouch, C. 22
cultural spaces 86

Davies, B. 84, 177, 184
democracy 64, 73, 80, 81, 83, 85, 93
Dewey, J. 81
diagnoses 175, 179–183
disciplinary power 160
disciplinary technology 158–170
discourses 8, 9, 79, 80, 114, 135, 159, 163, 175–179, 182, 185; theories 79
dispositif 7–10, 14
diversity 5, 26, 90, 91, 125
Duncan, Arne 87–90

190 INDEX

economic discourses 158, 165
economy 21, 22, 49, 52, 64–66, 69, 70, 73, 81,
  82, 85
educational/education: commercialisation 11,
  12, 99–105, 113–115, 118; commodities 12,
  101–103, 105, 108, 113, 114; economy 62–74;
  institutions 5, 73, 86, 135; markets 11, 102;
  policy 5, 64, 68, 99, 109, 114; products 12, 101,
  105, 106, 114, 120, 143, 147; programmes 175,
  181, 184; sector 11, 64, 67, 71, 73, 101, 106, 114
efficacy 101, 105–113; framework 11, 101, 105,
  106, 108, 114; mechanisms 107
efficiency 84, 105, 106, 109, 110, 121, 174, 175
Elliot, L. 20
emotional learning 13, 143
employability 159, 163, 164, 166
enterprising discourses 174–181, 183–185
Estonian students 164, 168, 169
Estonian University 159, 162, 165–167, 170
ethics 5, 7, 139
Europe 21, 45, 53, 83, 85
exchange-value 47, 48, 102, 103, 108

Fairclough, N. 163, 165
financial capital 46, 47, 51, 58
financial crisis 18, 21, 22, 46, 52, 53, 58
financialization 51, 52
financial sector 52, 57
focus groups 148, 149, 159, 160, 162, 164
Foucault, Michel 83, 84, 119, 131, 136, 158, 161
Furedi, F. 176, 180, 184

Gard, M. 146
Geer, B. 161
general upper secondary school for adults
  (GUSSA) 179, 180, 182, 183
Gledhill, J. 27
global city 62–74
global economy 22, 45, 63, 64, 69
global education industry 99–101, 114, 145
global higher education markets 158, 164
globalization 25, 64, 65, 67, 87, 92
Gourlay, L. 166
governmentality 6, 83–85, 132, 176
Greene, M. 80
Green Revolution 68

Hall, S. 30, 36
Harris, J. 23
Harwood, V. 180
Hay, S. 159
Hayek, F.A. 2
hidden dangers 144, 149–151
higher education 11, 13, 68, 69, 86, 92, 94, 159,
  160, 163–166, 169, 170; choices 162, 163;
  institutions 86, 89, 90, 158, 162
Hilgers, M. 30

Hogan, A. 106, 113, 127
Hughes, E. 161
Hyderabad 11, 62–67, 69–74

imagined reputation 112, 114
individual responsibility 13, 184, 185
instrumentalism 8, 9
international schools 70, 125
invocations, of neoliberalism 37, 38
irresponsibility 134–137

Jessop, B. 3, 111
Jones, M. 58n6

Kalb, D. 21, 35
Kapitzke, C. 159
Kennedy, John F. 81
Kingfisher, K. 27
knowledge 8, 9, 47, 102–104, 111, 136, 137,
  147–149, 152
knowledge-based economies 48, 52, 103, 104
knowledge brand 101, 108–112
Kumashiro, K.K. 89

Lazzarato, M. 136
liberal public education 80, 87
Lingard, B. 106, 119
London 20, 22, 50–53, 56, 57
Lucey, H. 181
Lynch, K. 110

MacLeod, G. 58n6
managerialism 6, 11, 91, 92
market discourse 121, 122, 128
marketing 90, 92, 113, 118, 120, 124, 126,
  144, 153
marketisation 5, 6, 11, 118–122
market language 123, 125
marking teams 167, 168
Maskovsky, J. 27
McLaughlin, K. 184
Melody, J. 181
Miner, B. 87
Molnar, A. 145
Mõttus, R. 162
Murphy, R. 166

national rankings 91
Nef, J. 64
neoliberal governmentalities 131
neoliberalization 3, 4, 6–8, 10, 11, 13, 14, 25,
  28–30, 32, 33, 35, 38, 43–45, 47, 48, 51, 58, 162;
  economic significance of 47–48
neoliberal positioning: of students 158–160
neoliberal reform 4–6, 10–14, 69, 73, 78
neoliberal regime shifts 44–47
neoliberal societies 91, 169

INDEX

neoliberal subjectivities 6, 10–13, 161, 185
neoliberal urbanism 72–74
New Labour 24, 51, 52
New York 20, 112
Nolan, J. 176
Nussbaum, M. 92

Oliver Wyman 57
Ong, A. 2
organic crisis 43–58
Orr, S. 160

Pearson plc 11, 99–115
Pearson's Efficacy Framework 101, 105, 109, 112, 114
Peck, J. 4
perceived affordances 149–151
performativity 6, 12, 132, 134–137
Pinochet 5
Pluim, C. 146
political economy 32, 33, 37, 48, 101
political rationality 83, 137
postcolonial state 64, 65, 68
power 109, 110, 113, 132, 133, 135–138, 140, 161, 163, 169, 176, 177; brokers 87; relations 27, 132, 133, 135, 136, 161, 163, 168, 170, 177, 182
Priestley, M. 144, 146, 147, 150
Pritchard, R. 169
private schools 5, 124, 125
privatization 3, 118–121, 127, 128, 145
public education 11, 71, 78–80, 85–88, 92, 94
public relations 91
public schooling 79, 85, 87, 94
public schools 79, 80, 82, 85, 87, 88, 92, 93, 119, 120, 123–125, 127, 128
public services 24, 45, 50, 64, 86, 109, 135, 138
public universities 72

quality education 102, 104

Ravitch, D. 80
reputation 101, 112–114, 164
resistance 5, 7, 10, 12, 14, 33, 35, 46, 47, 131–134, 139, 140
Robinson, S. 144, 147, 150
Robles, W. 64
Rose, N. S. 134, 176, 177, 183

Saar, E. 162
Sader, E. 22
schools: autonomy 12, 120, 121, 126; choice 5, 8, 9, 85; of education 78, 79, 88–92; leaders 93, 124, 144, 146, 148, 149, 152, 154; websites 121, 122, 124
Schugurensky, D. 86
self, care of 131–140
self-centredness 174

self-development 182, 183
self-improvement 182
self-knowledge 133, 182
self-making 182
self-mastery 182
self-realisation 175, 182, 183
self-reflection 182
Sellar, S. 106
semiotic/discursive strategy 107
Shiva, V. 74n7
social and emotional learning (SEL) 13, 126, 133, 139, 140, 143–146, 148–153, 165, 174, 176, 181, 183–185
social impact 49, 100, 101
socio-spatial reform 69–72
state policy 64, 65, 67
state revenues 53, 82
Stevenson, J. 166
student assessment 158–170
student discourses 159, 163
student experiences 13, 166
student outcomes 121, 151, 153
student performances 145, 161, 168
student subjectivities 160, 162, 163, 170
subjectification 159, 163, 177, 178
subjectivities 7, 10, 12, 131, 133, 159, 167, 169, 176–180, 182, 183
Sum, N. L. 111
Svensson, G. 164
Symcox, L. 92

Taras, M. 161
teacher agency 12, 143, 144, 146, 147, 153; achieving and articulating 152–153
teacher candidates 89, 93
teacher certification 89
teacher education 11, 79, 85, 88, 90, 91
teacher preparation 78–80, 85, 87, 88, 92
teachers 12, 88, 93, 132, 135–140, 144, 146–154
teaching subjects 132, 133, 136
Telangana 66, 67, 69, 71–73
Thatcher, Margaret 24–29, 32, 36, 85
Thatcherism 24, 45, 52
Theodore, N. 65
therapeutic discourses 13, 174, 176, 178–180, 184, 185
therapeutic education 176
therapeutic turn 175, 176
therapization 174–180, 182, 185
Tickell, A. 4
Torres, C.A. 86

UK University 161, 162, 168
uneven development 36, 43, 44, 48–52, 56–58; in United Kingdom 50–51
uneven geographies, of development 66, 67
United States 108, 112, 132

Upadhya, C. 75n10
urbanism 62–74
Useem, M. 86

value displaces values 137
value for money 109
vulnerability 168, 175, 180, 184, 185

Walkerdine, V. 181
Wood, G. 164
world market 43, 45, 47, 49, 57, 65

Yorke, M. 160
Youdell, D. 118